Effective Telephone
Fundraising

Effective Telephone Fundraising

THE ULTIMATE GUIDE TO RAISING MORE MONEY

Stephen F. Schatz, CFRE

WILEY

John Wiley & Sons, Inc.

Published by John Wiley & Sons, Inc., Hoboken, New Jersey.
Published simultaneously in Canada.

Cartoons, hourglass, and hand phone graphic © Jennifer A. Herman. Reprinted with permission.

For general information on our other products and services or for technical support, please contact our Customer Care Department within the United States at (800) 762-2974, outside the United States at (317) 572-3993 or fax (317) 572-4002.

Wiley also publishes its books in a variety of electronic formats. Some content that appears in print may not be available in electronic books. For more information about Wiley products, visit our web site at www.wiley.com.

Library of Congress Cataloging-in-Publication Data:

Schatz, Stephen F.
  Effective telephone fundraising: the ultimate guide to raising more money/Stephen F. Schatz.
     p. cm.
  Includes index.
  ISBN 978-0-470-56059-4 (pbk.)
  1. Telephone fund raising.   I.   Title.
  HV41.S247 2010
  658.15'224-dc22

                                                                    2009045995

Printed in the United States of America

10 9 8 7 6 5 4 3 2 1

*This book is dedicated to the person whom I most admire,
for her keen and penetrating intelligence, vast stores of knowledge,
hard work and perseverance, high moral and ethical standards,
selflessness, and for her support and faith in my efforts:
to my best friend in life's journey, my wife, Virginia Sacha.*

Contents

Foreword

In 1876, Rutherford B. Hayes, newly elected as the 19th U.S. President, became the first commander-in-chief to use the telephone. With Alexander Graham Bell at his side, President Hayes placed a call from Washington, D.C., to Philadelphia. Following the demonstration, an impressed President Hayes turned to Mr. Bell and said, "That's an amazing invention, but who would ever want to use one of them?" A Western Union internal memorandum from the same year stated, "The telephone has too many shortcomings to be seriously considered a means of communication."

Fast forward to 2009. I was sitting in my Philadelphia office working on my upcoming book about donor-centered planned gift marketing when I read an interesting post on GIFT-PL, the listserv for gift planning professionals hosted by the Partnership for Philanthropic Planning. Kaye C. Stackpole, Director of Gift Planning at Westminster College, wrote, "We reviewed our metrics last year and added a new category—Extended Phone Call (EPC) that can count the same as a personal visit. With travel budgets restricted last year, we discovered, for stewardship calls especially, donors appreciated our updates by phone and respected our efforts for implementing cost saving ideas."

The telephone is indeed an amazing invention. Unlike the executives at Western Union in the nineteenth century, today's development professionals recognize the telephone for the powerful communications tool it has become. Today, the telephone performs many varied functions in the nonprofit development office. One of the major applications of the telephone medium is solicitation, whether for annual donations, capital gifts, memberships, or planned gifts.

While fundraising phonathons of one sort or another have been with us for a very long time, telephone fundraising as we know it today can be traced back to the Yale University capital campaign. In 1977, the major-gift consulting firm IDC was brought in to help Yale develop a strategy to give alumni who could not be visited face-to-face an opportunity to support the campaign. Under the direction of Bill Freyd, IDC developed the first personalized methodology for the public phase of a capital campaign. Yale combined the use of letters and telephone calls to simulate the steps used in major-gift cultivation and solicitation.

In 1980, Steve Schatz and I worked together at Temple University during its Centennial Challenge Campaign. Temple was the first non–Ivy-type university to implement a professional telephone fundraising program. The approach that worked so well at Yale, asking alumni to donate 2 percent of their gross annual income for each year of the next five years, resulted in a great deal of foul language and hang-ups when tried at Temple. As you may guess, Ivy Yale and state-related Temple do not have much in common, culturally speaking. Steve and I worked tirelessly to effectively adapt the program implemented by Temple's consultant, Philanthropy Management Inc. By adopting donor-centered strategies, we were able to achieve great results.

Penelope Burk, in her book *Donor Centered Fundraising* (Burk & Associates Ltd., 2003) describes what she means by the term, "Donor-centered fundraising is an approach to raising money and interacting with donors that acknowledges what donors really need and puts those needs first. Donor-centered fundraising impacts fundraising success in three ways. First, it retains more donors longer, giving them time to develop their own philanthropic resiliency; second, it causes more donors to offer increasingly generous gifts; and third, it raises the performance of even the most active and loyal donors to a new standard."

In 1982, following our success at Temple University, Steve and I created Telefund Management Inc. which we later renamed The Development Center before selling it years later. We retained our innovative, donor-centered spirit. We were the first to apply professional telephone fundraising techniques to the museum world (*The NSFRE Journal*), and among the first to bring such techniques to the performing arts world, social service agencies, and, of course, other colleges and universities. Because we had very good competitors, we had to be innovative not only to survive but to thrive. We generated tremendous results for our clients and were ranked among the most cost-effective professional solicitation firms in the nation in various state attorney general reports. Along the way, we developed powerful telephone fundraising techniques, many of which are now so commonly utilized as to be taken for granted while other valuable tactics are less known and, therefore, less practiced.

In this volume, Steve shares the secrets for making the most effective calls possible. While acknowledging the different applications for the telephone and the different styles of calls, Steve writes with a particular point of view that, over years of crafting great campaigns and training excellent callers, we found to be the most fruitful. Regardless of the application or style, the most productive telephone fundraising will always be donor-centered at its core.

When I was a child first learning how to use the telephone, my mother instructed me to greet the recipient of my call, identify myself, and ask permission to speak. Guess what? Good manners still make sense. Just one of the techniques that Steve advocates is asking permission to speak. It is a simple technique. It is donor-centered. It leads to better conversations and, therefore, produces stronger results. Yet, so few telephone fundraising calls today start this way. Steve dissects the telephone fundraising call. In doing so, he provides many simple as well as complex techniques for enhancing the quality of your telephone fundraising efforts. He does so step-by-step and with humor. In all cases, his core strategy is donor-centered.

Today, there are over 1.5 million nonprofit organizations. Anthony Alonso of Advantage Fundraising Consulting has pointed out that over half of all nonprofit organizations in the United States use telephone fundraising. Americans donate over $1 billion annually to charitable organizations through telephone fundraising programs run by professional companies alone. Over 60 percent of all U.S. households were solicited for donations in 2005. In other words, a lot of people are receiving a lot of calls for contributions to a lot of organizations.

To be effective, truly effective, nonprofit organizations must make better calls. Simply put, good enough is no longer good enough. To secure more donors, raise more money, and build donor loyalty, nonprofit organizations must become better communicators. If your telephone program is already good, this book will help you make it better. If your telephone program is weak, this book will show you the practical steps you can take to make it stronger. If your organization does not yet have a telephone program, this book will help you create one that is highly effective from the start.

This volume will provide you with practical, fundamental information in an easily accessible way. You will learn things you are doing right, so you can keep doing them with confidence. And you will discover better ways to do other things. By taking you through the call process systematically, Steve reveals what has been proven to work best.

Steve and I are among the individuals who pioneered telephone fundraising. Over the decades, we have earned our gray hairs and have witnessed many changes in the development world. But one constant remains unaltered: Donor-centered fundraising produces the best results. To learn how you can harness this powerful approach to telephone fundraising, read on. My friend, former business partner, and fellow pioneer will be your guide.

Michael J. Rosen, CFRE
President
ML Innovations, Inc.
mrosen@mlinnovations.com

Introduction

Truth be told, I am writing this book more out of a sense of responsibility than my desire to write. As one's first opus, one may dream of penning best selling thriller, like *The Da Vinci Code*, or a revered book on philosophy *The Meaning of Existence: Finally Explained* (my *next* book).

A book on telemarketing? Perish the thought! So, I am under no illusions that this tome will be taken to the beach, each page turned with breathless anticipation as to what might happen next ... "Did you read how the caller turned around that 'I can't give because I have kids in college' objection? I can't wait until the next chapter! I just can't put this book down!"

I was in on the nonprofit telephone fundraising revolution pretty near its beginning. Over the span of close to 18 years I spent a good portion of my life trying to figure out what works and what doesn't in terms of making telephone solicitations. I have audited thousands of telephone solicitations. I have written and tweaked hundreds and hundreds of what you might call "scripts." In terms of raising money, I think we were pretty successful. We built a multimillion dollar direct mail/telephone fundraising service bureau that raised tens of millions of dollars over a period of more than 20 years. Tens of thousands of new and renewed donors were found for some of the nation's top nonprofit organizations. But more than that, we trained several thousand new fundraisers in the basics of raising money. Scores of these went on into fundraising, development, and marketing careers. That's probably what I'm most proud of.

Having been *off* the telephone fundraising radar screen for close to a decade, I thought, perhaps, the development profession had taken solicitation techniques to new heights of sophistication, and the quality of fundraising calls, thanks to experience and expertise, was better than ever. Unfortunately, being on the receiving end of many calls asking for funds, my impression is that the quality of calls is somewhat worse than it was 10 years ago. Moreover, pressed into reluctant service as a volunteer fundraiser for a couple of charities, I have found that the "old" techniques still work, that it is possible to make quality calls, engage prospects over the phone, state your case in a compelling way, and ask for and negotiate a pledge of support. And, yes, get hung up on as well. But in spite of the sheer volume of "junk calls" that irritate potential donors at dinnertime, I believe the medium still works and is valuable tool within the context of your overall donor development strategies.

So, here you are: a brain dump as it were. Apologizing in advance to my esteemed colleagues who may be authors themselves, I have never picked up a book on fundraising that I was eager to read or that I found particularly pleasurable or memorable. Since the subject of this book *especially* is not exactly what I'd call fascinating, or inspiring, or stimulating, I'll try to offer a humorous view to the proceedings, to take the sting out of the mundane, the arcane, the, well, less-than-appealing subject matter. No, this is not a book for the senior development professional, he or she with gray hair, $500 suit, and an air of gravitas. This is a book for those in the trenches. Make no mistake. Telephone fundraising is the "trenches of development." Regarding this metaphor, I've never been able to shake the vision of poor World War I soldiers, cowering in the trenches, under bombardment, waiting for the inevitable signal to charge across no-man's-land, and then the sergeant in charge blows his whistle, ordering the men over the top to face withering machine gun fire . . . *it's six o'clock, time to pick up those phones and start calling!*

In the "development" field (a nice euphemism, I have always thought) no job is harder, more challenging, and more thankless than picking up the telephone (or the headset) and making case after case for funding one's cause, and experiencing rejection after rejection en route to a goal.

I will never forget a client from a large educational institution who felt the responsibility to visit our facility on the first night of calling. As he said, many people like to eat sausage, but just don't want to know how it's made. He didn't want to be there, but felt he must out of a sense of duty to his organization.

For those of you who are in the "sausage business," who have had some experience as a telephone fundraiser or solicitor, some of this information may already be familiar to you. In that case, perhaps I will be able to frame the information or techniques in a broader context, so that what you already know may make even more sense. For those of you who, God forbid, make your living in some area that involves telephone fundraising, you have my condolences. In reading this book you may have the conviction that you know how to do it better. Perhaps you do, and I invite you to write your own book on the subject to add to the body of great knowledge in development books. By writing this book, I do not envision myself as any kind of "prophet" writing a "bible" of telephone fundraising. I'll leave that for you to do.

Scope of This Book

First, what this book is NOT about.

This is NOT a book about *telemarketing*, a term that in relation to fundraising and development, I loathe. This is NOT a book about running a call center; staffing a call center; hiring, training, and managing and motivating call center employees; evaluating their performance; or monitoring or analyzing the work output of calls. It is NOT a book about analysis and segmentation of data going into a fundraising call center and determining strategies in conducting a call center campaign. This is NOT a book about analyzing the statistical effectiveness of tele-fundraising campaigns, by individual solicitor or in aggregate. It is NOT a book about call center automation, power dialing, predictive dialing, or equipping or furnishing a call center. It's NOT a book about the relation of direct mail to telephone calls, either as effective introductions to calls, or the fulfillment process, although some comments will be offered on the subject. This is NOT a book about legal compliance to the various and nefarious state codes, statutes, and regulations. This is NOT a book about any aspect of management either as relates to the business of the development or the business of running a call center.

This is a book about FUNDRAISING TELEPHONE CALLS and how to effectively write scripts or "call outlines" (what we called "soft scripts") that aid telephone fundraisers to make effective calls to past and potential donors. This is a book on how the sausage is made, where the rubber meets the road, or whatever other metaphor you wish to use: a practical guide to writing effective telephone call scripts and outlines.

The call itself, that's what this is about. It's the call that raises the money. If you are making good phone calls, you will raise money. If you aren't, you won't.

There are two elements to a making a good phone call, only one of which is under the control of the person responsible for conducting a telephone fundraising campaign: the person making the call, the "tele-fundraiser," and the telephone "script" or the call outline. The former element can be controlled (with difficulty) through the recruitment, screening, hiring, training, monitoring, motivation, and management process. The other element, the message/call outline, and conducting an effective negotiation over the telephone medium *is* under your control. Only one word about the former: Hire the best tele-fundraisers you can and pay them more than you think you can afford.

The Characters

As most every good book has interesting characters, with the aid of a creative and talented illustrator, I've attempted to create a couple of characters that run through this book: Mr. Smith, our ubiquitous donor prospect, and Alice Jones, our plucky, intrepid telephone fundraiser.

MR. SMITH, Our Prospective Donor

Mr. Smith will be our prospective donor who we will be calling throughout this book. You may know Mr. Smith. Then again, you may not know him at all.

Mr. Smith is a large donor who gave last year, or Mr. Smith may have never given anything at all. Ever. Or Mr. Smith may have given a small amount of money, once or twice in years past, but has stopped giving altogether.

Mr. Smith may have felt strongly about your organization and your mission and may have strongly backed you in many ways, but then you did something to irk him or make him really angry—and you don't even know it. Or Mr. Smith may have only a casual acquaintance with you and may be largely indifferent to your needs.

Mr. Smith may have sold his tech business two months before your call for several million dollars, and may be considering a long sabbatical in the South of France. Or Mr. Smith may have lost his job the very day you are calling him for a contribution.

Mr. Smith may be closely affiliated with your organization. He may be a subscriber; a member; a volunteer; someone who signs up for your newsletters, goes to your website, and closely follows your organization's activities. Then again, he may never have even heard of your organization, although he may have some sympathy for you when understands what your mission is about.

Mr. Smith is "every man" and he is no one. Mr. Smith is your *prospect*.

ALICE JONES, Our Fundraiser

Alice is going to make calls for your organization. Alice may be a young, eager student who is working part time for your organization and who barely understands what the word *philanthropy* means, much less be able to spell it.

Or Alice may be a mature "hired gun"—a paid solicitor working for a company your nonprofit organization has retained to make calls on your behalf. She may be well trained and highly experienced, or this may be her first week on the job.

Or Alice Jones may be a volunteer who is coming to work for you 6 to 8 PM, Tuesdays and Thursdays for the next two weeks in your volunteer phonathon. She knows your organization well and may even know some of the prospects she is calling, but she's far from being a fundraising professional or experienced salesperson.

Moreover, Alice may have the natural "gift" of having people like her instantly over the telephone, with a smooth, engaging, suave telephone demeanor. When she calls, people just seem to want to give her money. She is one of your "stars."

Or Alice may not be the most articulate person in the world, who can occasionally mangle words and syntax and really has to work at persuading folks to listen to her, much less give her money—someone whom you question whether she has the fundraising "chops" to succeed.

Alice is everything you want and don't want representing your organization. She is your *telephone fundraiser.*

Acknowledgments

There are a number of people to thank for the knowledge to make this book possible. First, I'd like to thank the person who gave me my first development job. In 1980, Lee Wenke was Vice President for Development at Temple University. He hired me for my first job in development, even though I didn't know what the term *development* meant. Those students of our esteemed college campuses who have walked past the administrative offices with signs like "Development" or "Institutional Advancement" hung over them have probably scratched your heads trying to figure what went on behind those office doors. I guess Lee figured that if I could sell myself for a job that I didn't know anything about, I could sell Temple University alumni on the idea of giving to their school's first-ever capital campaign. He was at least partially correct, though he did eventually fire me.

Second, I'd like to thank Ron Erdos, who back in the 1980s owned a consulting firm called Philanthropy Management Incorporated. Spending a mere 20 minutes with Ron, analyzing Temple University phone calls in February 1981 gave me a foundation for how to think about phone calls, their structure, and the function of a good solicitation. Third, I'd like to thank my business partner of more than 15 years, Michael Rosen, who cofounded The Development Center. Together we shared an intellectual curiosity on what was involved in making good telephone calls. For us, it was not drudgery. Analyzing, experimenting, trying new things, and finding solutions that worked was a formidable intellectual challenge. Indeed, one had better come up with solutions fast if you were going to survive by raising money. Fourth, I would like to thank the two or three thousand employees who passed through the doors of my company, some full-time professionals in marketing, client relations, and data management, who contributed to our 20-year success. Fifth, I'd like to thank our many fine colleagues and ethical competitors in the telephone fundraising profession, a field that, in the immortal words of Rodney Dangerfield, "got no respect." Sixth, I'd like to thank Ted Hart, founder and CEO of the ePhilanthropy Foundation, for pulling me out of retirement and involving me at the birth of an entirely new medium of fundraising communication: the Internet. Seventh, hearty thanks to the great telephone fundraising companies who have contributed material appearing in the appendix of this book: Thanks to

Gregg Carlson, chairman and CEO of IDC, who contributed a great example of "talking points" for fundraisers; a tip of the hat to Joe White, president of Left Bank Consulting, for scripts and commentary he prepared (joe@left-bankconsulting.com), and to Mal Warwick for material that has been reprinted with permission from *Mal Warwick's Newsletter: Successful Direct Mail, Telephone, & Online Fundraising* (http://ga1.org/malwarwick/join.html; Copyright ©2008 by Mal Warwick); thanks also to Steve Brubaker, senior vice president for Corporate Affairs at InfoCision, who contributed an insightful guide to writing successful scripts, along with information about the Taylor Institute for Direct Marketing; and thanks to Anthony Alonso, president of Advantage Consulting, for an excellent and innovative example of an effective telephone fundraising script. The companies represented are among the most established and respected in the telephone fundraising sphere. Eighth, I would be remiss if I did not add profound thanks to Susan McDermott of John Wiley & Sons for having faith in this project, and to Judy Horvath, my editor, for her encouragement and painstaking corrections of a very green, novice author. Last, and most important, I wish to thank my wife and daughter: my wife for her love, unflagging loyalty, and friendship, and my daughter for her smiles that radiate like sunshine, and at age 15 for teaching me new dimensions to the process of negotiation.

About the Author

Steve Schatz hails originally from Terre Haute, Indiana, and the small Midwestern farm community of Hoopeston, Illinois. He dual majored in business marketing and music theory and composition at Indiana State University and as an undergraduate had no idea what the word *development* meant. One day, in the midst of severe right versus left brain attack, he missed an exit while traveling east down Interstate 70, and ended up in Philadelphia, Pennsylvania, where he completed a master's in music at Temple University, concentrating in history, musicology, and some theory.

Accepting that he had talent only for teaching, and not having the fortitude to continue on for a PhD, he applied for gainful employment in Temple University's first-ever capital campaign, where he was thrust into the position of managing an in-house telephone outreach effort.

After achieving more success than was thought humanly possible, and believing that if he could raise money from Temple alumni, he could raise money from anyone, he and a partner, Michael Rosen, struck out on their own in 1982, founding a firm that eventually became The Development Center, a direct mail telephone outreach fundraising firm based in Philadelphia. For over 20 years TDC served educational institutions, arts organizations, museums, health care, and cultural institutions nationwide.

Their company was acquired by the Communications Services Group in 1997, and in 1998 Steve left to take a long sabbatical.

In 2000, Ted Hart, founder of the ePhilanthropy Foundation, dusted Steve off from retirement, asking to help him get a new nonprofit organization off the ground: the ePhilanthropy Foundation, with the mission of providing ethical standards and best practices for nonprofits navigating the new medium of the Internet. Steve served as COO until that organization was acquired by Network for Good in 2007.

Steve lives in Philadelphia with his wife, daughter, and cat, and stays out of significant trouble through ownership and management of some historic residential properties. He serves on several boards and volunteers more than he should. But currently his real passion is spinning, the stationary bike cardiovascular exercise. Steve is a very popular spinning instructor in Philadelphia and is known for his very eclectic music, ranging from thirteenth-century polyphony to contemporary heavy metal. But his real favorite music to spin to: the great orchestral masterworks from Haydn to Bernstein, and we hear he can do a real mean spin to Beethoven's Seventh.

You can reach Steve at steve@effectivetelephonefundraising.com.

The Nature of the Telephone Medium in Fundraising

Long before you pick up the phone to solicit funds, careful thought must be given to what you want to accomplish, how much you can invest, and how the telephone fits into your overall fundraising strategy.

Contacting Your Database of Constituents

Most nonprofit organizations, at the core of their annual giving and capital efforts, have a database of prospects: donors both current and lapsed who have some kind of track record of giving to their institution, and other constituents who have shown some degree of interest or affiliation, however tenuous.

As fundraisers, wouldn't it be nice to simply sit in your office and have donor checks arrive unsolicited in the mail, your major donors coming out of their way to personally drop off their checks on your desk, or other donors calling you to ask how much they can give to your organization? Well, we can at least dream of such a fundraising utopia.

The fact of the matter is that successful fundraisers take the initiative and *solicit* their donors and constituents through a variety of means. Regrettably, the Latin root of the word *solicit* is *sollicitare*, meaning ''to disturb''—a rather disturbing thought in itself!

According to Merriam-Webster, as a transitive verb in modern English, *solicit* can mean to approach, to entreat, to request, or to plead—all-important dimensions of the fundraiser's job. As a verb, *solicit* also carries some stronger connotations: to urge strongly and to try to obtain by urgent requests or pleas. It is this dimension that is most commonly thought of in connection with charitable solicitation (leaving aside the darker connotations of the verb: ''to entice or lure especially into evil''). Hmmm, as ethical fundraisers, we'll lay that dimension aside.

So, if we have to take the initiative and approach, even "disturb," our prospects, what are the most effective means to do so? Let's look at the major direct marketing "arrows in the quiver" of fundraisers: face-to-face solicitation, direct mail, e-mail, and, last, the telephone. And for each one, let's evaluate the unique qualities of each medium of communication according to a number of parameters:

- Degree of Personalization
    How does the medium lend itself to "personalization," the ability to create a message tailored to a specific prospect? The axiom is that the more personal the solicitation, the more likely you are to achieve results.
- Type of Channel
    Does the channel afford one-way or two-way communication with the prospect? (I suppose in the Internet age, you also have to consider multidirectional group communication via chat rooms and social networking sites!)
- Degree of Interruption
    What is the "interruptive" quality of the medium? Does it divert the prospect's attention from something else, or does the prospect freely allot the time necessary to receive the communication?
- Message Timing
    How quickly does the prospective donor receive the message from the time it has been sent? How significant is the delay? And from the time the prospect receives the message, how long does it take before you know a decision has been made, if ever?
- Dimensionality
    Does the communication channel enable to you to communicate through one or more senses? Is it an aural or visual medium—or both? Other than a handshake, so far, I have yet to see "tactile" or "olfactory" dimensions in fundraising, unless it's a result of a personal visit—a field trip, perhaps to a clinic.
- Time of Attention
    How long, relative to other channels of communication, can the medium hold the prospect's attention? The axiom here is the more time the prospect invests in hearing your message and evaluating your proposal, the more likely you are to have a positive result.
- Reliability
    How reliable is the medium in reaching its target? How do you *know* if your message was received, much less considered?
- Ability to Reach Large Numbers of Constituents
    Can the medium reach a large number of constituents in a short time, perhaps the course of an annual appeal?

- Cost

  What is the bottom line cost of the medium relative to another?
- Flexibility

  How flexible is the medium in allowing you to change message and strategy midcourse, to fine-tune, tweak, and alter strategy?

Weighing these factors can help you develop a strategy in choosing to communicate with your constituents. You may choose one, more than one, or a mix of media to achieve your fundraising goals.

Face-to-Face Soliciting

Arguably the most *effective* solicitation medium has been and will continue to be face-to-face. In most cases, we think of face-to-face solicitation as being accomplished by senior development officers or highly dedicated volunteers making an appointment with a prospect and visiting him or her at home, the office, or an agreed location. There is also the "cold call" face-to-face soliciting dimension that can involve door-to-door prospecting and on-the-street solicitation of passersby, but these techniques are not feasible for soliciting *existing* constituents in your database.

Considering the dimension of personal solicitation of prescreened prospects at their home or office, there are a number of dimensions to consider in the nature of the communication.

Degree of Personalization: High

Face-to-face soliciting is undoubtedly the most personal of all media available to fundraisers. Usually the prospect has agreed to the visit beforehand and has time set aside to meet with the fundraiser. In this way, face-to-face fundraising is the "least disturbing" of all the communication media available.

In most cases, the fundraiser will have had time to research a prospect's donor record, say a "Mr. Benton Smith," and determine his interests and degree of affiliation with the organization. Good fundraisers will then be able to tailor a proposal best suited to him. Moreover, the fundraiser is no mere "solicitor," but is a human being with a name and a face. Also, the prospect is more than a name with a donor record as well. He or she is a live human being. The warmth and immediacy of human interaction can itself set the atmosphere for a positive exchange and a positive result.

Type of Channel: Two-Way

Unlike broadcast media, direct mail, or e-mail solicitation, the prospect and the fundraiser engage in a verbal exchange. Each speaks, each listens (hopefully), and questions are posed of one another and are answered.

Perhaps there is a third party involved in the decision by the prospect, a partner or a spouse. In this case, you may find three-way or more directions of communication. Questions can be answered, and objections can be immediately dealt with.

Degree of Interruption: Noninterruptive and Focused

If the donor prospect has indeed set aside the time in his or her schedule to meet with you, you are not interrupting that person in the middle of another task or activity that can distract your appeal. Therefore, the communication can be more focused, potent, and effective. Of course, there may potentially be outside forces that can interrupt the two of you: the emergency call from home, the latest minor crisis in the office, the secretary who enters the office to inform her boss that the building is on fire!

Message Timing: Immediate

Once a prospect agrees to a meeting, the communication exchange that takes place is immediate, without delay. The fundraiser makes an appeal, he or she urges, entreats, requests, or pleads. And when the solicitor makes the "ask," he or she will likely know the result: a yes, perhaps a deferred yes, or a no. Sure, some further follow-up might be necessary in order for a decision to be made that further extends the process. But the fundraiser, at the minimum, will be able to gauge where in the process the prospect can be placed and the likelihood of receiving a gift.

Dimensionality: Multidimensional (Aural and Visual)

A face-to-face meeting is not merely an aural/verbal medium, it is also a visual one as well. Good fundraisers, of course, will carefully listen to what a prospect has to say and how he says it, his tone, and manner of expression. But really good fundraisers can key on a variety of nonverbal cues as well: facial expressions and body language.

For example, if your prospect, "Mr. Smith," visibly pushes back from his desk with your $25,000 request, his lips narrowing in a mild grimace, you might guess that you've asked for too much. (Please note that prospects can also pick up on visual and aural clues as well—for example, if you lack confidence and resolve in making your solicitation!)

Good fundraisers will also notice other visual clues: the kind of car the prospect drives, the size of the office you may be visiting, and the details of the room where you are meeting, from the diploma on the wall to the pictures on the desk, and so forth. These clues can help you complete the "picture" of the prospect.

And from the fundraiser's standpoint, he or she can augment the verbal presentation with a variety of visual aids, from pictures and printed literature that help reinforce the purpose of the appeal, to a brief multimedia aid like a PowerPoint presentation.

Let me note one simple solitary dimension available in the personal medium as well, one unavailable in any other medium, a *tactile* one: the nature and firmness of the prospect's handshake upon meeting and departing.

Time of Attention: Long

The face-to-face medium affords the solicitor more time to make the appeal than other channels because both the prospect and the fundraiser have set aside the time to communicate. It represents an *investment* by both to come to some kind of resolution.

Mr. Smith will have invested enough time to determine whether your cause is worth supporting. You will have invested the time and the energy to tailor a solicitation appealing specifically to Mr. Smith's interests. Perhaps that investment is only 15 minutes. Perhaps it is an hour meeting at the prospect's office. Perhaps it is a long afternoon lunch (with a martini or two). The axiom here is the more *time* Mr. Smith is willing and able invest in getting to know you, your organization, its programs, and its mission, the more successful you will be in receiving a gift.

Reliability: Very High

Unless Mr. Smith, unbeknownst to you, has become suddenly unconscious, in a personal visit you *know* your message has gotten through, without delay, and is not subject to the multiplicity of filters.

Ability to Reach Large Numbers of Constituents: Low

Perhaps a lone development officer can arrange four or five personal visits in a single day, if he or she is superhuman. But if your database numbers are in the thousands, it could take many years to reach a majority of your constituents, necessitating other means of communicating to them.

Cost: Very High

Moreover, because so few people can be reached in a short time, the "cost per contact" is very high. Couple this with the fact that many organizations' constituents are widely dispersed geographically, huge travel costs may come into play, further decreasing the number of them that can be practically reached and increasing the costs. While some organizations have had success in donor prospecting by door-to-door or on-the-street solicitations, cost-effective personal visitation is usually reserved for the most highly rated giving prospects, the ones that have an interest or affiliation in your cause and who can write a big check.

Flexibility: Very High

An effective solicitor who either visits Mr. Smith alone or with a colleague should undoubtedly have a strategy going in on what to say and generally how to approach Mr. Smith to gain his interest and involvement in his or her cause or project. But it may be apparent during the course of the meeting that a new strategy is needed. Effective fundraisers can tack and change course as they sail—emphasizing new details of the fundraising efforts to Mr. Smith, based on his questions and demonstrated interests.

Direct Mail Soliciting

A medium of communication that has been in existence for many years is direct mail. Nearly all nonprofits engage in direct mail soliciting to some degree. Perhaps it's for that reason that its effectiveness has somewhat diminished over the years. There's a lot of direct mail.

Degree of Personalization: Low-Medium

The degree of personalization in direct mail ranges from completely impersonal to somewhat personal. Only handwritten notes with text that is tailored specifically to the prospect can be considered in the very personal range. And unless you have a staff of handwriters, or you yourself are extraordinarily fast and not prone to writer's cramp, handwritten notes in the realm of fundraising are relegated more to thank-you notes. It's generally impractical to reach a large number in your database in this fashion.

At the other extreme you have bulk mail, mass-reproduced letters with address labels on envelopes, and somewhere in between, first-class, stamped, word-processed personalized letters.

Here the degree of personalization can vary to simply including the prospect's address with a cheery "Dear Mr. Smith" salutation, to dropping into the body of the letter various fields from the organization's database, like Mr. Smith's last gift or his year of graduation. However, a savvy public is not likely fooled into thinking word-processed letters, no matter how personalized, are typed and mailed individually, therefore decreasing their potential effectiveness.

Type of Channel: One-Way, Written Communication

As fundraisers you have a need, a story, and a strategy to raise funds. This is communicated to a letter writer who in the course of a one-, two-, three-, or more page letter makes a compelling case to the prospects. But the story, the "pitch," is going one way; there is no way for Mr. Smith to ask questions, raise objections, and have them immediately answered other than by taking the initiative to write back or call. It is a noninteractive medium.

Degree of Interruption: Noninterruptive

Generally speaking, the time involved in receiving, scanning, and reading mail is allocated at the discretion of the prospect. Mr. Smith may go out to receive the daily mail or have it dropped on his desk. Mr. Smith will scan the exteriors of the envelopes and decide which he is going to open. While it is true he may be irritated by the quantity of the mail and the unwanted bills and fundraising letters, it's generally a mild irritation—unless it's a summons or a formal legal complaint that could really get Mr. Smith's ire up!

Message Timing: Delayed

The time at which your letter is sent to the time it is received can range from a few days (in the case of first-class mail) to a few weeks (in the case of bulk mail). And once the message is received and the letter is scanned or read, it may be days, weeks, or months more before Mr. Smith responds. The fundraiser has no idea how far along the channel an individual solicitation may lie.

Dimensionality: Single Dimension—Visual Written Communication

In a mailed solicitation, you are reaching Mr. Smith through only *one* channel—what he can see and read. Your appeal might be made more interesting and attractive through pictures, but it's the written word that is most likely to touch Mr. Smith and move him. You cannot see Mr. Smith's reaction to your letter or sense its effect. Indeed, you don't even know if he received or read it.

Time of Attention: Short-Medium

The time Mr. Smith invests in paying attention to your message can vary from none to a medium length of time. Upon receiving your envelope Mr. Smith might simply glance at it and relegate it to the circular file for immediate recycling. Or he may open the letter, determine it's just another solicitation letter, and toss it as well. Then again, something might catch his eye, pique his interest, and have him sit down and read it word for word. Perhaps he will be inspired enough by your call to action that he will actually reach for his checkbook or credit card.

Reliability: Low-Medium

The only way you have of knowing if your message was received and read is if you receive a return envelope with a check! Moreover, prospects constantly move, and much of your mail will be returned and not forwarded. And today, with the plethora of junk mail and multiplicity of solicitations of all kinds, your envelope will usually be just one of many. There is no assurance that, even if your envelope is delivered, it will be opened.

Ability to Reach Large Numbers of Constituents: High

As long as you have an address, you can send a direct mail piece. In a matter of days, either through your own in-house mail capability or sending the work to a direct mail house, you can reach out to tens, even hundreds of thousands of constituents or potential constituents with your message.

Cost: Relatively Low

On a *per piece* basis, the costs of reaching out to a large number of prospects is, relative to personal visits or the telephone, much lower, the main variable being the degree of personalization you want to invest in.

By personalization I mean investments you make to tailor the piece to the individual prospect. Personalizing a direct mail piece can include the appearance of a typed envelope rather than using an adhesive address label, the use of postage stamps rather than metering, and having the letter include an inside address and/or other variable fields that can help further personalize the letter to the prospect. Even if the letter you write is word-processed, you can choose to personally sign each letter that goes out, as opposed to duplicating a facsimile, and even include handwritten notes in the margin. After several hundred of these, however, you may need to put your arm in a sling for a while!

The general rule: the greater the degree of personalization, the greater the cost. And the corollary to that rule is, the better the giving potential of the prospect as measured by his or her past giving record or demonstrated affiliation or support for your cause, the more likely your investment in personalization is to pay for itself.

After all, your more valued prospects are more likely to feel less valued if they receive a form letter, more valued if they are treated more personally. On the other hand, spending huge sums to personalize a solicitation letter to a list of prospects that you have purchased from a mail house, prospects who may or may not have an interest in your cause, is unlikely to pay for itself.

There are creative costs to consider, too. You can choose to have the letter professionally written, which can be a substantial expense. Furthermore, your administrative time in managing the process and either in recruiting a constituent as signatory or drafting the letter yourself and getting it through the approval processes can be extensive. In a perfect world, the approval process would merely consist of one person: you. In the real world, it can involve superiors, separate departments, and committees. Oftentimes creating a solicitation letter ready to mail can be an underestimated challenge that can take days or months.

Flexibility: Low

To keep costs low, generally a large mailing is a one-size-fits-all approach. To segment your database and send different letters to each based on their interests or other variable criteria can increase costs substantially.

Furthermore, generally speaking, when you have an approved letter and it is dropped into the mailbox, there's no turning back.

Even with extensive editing and approval processes, mistakes slip through: that typo that no one caught, a factual mistake, either major or minor, like the year 1935, the year you say your organization was founded, when it was really 1925; or most embarrassing, misspelling a major board member's name, say Jennifer Adams as opposed to Genifer Edems, and then sending her letter in Mr. Edenstein's envelope—ouch!

Also, let's say your strategy in the letter was a bomb. Far fewer checks are appearing in your return mail than you had anticipated. YOU thought your constituents would be interested in building a new student center, and instead you find there were probably three or four other campus projects or causes that would have excited them more. Oops.

After a letter drops, with direct mail, there is no Roseanne Rosanna-danna to say to your prospects: *It just goes to show you, it's always somethin' . . . if it's not one thin', it's always another*—or simply: *"Never mind!"*

E-Mail

The advent of the Internet and wireless communications devices has created a number of channels to communicate with each other. We live in an age of web sites, blogs, message boards, chat rooms, e-mails, texting, Twittering, and online social networking services from MySpace and Facebook to LinkedIn. By the time this book goes to print, there may be yet another online innovation *de jour*.

But of all of these electronic channels, the one that has emerged as a very effective and inexpensive solicitation medium through which you can target a message to large number of constituents that is your database is soliciting through e-mail.

Savvy organizations have expended considerable effort in augmenting their constituent databases with e-mail addresses, such that e-mails are becoming as common a feature as addresses or telephone numbers in donor and constituent records.

An early impediment to communicating by e-mail has largely disappeared. Early e-mail addresses were often the donor's business e-mail addresses, which could change as frequently as a donor changed jobs. But today, nearly everyone has at least a semipermanent e-mail address through one of the plethora of free or paid services that are available throughout the world. And even if someone chooses to change e-mail services, a web-savvy public is skilled enough to arrange forwarding from the old e-mail address to the new one. In this way e-mail addresses can be longer lived than a donor's physical address.

Degree of Personalization: Low-Mid

On the whole, e-mail messaging is a less formal, more casual medium than direct mail. Today's modern applications built for e-mail solicitation campaigns have the abilities to personalize an e-mail solicitation in many of the same ways that word processing is able to accomplish. Again, a savvy public knows what can be accomplished electronically these days, and no one believes the e-mail she is receiving is really directly from the organization's president, or *the* president, for that matter!

Type of Channel: One-Way Channel

Just as with a written fundraising appeal, you still need a compelling story to raise funds. How one does this in the medium of e-mail has spawned an entirely new creative niche in fundraising, allowing the prospect electronic interactivity to information your organization may wish to make available through hyperlinks. However, in the final analysis, for all the bells and whistles you may wish to embed in an e-mail message, it is still one-way communication, even though the prospect may respond or ask a question with cyber-ease, an hour, a day, or a week later.

Degree of Interruption: Noninterruptive

Those of us who cut our e-mail teeth with America Online remember the cheerful "*You've got mail!*" as mail appeared in our inbox—so long as we were dialed up! In those days, e-mail was relatively new, and each e-mail received was a minor event, if not cause for excitement—at least we were not disturbed by their appearance!

These days many folks are online constantly and the stream of electronic messages into their inboxes is continuous. People generally look at their e-mail as they are ready to do so, either on a schedule, or as schedule permits, so when they go to their inbox, they are consciously setting aside time to review messages—even if they are on-the-go and checking through a hand-held wireless device. So, your e-mail solicitation is unlikely to be interrupting something the prospect was doing.

Message Timing: Somewhat Delayed

While preparing a physical mailing can take weeks and days, and days more once the mailing is taken to the post office, a large e-mail solicitation can be sent with cyber-ease with a click from your office. From that moment, your mail will be electronically delivered in seconds anywhere in the world.

The delay occurs at the prospect's end. Perhaps Mr. Smith is on vacation, thankfully to some bucolic place without Internet service, and is unable or unwilling to check his messages. Yours will have to wait until he gets back and is greeted with 742 new messages in his inbox. Ouch!

And once Mr. Smith does check his e-mail, he may do a quick sort, responding only to those messages that he deems at a glance are most critical, yours continuing to sit, unread in the inbox. Or Mr. Smith may be one of those "always on" communicators, eagerly getting to and responding to every message as it comes into his inbox, even those to his wireless device as he is traveling in the cab to the airport. Good for you. At the other extreme, Mr. Smith may be among the cyber-cynical who look at the computer, shake their heads, and wonder if it really does represent advancement to mankind's quality of life. That Mr. Smith may be determined to check and respond to his e-mail once or twice a day, resolved to win the battle of man versus machine. However, even that may be an improvement over his once-a-day review of snail mail.

Regardless, once Mr. Smith gets to *your* e-mail, he will either respond or he will not. That response could be as instantaneous as a quick click, and the entry of his credit card information. Or he could set the e-mail aside, check a third party who may be involved in the decision (spouse or partner), and defer decision for days, weeks, or months.

Dimensionality: Multidimensional Potential

Generally speaking, it is what you write in the e-mail, like a letter, that will touch Mr. Smith and impel him to take action. However, your message can be augmented through the flexibility and power of the Internet to give him access to pictures, audio, even audiovisual information that helps support your case. Each click may pique his interest further, causing him to drill down into the web of hyperlinks you have made available through your e-mail.

This can be compelling, but hopefully not too distracting. The one click you definitely want him to make is that link enabling him to enter his credit card information. Do not let Mr. Smith lose sight of the forest for the trees!

Time of Attention: Short-Medium

If Mr. Smith receives a very large number of e-mails, the time he takes in reading and responding to each one is generally an inverse to the number of messages he receives. Some busy executives receive hundreds of e-mails a day and need to quickly assess, at a glance, those that are urgent and need attention. Moreover, it's a good bet that the better a prospect Mr. Smith is for you, the higher his giving potential, the more messages he's got in his inbox.

Therefore, his review of your mail may range from a glance at the "From" box and the "Subject" line, to a brief scan of the contents of your message, to actually taking a minute or two to read the basics and maybe make a few clicks to the hyperlinks you have provided.

Reliability: Medium

E-mail solicitation by nonprofits is generally directed to those who are identified as being constituents and whose e-mails the organization has acquired through various ethical means: personally through events and face-to-face contact, through direct mail forms that have been returned and filled out, or through the organization's or partner organizations' web sites where prospects have entered their e-mail information and have opted in to receive additional information. Donor prospecting through the purchase of e-mail lists of individuals who have no prior connection to your organization, and who have not explicitly elected to receive electronic communication from you, presents serious ethical questions.

Therefore, when you solicit by e-mail you're usually soliciting a constituent in some way, either a prior donor, someone who is affiliated in some way with your organization, or someone who has a demonstrated interest in your cause. If Mr. Smith is already a part of your extended family, hopefully he'll recognize the "From" line on the message, see the name of your organization, and be willing to open it.

Many argue, however, that with its low cost, the sheer volume of e-mail generated by commercial enterprises and nonprofits alike has led to diminishing returns and much lower open rates. They assert that legitimate communication is blended with spam in such volume that the medium has been compromised to the extent that prospects may be less willing to open *your* e-mail message and give it due consideration. In this way, the age of e-mail is at the same stage as the junk mail phenomenon of years past.

Indeed, there has been much written recently to combat this, techniques to get *your* e-mail opened: from personalizing the subject line, to creating short, creative, and compelling subject lines that induce the prospect to open the e-mail to lead to your compelling message and call to action.

Regardless, there is no assurance that once your e-mail message has been sent that it will be received. The e-mail address you have today may no longer be valid, or it could be entered incorrectly and could bounce back. It may fall victim to Mr. Smith's spam filters or be filtered by a family member or administrative assistant tasked with weeding out nonessential communication.

Last, once your e-mail is received, there is no assurance that Mr. Smith will open it or read it, much less act. Perhaps you have sent so many e-mails that you have worn out the welcome mat to Mr. Smith's inbox.

Ability to Reach Large Numbers of Constituents: High

As long as you have a valid e-mail addresses, and some assent by your constituents to receive electronic communication, you can easily reach as many of them as you wish: hundreds, thousands, even millions! And this is easily accomplished through a few clicks of a program at your end. Your ability to reach your constituents electronically is limited only by your diligence in augmenting your database with current e-mail addresses and by the constituents' agreement to receive e-mail from you: their opt-in.

Cost: Low, Low, Low

Pixels are cheaper than paper; e-mail solicitation applications and software less expensive than mail house equipment; and all of that is far less expensive than airline tickets, gas, cab fare—and lunch at Delmonico's. Most of the cost involved in e-mail soliciting is *your* time: the administrative overhead in managing this aspect of your fundraising effort and the staff creative overhead in getting a program and strategy approved and implemented.

Flexibility: Low-Medium

Because it is a low-cost electronic medium with virtually no costs of duplication, it is easier and more feasible to test messages in batches than direct mail and see how your constituents or certain targeted segments respond to a given message. You can test, fine-tune, and tweak prior to sending out a final database-wide "blast."

But you've heard the expression, "Diamonds are forever"? Well, so are e-mails. Once you make that click and your e-mail messages are sent off into the cyber-ether, there's no taking them back, no second chance. In this way, issues of accuracy are just as important as with the direct mail medium.

And once your e-mails are out there, those messages can live *forever* on the web. So, every message you craft, every paragraph, word, pixel—be prepared for it to find its way from someone's inbox into a broader electronic milieu like a blog or message board and live on into eternity.

A book could probably be written about problems with e-mail messaging; the most egregious examples are usually in one-to-one communication. It's one of the fascinating phenomena of this new electronic medium and the web in general that people write and say things they would never think of expressing personally or in physical written form: the angry e-mail one might send to a friend (or enemy) complete with expletives, the overly candid pictures that someone posts on his or her MySpace page, the highly opinionated entry he makes on a controversial blog that someone can pull up with a search engine. Remember: The web is not a private space. It is a public one.

The Telephone Medium

Visiting prospects personally, sending them mail, sending them e-mail: choices, choices, choices! So, where does the phone fit in—the fourth "arrow" in your quiver? What's good about it? What's bad? What, if anything, makes it unique and sets it apart from your other choices?

Degree of Personalization: High, Personal: One to One

Well, at least it *can* be very personal, if you choose to make it so. Like a personal visit, the communication is one to one. You have a human being, perhaps yourself, informed about the mission of your organization and its needs, ready to make a compelling case for funding and ready to make a proposal to a prospect or a constituent. At the other end is a human being, an existing constituent or a potential one. The telephone allows for a personal, human, verbal exchange.

Furthermore, even in a telemarketing setting where a solicitor dials prospect after prospect, while the phone is ringing, a good fundraiser can glance over Mr. Smith's record to get a clearer picture of who he is. Perhaps Mr. Smith graduated in 1973—wow, he must be close to 60 years old, in his prime giving years, economically secure, but not yet retired "on a fixed income." Or, you may notice from Mr. Smith's record that he has been a subscriber to your theater since 1982 and shares with his wife some of the best seats in the house. Hmmm, do you think he might be able to give more than, say, the new subscriber with seats far back in the theater? Or perhaps Mr. Smith has been giving every year for the last five years, starting out with modest gifts, but last year he gave over $100. And to top it all off, he signed up to receive the urgent "Environmental Alert" e-mail blasts. Does that give you any clue, as a fundraiser, as to his sense of affiliation and commitment to organization?

If you're a fundraiser using the telephone to communicate, the several seconds you have to review a constituent's record as the telephone dials, or the few seconds early into a call after your predictive dialing system has connected, can help you develop a mental image of Mr. Smith, anticipate what his giving potential may be, and then tailor your generic fundraising approach to appeal to him as an *individual*.

Type of Channel: Two-Way Channel

Well, at least in the telephone medium, it *can* be a two-way street—if you are not using a simple sales pitch you must read word for word, while Mr. Smith, drumming his five fingers on the kitchen table, graciously waits for you to deliver your spiel and does not hang up on you.

Ideally, the telephone affords *two-way* communication, just like a personal visit. You can use the telephone to inform and express and to communicate the needs of your organization in a compelling way in order to move Mr. Smith to action.

But also consider the fact that the telephone, like a personal visit, enables a good fundraiser to listen and hear. Mr. Smith may have something he wants to say. He may want to offer an opinion or take your call as an opportunity to express his views about something he thinks is important to a representative of the organization of which he is a current or prospective constituent.

Moreover, if you consider fundraising as "The Art of the Ask," a good fundraiser sooner or later in the course of a telephone call is going to be asking a question. Indeed, even hardcore telephone pitches begin and end with a question: *May I speak to Mr. Smith?* And *Mr. Smith, can you give just $25?*

Why not use the telephone medium to ask the prospect questions from the beginning and lead the prospect to your desired conclusion by asking questions? Good fundraisers, like good salespeople, can control a call, or a visit, by the art of asking good questions. That's why the most effective telephone fundraising calls, either personal or by phone, are ones that establish dialogue with prospects and create goodwill.

As I used to demonstrate in trainings to hundreds of telephone fund-raising trainees over the years, holding up a telephone so everyone could see, "Look the telephone has *two* parts, a mouthpiece *and* a receiver. Good fundraisers use both, so please, whatever you do, please *listen* as well as speak!"

It is only by listening to prospects that a fundraiser can uncover clues to Mr. Smith's giving potential that may not be apparent in his donor record. By listening for those clues, the really good fundraisers will be able to ferret out the prospects that can give $1,000 from those who can give only $25—or nothing at all.

Degree of Interruption: Interruptive

It's unfortunate, but other than showing up at a prospect's door un-announced, the telephone is the mostly highly interruptive of all the media available to fundraisers to solicit gifts from prospects. Sure, sending a precall letter or postcard can seek to ameliorate the interruptive quality of a ringing phone to some degree by letting the prospect know in advance that a phone call is coming.

But in the final analysis, when the phone rings, Mr. Smith is involved in doing something else. Picture all of the possibilities. Mr. Smith may be snoozing on the couch after a grueling five-day business trip, awakened by the ringing phone. He may have just rushed into the house, fumbling with his keys, to catch your incoming call on its fifth and final ring, dropping a bag of groceries in pursuit. He may be in the middle of his favorite cable news program, intensely focused on some life-or-death issue of national impor-tance. He may be upstairs, putting his two-year-old child to bed, singing her favorite lullaby, and the seventh time through, she was almost asleep! He may be on his cell phone, rushing through traffic to get to the airport, having just been cut off by a crazy cab driver. Or, that favorite and most common circumstance, you may have interrupted Mr. Smith at the dinner table, right in the middle of his favorite Wednesday night dish: meatloaf.

Talk about awkward! But there is no way around it. That's why the precious early seconds of a phone call are critical to its success or failure. You want to get Mr. Smith to drop what he is doing, at least for a bit, and talk to you.

But one way *not* to ensure success: talking as fast as you can to get through your pitch. How many times have I heard a fundraiser, upon being informed by the prospect that he had just been interrupted, then lurch forward, *That's okay, Mr. Smith, I'll be brief* . . . and then begin to talk at a speed that is barely intelligible!

So, the telephone medium is particularly vulnerable to the vicissitudes of prospects' mood of the moment. If you've interrupted Mr. Smith from something he liked doing, it is a hurdle to overcome.

Message Timing: Immediate

On the positive side of the ledger, you *know* if your message has been received.

Yes, you may have difficulty in reaching Mr. Smith, making multiple dialed attempts that result in no answers, busy signals, answering machines, or third-party contacts saying, *I'm sorry, he's not home right now!*

But ultimately, either you will speak to Mr. Smith or you will not. And once you have spoken to him, you more than likely will know the result. At one extreme, Mr. Smith may hang up on you. Or, more graciously, he may simply decline your invitation to participate in the annual giving program this year. At the other extreme, you may have negotiated a pledge for $100,000—and Mr. Smith agrees to put it all on his "Prestige Platinum" credit card, right now. Oh joy!

Dimensionality: One-Dimensional

As video phones are not yet in common use (and hopefully never will be), the telephone fundraiser must rely on one sensory dimension to communicate his or her message: verbal, spoken language between two parties. Yes, some telephone fundraising programs have experimented by augmenting the verbal with special recorded messages: *Mr. Smith, can you please wait for a special message from our party chairman?* That tactic may serve to buy some credibility for a lowly telephone fundraiser. Moreover, perhaps that is even augmented with Hollywood production–style music and sound effects. But in the final analysis, it's the verbal interaction of fundraiser and prospect that will either raise funds for your organization or will not.

That said, skilled fundraisers can use the one dimension they have to their best advantage. For example, let's say that you're trying to reach Mr. Smith, a mature-sounding woman answers the phone, agrees to put you through to the prospect, and you hear in the background: *John, the telephone is for you, it's XYZ organization.* If you know from the donor's record that Mr. Smith is not of school age, one might reasonably conclude that it's the prospect's spouse who answered.

Or perhaps a teenager answers the phone and you hear him say: *Pop, it's for you! Just a minute, he's coming.* Perhaps you are calling the prospect at home, and you hear in the background the din of a large number of people, some laughing, levity, and the sound of a piano. Perhaps Mr. Smith is having a party! Or Mr. Smith may answer the phone himself, but you can hear the sounds of a television in the background and hear an announcer say: *It's World News Tonight, with Charlie Gibson. Top story tonight, the jobless rate is up, and the economy is down.* Gee, couldn't it have been good news for a change?

Or perhaps Mr. Smith sounds particularly short and even more irritated when he hears you announce the name of your organization, or conversely, he sounds excited and happy to hear from you: *I'm really glad you called—I need to upgrade my membership this year!* Hey, it *does* happen.

So, good fundraisers are good listeners. All of these things you hear, from background noise to the prospect's tone can provide valuable clues to Mr. Smith's mood of the moment that can help you tailor your approach to him.

Let's consider a possibility, further into the call, when you ask Mr. Smith to consider making a large gift to XYZ organization, perhaps $1,000, and you experience a long pause in response, the prospect taking in a deep breath. Doesn't that mean you asked for so much money that you've knocked the wind out of him? Or does it mean that he's thinking about it, mulling it over? Rather than bulling ahead with your pitch, perhaps you simply wait for Mr. Smith to respond—or ask a follow-up question if it's not clear what he means. What you hear can provide valuable clues as to Mr. Smith's giving potential.

In the final analysis, unlike a personal visit, which has a distinct visual dimension and the opportunity for both fundraiser and prospect to communicate both visually and aurally, the telephone medium has only the verbal/aural. Use it to your best advantage.

Time of Attention: Medium

Setting the interruptive nature of a telephone solicitation aside, once you have Mr. Smith on the line, and he agrees to speak with you, you can focus him on your message more clearly, for a longer time than any other medium short of a personal visit.

He may glance at your letters or your e-mails, perhaps even reading them and, most desirably, devoting a couple of minutes or more to consider your appeal and to respond.

Sure, Mr. Smith may answer the phone, hear the name of your organization, and blurt out *I don't accept telephone solicitations—take me off your list!* And then proceed to hang up on you.

But barring that, a skilled fundraiser can usually hold Mr. Smith's interest, lengthen a call that may early on have been shortened by the prospect with an perfunctory, *if this is a fundraising call, I'm not interested!* Every second that Mr. Smith invests in continuing to communicate with you helps you create a dialogue, develop rapport, establish a two-way channel of communication, and thereby lay the foundation for you to make an ask.

Granted, the nature of the medium will not permit you to chat with Mr. Smith for 45 minutes or an hour, the way a personal visit can. Nor would you want to spend that long—you have too many prospects to reach.

But the longer you can expand Mr. Smith's attention beyond 10 seconds, beyond 30 seconds, and into the realm of a couple of minutes, perhaps more, the more likely you are to achieve a "yes" as opposed to a "no." Each prospect has that optimal time limit—a window through which you can establish a relationship and make a successful appeal that will be the maximum possible, considering his or her ability and willingness to give to your organization. Find it.

Reliability: High

In the telephone medium, you *know* if your message has gotten through, if it's been received. And most usually, you know the outcome.

E-mails may bounce, direct mail may be returned—and you generally know if that has happened and can update your records accordingly. However, if either letters or e-mails are received, there is no assurance they will be opened, read, or considered. You will never know. At a risk of an inappropriate metaphor, with the telephone, you know if your arrow has struck its target. In a personal visit, you can see it. In the telephone medium, you can hear it.

Ability to Reach Large Numbers of Constituents: High

Depending on the technology available to the office or agency doing the soliciting, the accuracy of the phone list, the length and type of the script, and the degree of affiliation of the targeted constituents, a single telephone fundraiser can reach between 3 and 20 prospects in an hour. If you have a staff of 20 fundraisers, over the course of a month you can reach thousands of prospects, with ease and a speed that is simply impossible in face-to-face meeting.

Of course, you won't be able to reach *every* prospect on your list. Inevitably, there will be a large number whom you can never seem to catch at home or who screen out your calls with their answering machines (or another household member). Furthermore, no matter how updated your list of telephone numbers may be, even with prospects who have been constituents of your organization for years, there will be a percentage of wrong numbers without a forwarding number and numbers not in service.

So, even in the best of circumstances, you'll only be able to reach a bit more than half of the names on your list, though list penetrations of close to 80 percent are possible (at a higher cost) for selected segments of donors, whose telephone numbers are long established and who are receptive to speaking to a representative of your organization.

You've heard the expression that "man does not live by bread alone"? Well, good fundraising campaigns do not rely on "phone alone," but include it in a mix of media, part of a broader strategy to reach out to your constituents in a variety of ways.

Cost: Moderate

Unlike e-mail, which costs pennies to reach individual prospects, or direct mail, which can cost several quarters, the cost of soliciting by phone is usually measured in dollars. But it's still a lot less than a "sales" call, which, depending on which study you look at, can range from an average of about $100 to over $300.

Telephone long distance rates used to be a big cost factor. But with competition by long distance carriers and the new option of using the Internet (VOIP, Voice Over Internet Protocol), telephone expenses are no longer such a limiting factor.

The big cost is labor—that is, the cost of paying for a staff of telephone fundraisers. Of course, you can save on that expense by recruiting a group of volunteers. Using volunteers has some distinct advantages, since they are usually knowledgeable and committed constituents themselves, require less training as a consequence, and can communicate with other constituents comfortably and genuinely.

Moreover, such volunteer efforts frequently use existing facilities: the organization's development office phones that are used administratively during the day or perhaps professional offices donated by a constituent, like a law office with many phones. This eliminates the necessity of an up-front capital expenditure on office and telephone equipment, expenses that can run into the tens and hundreds of thousands of dollars.

But phonathon outreach efforts are usually ill suited to reach out to the thousands or tens of thousands of prospects many organizations seek to solicit. Volunteers simply don't have that much time or fortitude.

This leaves an organization seeking to incorporate the telephone as an essential element of a development strategy with a dilemma: Do I undertake the investment of creating and staffing my own phone center or do I farm it out to a fundraising or a telemarketing company with the facilities and expertise to contact my constituents on my behalf?

Creating, managing, and staffing a professional call center is an ambitious undertaking (along with the mail house capability for precall letters or postcall confirmations). It is an expense so significant that it is unlikely to repay its overhead unless it is operated year-round—requiring the organization to have a list of sufficient size to warrant it.

Most organizations with lists numbering less than 100K, but too many for a volunteer effort, usually opt to contract with an ethical, trustworthy outside agency experienced in telephone fundraising. Such an agency's staff will already have been trained and experienced in various fundraising and marketing techniques. But the staff will need to be trained to know your organization's mission and the objectives of the fundraising campaign and be able to communicate that to your constituents.

Furthermore, an outside agency will have facilities and equipment necessary to conduct a truly professional telephone campaign. The list of such facilities is quite extensive: phones, dialers, predictive dialers, call center software and computer technology, agent computer terminals and/or systems, telephones, headsets, evaluation software and reporting, agent stations, soundproofing, chairs and other furniture, break facilities, mail house center equipment and staffing, and administrative structures to support all of the above, from training, management, accounting, creative staff, clients services, and so forth.

The cost and complexity of creating, maintaining, and managing a quality call center, with dozens, hundreds, or thousands of employees, is substantial indeed.

Flexibility: High

Let's say that it's the first night of your telephone fundraising program. Your telephone fundraising staff is using a script that emphasizes giving to the Century Fund endowment campaign, with a first ask of $1,000. After two hours and monitoring the constituents' reactions, you have only three pledges, two for $25 and another for $50—far less than you had anticipated. Back to the drawing board! On the fly, your phone managers do some tweaking, emphasizing "student scholarship" rather than endowment, and they begin the negotiation with a first ask of $500 instead of $1,000. It works! Pledge rates shoot up, with a healthy average gift. Such strategic shifts, on the fly, are possible only in the telephone medium—and you may have found that you burned less than 5 percent of your total list to find the right formula.

The telephone can also enable tactical, prospect-by-prospect shifts as well. In this way the telephone is nearly as flexible as a personal visit. As we mentioned earlier, because the telephone is a two-way communication channel, the prospect himself or herself may give you implied or explicit clues about his or her interests, involvement with your organization, and giving potential.

What an individual fundraiser hears can provide the information that fundraiser needs to alter his or her approach to the prospect and change from a standard pitch to something more personal and appropriate for Mr. Smith.

Let's say that you make a call, the purpose of which is to emphasize the funding of student scholarships, but in the course of your conversation, you find that Mr. Smith has no interest in that, but instead, only feels a sense of affinity and loyalty to the biology department from which he graduated. Well, if your organization permits, rather than no gift at all, why not allow Mr. Smith to designate his pledge to the biology department?

Or let's say that Mr. Smith, in response to your proposal for a $500 gift, says something to the effect: *I just can't do quite that much, right now.* So, Mr. Smith *"can't do that much right now."* Does that mean he could do that much *later*? How much later? Does it mean he could do $250 now, and then, three or six months later, give another $250? As a good, sensitive, perceptive, listening fundraiser, perhaps you should find out!

In states that permit monitoring of calls by a third party for training purposes, the telephone affords another unique advantage. For example, let's say a manager is listening to a telephone call. The fundraiser, a young woman named Elaine who was hired only two weeks ago, is making a call on behalf of a symphony orchestra that has been awarded a challenge grant. Elaine calls one of the orchestra's loyal donors, Mrs. Benton Smith. As the phone is dialing, Elaine notices Mrs. Smith's donor record: She has reliably given $1,000 each year, *except* for last year.

While monitoring your fundraising staff, you notice Elaine is stuck in negotiation by an obstreperous Mrs. Smith, who is refusing to give anything at all this year because, in her words, *the orchestra plays too much damn modern music!* What is poor Elaine to do? She doesn't want to lose what has been a great donor, but doesn't have the experience or knowledge to turn the situation around. Obviously, she can't say, *Mrs. Smith, I'll ensure next season the orchestra will play only Beethoven and Brahms.* That would not be truthful, and besides, might get her fired if her manager is listening!

Well, the manager who *is* listening comes to the rescue! He hears the situation over the monitor and goes directly to Elaine's station and whispers in her ear: *Tell Mrs. Smith that her opinion is VERY important to us, and I'll make sure the executive director knows how she feels . . . but it would be a shame to lose your support this year, especially with the challenge grant. Can't she at least renew her $1,000 gift?*

Mrs. Benton Smith, her blood pressure slowly coming down, thanks to Elaine's cheerful demeanor and willingness to listen, is so happy that someone finally listened to her complaint. At long last, she had the chance to register her dissatisfaction, a dissonance that will be resonate up the chain of command. She relents and sweetly says, *well dear, I think we can make it*

$1,500 this year. Score one for the home team. Or perhaps we should say, what a lovely coda!

Strategies for Using the Telephone in Fundraising Campaigns

The telephone, while not cheap, is not outrageously expensive either. Moreover, it is highly personal, flexible, reliable, and can give you immediate results. So, why not just phone everyone on your list?

Well, first of all, while it is less expensive than personal visits, you may simply not have the budget to place a call to everyone on your list. Also, as we have said, you won't get through to everyone, maybe only half or less. Most organizations want to give everyone on their list some kind of opportunity to give.

Let's examine different organizational objectives and strategies for using the phone.

Strategy: Budgetary Limitations

Let's say your development budget will enable you to send out a bulk mailing to 15,000 nondonor constituents, word-processed letters you can produce at your office to 1,500 past donors (which you'll try to hand sign), but that leaves only $1,500 left for anything else in your direct marketing effort. You've sent out requests for proposals (RFPs) to telephone fundraising firms in the past and know that to call the 10,000 or so records for which you have phone numbers will cost over $30,000. You don't have it.

Why not consider a volunteer or even a staff phonathon to reach out to the 400 or 500 past donors that don't respond to your word-processed direct mailing? The $1,500 left in your budget would more than cover the telephone expenses and leave plenty of room for refreshments and prizes. To break even, all you need to do is renew three $500 donors who didn't respond to the mail solicitation. So, even in this context, the phone can play some part in your overall strategy.

Objective: Increase Participation

Your organization, say a public university, has just been awarded a $100,000 challenge grant by a well-known foundation with the goal of increasing alumni participation to the Annual Fund. You're the director of the Annual Fund and have a list of 50,000 alumni who have *never* given, despite having received a bulk mail solicitation every year.

In order to get participation up, your boss, the Vice President of Development, is willing to break even, perhaps even take a small loss, on the investment to more personally solicit these nondonors. He wants to make sure as many prospective donors as possible know about the unique opportunity and help the organization take full advantage of the challenge. The thinking goes, *if we can get 'em on board this year, maybe we can renew them next year.*

You budget sending out a bulk mailing, as you normally do, but this time highlighting the challenge grant. In it you include a return envelope and suggest that if they don't respond, a representative of the school might call. This time, response is better; 2 percent send in their first-ever gift—a total of 100 checks in the mail.

To back up the mailing, you have received a proposal from a telephone fundraising firm to solicit the nonrespondents, the remaining 30,000 for which you have phone numbers, at a cost approaching $100,000. It's quite an investment, but even if the program achieves breakeven results, you'll more than cover it when you consider the impact of the challenge grant monies.

It's the first night of calling; you help train the telephone fundraising staff and go back to the call center to see what happens next. You are nervous, perspiring, worried that the risk won't be worth it, that the program will bomb. Frankly, you're worried about your job.

But just 10 minutes after calling begins, a caller raises his hand to indicate he has a pledge. It's only $25, but at least that's a start. Another hand goes up for $50. Then another for $100. Just an hour later, the call center's best fundraiser, a young woman named Claire, raises her hand—she has a $1,000 pledge. Hooray—you hug your assistant and a do a little dance and go back out to congratulate the fundraiser. Hey, you think, this thing might actually work!

You watch the daily reports come in and five weeks later have the bottom line:

30,000	Number of prospects
12,000	Number contacted with decisions
2,640	Number of pledges (22 percent of those contacted)
$65.00	Average pledge
$171,605	Total amount pledged

Whew, even with a collection rate of 58 percent, we'll break even on this! Enter the hero.

Objective: Upgrade Gifts

You are a large organization with thousands and thousands of donors. You ask your IT department for an analysis: How many donors over $25 but under $1,000 have been stuck at the same level for the last three or more years? Your report yields the following data:

$25–49	11,239
$50–99	8,427
$100–249	2,102
$500–999	572

Furthermore, your organization has recently decided to implement "donor recognition" levels that afford the donors with some nominal "benefits" to recognize and thank them for their generosity.

You send a direct mail piece out, explaining the new donor recognition levels, inviting each to upgrade to the next giving level. The direct mail has modest success: of the 22,340 donor records, 55 percent merely renew their previous gift, but about 7 percent, a total of 1,564 donors, send in larger gifts than they had the previous year—a modestly successful result. The remaining 8,490 donors do not respond.

You have a choice. You can mail another follow-up letter imploring the past donors to merely renew their gift once again, or you can invest a bit more money and telephone the prospects to personally thank each of them for their past generosity and invite each of the to join a new, higher, more prestigious donor group. You choose to go for the gold. Perhaps your donors haven't responded or become more substantially committed to your cause because they've never been personally asked!

You launch your upgrade phone campaign to those 8,490 who didn't respond with any gift at all. Six weeks later, you get the final report:

8,490 prospects called

4,924 contacts/decisions

4,037 pledges (82 percent)

1,537 upgrades (38 percent of the pledges)

$149 (average upgraded gift, versus $89 prior average gift)

Not too bad, you say! Making a personal visit by telephone instantly recovered the vast majority of the regular donors who did not respond to the first direct mailing, and of those who renewed, more than a third upgraded, against only 7 percent through direct mail. And the average upgraded gift was nearly 60 percent higher!

Objective: Capital Commitment

Your organization has hired a consultant and has determined the feasibility of conducting a $5 million capital campaign. Of your 9,000 or so constituents, they determine that perhaps 500 should be targeted for personal visitation, each potentially capable of giving four or five figures or even more. Of the remainder, many have been loyal contributors to the Annual Fund, some even giving as much as $1,000.

The nature of the commitment you are seeking is over the five-year period of the campaign, over and above the amount they give annually. And because the capital campaign has a number of dimensions and is a once-in-a-generation event, to ensure maximum participation and enable everyone to participate, you want to approach each individual constituent as personally as possible.

Since it's simply not feasible to visit each one at his or her home, why not visit each by phone? Through the telephone medium, a representative of your organization will be able to reestablish ties, build rapport and create an atmosphere of goodwill, answer the prospects' questions and objections about the campaign, and then actively negotiate a financial commitment, which can involve installments and arrangements over a number of years.

General Strategies/Rule: Least Expensive to Most Expensive

As a general rule, most organizations want to solicit all of their constituents in one way or another, giving everyone an opportunity to participate. With such a goal, it makes sense to achieve results with the least expensive media first:

1. E-mail solicitation to all those prospects with e-mail addresses.
2. Bulk direct mail to those prospects without e-mail addresses.
3. Personalized mail to prospects determined to have higher giving potential (current donors, or/or high-level lapsed donors).
4. Telephone follow-up to prospects who have not responded to 1, 2, 3—best prospective donors first, as budget will allow.
5. The remaining prospects who do not respond, sending out Jake, a 6-foot, 3-inch tall, 240-pound bouncer and ex-longshoreman to the prospects' homes for "personal persuasion." (Joking, though I know many of you have thought about it at one time or another.)

Summary

So, where should the telephone fit into your overall strategy to raise money? It depends on the mix of media you are currently using to reach constituents to solicit them and your organizational objectives. If you have an in-house phone facility, your managers may be eager to solicit nearly everyone by telephone. At the risk of an inappropriate metaphor, "when the tool you have is a hammer, everything looks like a nail," you can manage to telephone nearly everyone and achieve an impressive top line revenue figure—at a cost.

At the other extreme are development officers who are so telephone averse that they envision that "hammer" as something figuratively hitting the heads of their prospects, leading to more headaches for everyone. They don't want to phone anyone.

But each medium, snail mail, e-mail, personal visits, and the telephone, has its strengths and weaknesses. Each, used properly in a carefully evaluated, coordinated campaign, can help you achieve your development objectives, be they for this year or over a multiyear strategic plan.

CHAPTER 2

Scripting Strategies

In direct mail, you have an extraordinarily wide variety of options in deciding how to approach your constituents. You can send a one-page, two-page, three-page (or more) letter. Or you can choose to send a postcard instead. You can send a mailing out metered bulk, stamped bulk, or first-class stamped or metered. You can send letters out on regular business-size stock, on personal stationery, or using some other special size paper. Your mailing might simply be duplicated through offset printing, or each letter can be produced through laser or ink-jet printing, with a wide range of personalization.

The signatory can be you, your boss, the president, a respected constituent, or a well-known celebrity or personality. The style of the text can range from a formal, institutional request to more a more casual, informal style of writing that may mimic the way the writer speaks.

You may choose to hand sign all of the letters, or only some of them, further personalizing some by writing a special note in the margin of the letter or as a postscript to make the prospect feel that the communication is personal.

Moreover, your mailing might have a variety of inserts, from simply a pledge card and a reply envelope, to some self-contained form for donors to return their checks or provide their credit card information. Your mailing might further include an insert of some sort, perhaps a brochure and explanation of donor recognition levels from which the prospective donor can choose.

Bottom line, the range of mailings you can choose to produce is varied and vast.

In the world of telephone fundraising, it's a bit simpler: You have a caller, you have a telephone, you have a prospect, and you have some kind of *written text* that guides the caller in making fundraising solicitation. Regardless of what kind of written text you produce for your caller, whether it's provided on written sheets of paper, or whether it's provided through a computer system monitor, the product of sophisticated, logical branched scripting, it is just that: text that either guides a fundraiser and/or text that will be vocalized.

Prescriptive versus Nonprescriptive Scripts

The approach that one takes in providing that text for a telephone fundraiser falls in a continuum from being totally prescriptive to nonprescriptive.

Prescriptive text that fundraisers are required to read, virtually word for word with little deviation or questions, is generally known as a script—or a hard script.

At the other end of the continuum is a call guide—a written list of instructions for a caller, suggestions on approaching a prospect on the telephone, a list of things to remember to say, some suggestions of points to emphasize, and some guidance on how to ask for a gift and confirming one if the reply is yes.

Every person who has been charged with the unenviable task of producing the text that telephone fundraisers will use in soliciting prospects will have their own preferences based on what kind of text, or script, he or she will use and what form the text will take.

First, what each person writes may be influenced by his or her own perceptions of what will push the hot buttons of constituents and his or her own style of speaking or writing. The scriptwriter then translates that into text she believes will be compelling over the telephone medium. The effectiveness of what she writes is further colored by her own experience in prior fundraising positions, maybe even her own experience as a telephone fundraiser. (Many of the best development officers today got their first experience in the trenches!)

The kind of script she uses may be further influenced by what the organization has done in the past. Indeed, the writer may have no choice in the matter at all, the scripting decision being made by a superior or, gasp, a committee. Finally, the writer may not have to worry about writing a script at all, choosing to trust the expertise of the outside telephone fundraising firm, needing only to review the draft for tone and factual accuracy.

The actual physical form the script takes depends on the technology available. Most often, it's simple, word-processed sheets of paper from which the telephone fundraiser reads or is guided. Professional telemarketing firms, or high-tech inside fundraising bureaus, have computer applications that allow fundraisers to view the script from a screen and toggle between sections. Sophisticated applications even involve "logical branched" scripting, where different text appears for the caller based on the input of the prospect's responses or objections.

One End of the Spectrum: The Hard Script

Here, the scriptwriter drafts a text for ALL of the telephone fundraisers to read, word for word, or virtually so. Of course, good fundraisers using a hard script generally do better if they don't *sound* like they are reading, in a stilted manner.

Advantages

There are some distinct advantages to using a hard script in some circumstances.

Uniformity One of the great challenges of managing a telephone fundraising program is that callers are individuals, and when involved in a dialogue with a prospect, they can veer off course and may even provide information that is inaccurate or engage the prospect inappropriately. By requiring callers to deliver only the text you have created, *you* control the message, its quality, tone, and accuracy.

Control In addition to control of the message that you're putting out, dialogue and interchange with the prospect are also controlled. With the conversation being mostly one-way, there is less chance for the prospect to gain control and lead the fundraiser astray. Sure, there can be dialogue even in hard-scripted situations. But such dialogue occurs "off the script."

Testing If you're controlling a single message that's being delivered, you can quickly see the results. Through monitoring calls, statistical evaluation, and agent feedback, you may find that you're not getting the results you anticipated with your script. To improve results, you can adjust the script on the fly, fine-tune it with edits and improvements, or test an entirely new message altogether.

Training Because the message is precise and controlled—and there is more limited conversation and dialogue demanded with a hard script— less agent training and prep time is necessary to get a telephone fundraising program up and running. Each individual fundraiser doesn't have to be the most talented rapport builder, drawing on innate qualities to develop relationships over the phone: the ability to schmooze. Nor does each agent need to be fabulously articulate, inculcated with vast quantities of background information on the institution, or the most experienced and cunning negotiator. The fundraiser's job is to deliver the script.

Time-Saving Not only does a hard script save time in training, it saves time in the phone calls. Hard-scripted phone calls are usually shorter, since there is less dialogue, and an individual telephone fundraiser, regardless of whether he is punching a touch-tone telephone or is connected to live prospects with the latest predictive dialing technology, can reach more prospects per hour with a succinct, focused script. And the thinking goes, the more prospects you contact, the more money you raise (setting aside the issue of pledge rates and average gifts).

Less Costly   Of course, time is money. If your agent time per contact is less, so is your cost. Telephone fundraiser salaries are the single greatest expense in a telephone fundraising effort. Using focused scripts gets your callers through the database in fewer hours.

Disadvantages

So, does it sound like the hard script is the way to go? Well, there are some real disadvantages as well.

Impersonal   Because the direction of the communication is essentially one-way, and the solicitor asks few if any questions other than "*Will you give $x?,*" prospective donors view the call as only a solicitation of them; they perceive they are simply another prospect on a telemarketer's list.

Neutral or Negative public relations (PR) factor   The nature of the telephone affords *two-way* communication. You are using mostly *one*, and not using the telephone as a friend-raising as well as fundraising vehicle. Doing so may save money, but also can represent a lost opportunity that can help solidify a donor relationship for the long term.

Limited Negotiating Horizon   Because so little time in the phone call is invested up front to develop rapport or to reestablish a prior relationship of the prospect with the nonprofit, prospects are likely to grant the solicitor less time, resulting in "one and done" and "two and out" negotiations.

One of my more hardcore solicitors, let's call him Nathan, had a substantial amount of telemarketing sales experience prior to joining our staff. Once, after I implored him to do a better job of building rapport with our client's prospects, Nathan countered with his no-nonsense approach. Nathan, pushing up his horn-rimmed glasses, leaned back in his chair, put his feet up on the desk, and looked up at me with the back of his head cradled in his hands, and said laconically, "It's not like we're trying to get them to drink their milk and cookies; they know we just want their money!"

Well, that's one view, and he *was* very successful, statistically speaking.

Less Optimal Pledge Rates and Average Gifts   Because of the shorter, more concentrated negotiating horizon in a one-way solicitation, pledge rates and average gifts are arguably lower than in a format that would lay groundwork for more extensive negotiating on an individual basis.

Fundraiser Morale   You are the experts who have provided what you will believe is a winning script. So, what you are insisting your solicitors read better be good. If what you've written does not work, that is, it creates lots of refusals, either your fundraising staff will jettison it and start doing their own thing or become very frustrated because they can't. Nothing is more demoralizing in life than to endure refusal after refusal after refusal.

So, what does a hard script look like? For a sample please take a look at the Appendix, Section B.

The Other End of the Spectrum: The Call Guide

Call guides can take a variety of forms. Some are just a list of instructions to a caller with information that aids and enables them to make solicitations on their own, in their own words. Others are a little more focused, providing a checklist of things they should remember to say, while still giving callers wide latitude on how to say it. Others are more focused still and provide an outline of an effective call process, with suggested prompts—words and phases that a caller can use verbatim or put into his or her own words.

Advantages

Sounds like call guides are pretty loosey-goosey? Well, there are some distinct advantages.

Potentially More Personal   Because the caller is using her own words, she has the opportunity to engage a prospective donor one on one with two-way conversation. Indeed, the entire call can be more conversational and sound less like a solicitation. This can lead the prospect to be a little more interested and engaged than if he was simply listening to a pitch.

Positive PR Potential   Frequently, call guides suggest the caller do some friend-raising as well as fundraising. For example, volunteers, say, members of the Class of 1983, might be making calls to their fellow classmates to solicit a class gift for the upcoming alumni day. The call might be a chance for two old classmates to recollect the good old days or perhaps share a story about the infamous biology professor, Dr. Phoebes, who used to flunk all the incoming freshmen. The chat they have can lay the groundwork for a gift, perhaps even a substantial one, to honor their class, or perhaps the We Survived Phoebes Fund.

Fundraiser Morale: Potentially Exploits Their Natural Verbal Skills   Call guides are frequently used in situations where you have a core group of volunteers who are already familiar with the organization for which they are raising money, so they don't need a lot of training on the background of the institution. Furthermore, these volunteers are committed to the objectives and success of the fundraising program; otherwise, they wouldn't be there in the first place. To force them to read a verbatim script and to treat them as mere solicitors might make them feel less valued.

Providing a guide and then "letting them loose" shows you have confidence in their natural abilities and provides them some element of self-esteem, especially if they are successful. That makes call guides a particularly useful tool in peer-to-peer fundraising (arguably the most effective format) and allows volunteers to connect with their fellow constituents person to person.

Disadvantages

In many situations, however, the negatives of call guides can outweigh the positives.

Uniformity of Message   With a call guide, your callers will know the general thrust of the fundraising campaign, but each will emphasize what he or she thinks is important and will put that into his or her own words. If you have a dozen callers, you may have a dozen different messages, each with its own set of facts and its own tone.

Control and Testing   For example, let's assume you are the development director for a museum, and you feel, based on your experience and your intuition, that your membership will be most interested in funding educational outreach programs.

Some of your volunteers, however, are really vested in the Keep Museum Sundays Free initiative. With volunteers, it will be hard to bend them to your direction. Moreover, if you are using a call guide approach with professional fundraisers, the same thing applies—each may willfully go his or her own way to achieve results. If some callers aren't reaching hoped-for response rates, it's extraordinarily difficult to get some of them on track, because there are so many tracks they can follow. So, from a management standpoint, you have far less control than requiring simple adherence to a pitch.

Time and Effectiveness   Some of your callers will have the gift of gab and will spend 20 minutes, 30 minutes, or more gleefully chatting with prospects about the organization or even matters totally unrelated to it. A few others may cycle through the lists of prospects at high speed, but with little success. Generally speaking, you will usually find that you'll make fewer telephone solicitations per hour than you would with a more focused vehicle than a call guide, and that the fewer, better, more naturally gifted callers will achieve dramatically better results and a far wider variation in overall caller performance.

Training   Some callers, particularly volunteers using a call guide, will be particularly adept at making friends and doing positive PR for your organization. But when it comes to the ask, their toes curl and their tongue gets stuck in their throat. With some individual coaching, you might be able to get them to ask, *Mr. Smith, can you give a little something this year?* Others, volunteers or new hires, will be congenitally unable to ask for a specific dollar amount on their own. That's simply the facts of fundraising. However, even those so congenitally disabled may at least have the capability to be trained to read a simple script with a stipulated dollar ask.

Sample Call Guide

So what does a Call Guide look like? We've provided a sample in the Appendix, Sections B and C. The names and places have been changed to protect both the innocent and the guilty.

Somewhere in the Middle: The Hybrid Soft Script or Call Outline

Somewhere in the middle between hard scripts and call guides are vehicles that seek to have the best of both worlds, allowing callers to engage prospects in dialogue and two-way communication without completely losing control of a call.

This is typically accomplished by incorporating questions in a script, borrowing from a sales process to lead the prospect in a desired direction, ultimately a pledge. And with soft scripting the author will try to provide some focused, pithy text that callers may be able to read virtually word for word in a conversational way to help them get back on track if two-way dialogue leads them astray, or to segue from one section or stage of a call to another.

This format gives an individual caller some freedom to conversationally engage the prospect and also permits, even encourages, prospects to ask questions and voice their own opinions and comments.

Advantages

Personal   Because there is dialogue and two-way communication is encouraged, the call will seem more personal to the prospect. Calls can even be tailored to the prospect, based on known variables in the organization's database. Perhaps the prospect, Mr. Smith, gives regularly to the Endangered Species program at the local zoo. Rather than merely thanking him for his past gift, you could thank him specifically for that, and update him on the good work you're doing in that area. Perhaps Mr. Smith has shown a willingness to respond to your advocacy organization's Action Alerts. Great, after you thank him for that, ask him what he thinks is the most important work your organization is doing, from two or three options.

Good fundraisers can even take the scripted segues of a call outline and make them seem natural and conversational, so Mr. Smith doesn't perceive he's just getting a pitch.

Positive PR Potential   By using the phone medium not just to hawk your organization's needs or tell what you think is important, Mr. Smith will feel he has a voice, and that voice is valued by your organization. This can put your organization in a very positive light, in his eyes, and help cement a relationship for the long term. That means more gifts and higher gifts in the long term.

Fundraiser Morale: Exploit Their Natural Skills   Your fundraising staff will be expected to listen, as well as speak. Adding the friend-raising and PR dimension to their job description can make them feel more important and valued as well.

Control and Uniformity   Using a soft script can help you maintain better managerial control over the message that you're putting out as opposed to a general call guide. If you decide that you want to emphasize the Museum Free Sundays program as opposed to the Educational Outreach Program, so be it. If you decide that you want to shift gears and emphasize something else or begin the first ask at $500 instead of $250, the soft script will afford you that measure of control.

Testing   And because you have a measure of control over the message, you can decide to change strategies, one against the other, in a controlled statistical evaluation. For example, you could divide half of your fundraisers with a student scholarship case statement, the other half emphasizing better funding of the library instead. That's hard to do in the environment of a general call guide.

Results   Because you are adding a PR component, and there is interactive dialogue that makes Mr. Smith feel like something more than a mere fundraising target, hopefully you'll experience higher pledge rates and, through a potentially more extended negotiating process, higher average gifts. At least, so you hope in order to justify the additional expense!

Disadvantages

Time   The friend-raising part takes phone time. By permitting, even encouraging Mr. Smith to speak, calls will be longer, caller control will be more difficult, and you'll be making fewer calls an hour as opposed to using a shorter, more focused hard script. You may be adding from a half minute to two minutes to a call. Furthermore, there will be a wider variation in call length. Some will be less than 30 seconds, but some may extend to 4 or 5 minutes, depending on the length and strength of the rapport-building process and how drawn out the process of negotiation is.

Training   First of all, you'll need fundraisers who can listen as well as speak, think, and react in addition to being able to deliver a compelling case. Finding fundraisers who can operate in this dimension effectively may be a challenge. And, because there is more risk in callers deviating from a straight-line call process due to dialogue and interaction with the prospect, more sophisticated training in techniques may be necessary to help them control the overall process of a call.

Costs   Longer calls, more training, possibly a higher level of communicator to boot = increased costs. And if you're a call center that needs to begin and end a client's program on a tight schedule, the longer you spend on the phone = the longer the program sits in your call center = higher administrative and fixed asset overhead.

Furthermore, many of the clients of professional telephone fundraising call centers, as you are well aware, are not that concerned about the long-range friend-raising dimension of their development programs. Their attitude may simply be: Show me the money! Now! With high turnover in the field of development, development professionals rapidly change jobs. Your phone room manager, or your client contact if you're a professional fundraising firm, might not be around for the aftermath.

Sample Soft Script

So what does a "soft script" look like? We've provided a sample in the Appendix, Sections B and H.

Final Analysis: Which Script Approach Is Best?

Well, the short answer is: It depends. A variety of issues weigh into the decision, including the giving potential of the prospect database, their degree of affiliation with their organization, your organizational values and tactical goals, and the reality of the kind of telephone fundraisers who will be making the calls.

Short-Range versus Long-Range View

Some organizations are perpetually in crisis mode and don't have the predilection or luxury of using the telephone as a cultivation tool. They simply need to make a lot of calls to as many records in their database as they can as fast and cheaply as they can, to add the revenue to *this year's* bottom line. They'll worry about next year, next year. This may augur for the use of a highly focused, high-energy hard script.

Just make sure that in using the telephone, your organization is not so overly aggressive that you are dragnet fishing your database, scraping the bottom of the philanthropic ocean bare, leaving nothing for future years.

Persnickety Prospects

Some groups of prospects, or perhaps your whole database, may loathe to be telemarketed—especially by *you*. Or perhaps your board or upper management is highly uncomfortable with the idea of being so aggressive as to interrupt constituents at dinner with a telephone fundraising call.

Who wants to deal with the complaints? "The telemarketer was short with me." "She didn't want to listen to what I had to say!" "The solicitor you hired couldn't answer even basic questions." "He was so inarticulate, not the kind of person you want representing us." Or even worse, "He hung up on me!" Ouch!

With these kinds of fears and premonitions perhaps you want to ease into the use of the telephone medium by recruiting a group of dedicated volunteers, like parents of alumni of a private school in an Annual Fund campaign, with a friendly, light-touch, call-guide approach. Or, barring that, explore contracting with a telephone fundraising firm that has experience in more hybrid scripting approaches, with communicators who may be able to develop rapport with your prospects.

With a phone campaign, you can see if there are any problems through monitoring and agent feedback, then fine-tune your approach to prevent prospect blowback or choosing to pull the plug on the telephone program altogether.

More Ambitious Objectives

Let's say you've been using the telephone successfully with a large group of prospects who give year in and year out. However, many are stuck in the $25 to $49 range. A few more have yet to crack the $100 plateau. They give, but using the conventional hard script, they aren't upgrading.

Why not experiment with a more hybrid call outline approach, do a little more PR up front, develop rapport, ask your constituents some questions about what *they* think is important or what interests *them*, and on that foundation, go for your upgrade? Hey, what you've tried before isn't upgrading them. Try another approach.

Or let's say you have a sizable group of Annual Fund donors and an even larger group of nondonors who, nonetheless, have an identified relationship with your organization and have at least some vested interest in your success. Your organization decides to mount a capital drive for building and endowment.

Given that you are seeking a *capital*-sized commitment over a number of years and not merely an annual one, the needs of your organization and the objectives of your campaign along with the constituents' stake in it cannot be explained in the course of a 90-second telephone pitch. Here dialogue and more extensive negotiation are essential to success. A more interactive approach is demanded.

Budgetary Issues

You may *want* to use the telephone to cultivate your nondonors, but you just can't. You have just enough money to send them direct mail once again, and then call maybe a quarter of them with a highly focused, short hard-script approach. The simple fact that someone has called personally, perhaps for the first time, may be sufficient to convert nondonors to donors. And once you have a few of them in the plus column, you can bestow on them the laurels of further cultivation.

Statistical Objectives

All other things being equal, you may simply choose the approach that achieves the statistical results you're looking for.

If your goal is to maximize *gross* income from a finite database, you will need to take maximum care to convert every nondonor and renew and upgrade every donor. So, you may wish to test a soft versus a hard script. If your goal is to maximize either pledge rates or average gifts, you may wish to do the same. Maybe your goal is to make sure everyone in your database gets a call, so that you can say as many people got an opportunity to give as possible. In this case, perhaps a short script is the way to go.

Perhaps your goal is to maximize *net* income, based on your investment, surely a pleasing thought. You may choose one instrument over another, perhaps even soliciting a portion of your database, rather than the whole thing.

Different tools can and will produce different results.

Quality of the Communicators

The general rule: the *less* prescribed the script, the *higher* the quality of communicator you will need to achieve optimal results. It stands to reason that the more you rely on an individual fundraiser's own verbal and persuasive skills, the better he or she should approach the ideal "Telephone Fundraising Superman''—or "Superwoman,'' as the case may be.

If you were going to envision the ideal telephone fundraiser for your organization, she might look something like this:

- Is herself a substantial donor.
- Has been dedicated to your mission for years through volunteerism and other involvement and knows your organization and mission inside out.
- Knows many of your constituents personally, has met many more, and has a good grasp of what the people are like in your database.
- Is willing to work for free.
- Has unlimited time to devote to you.
- Is warm and has a sunny disposition; even people who don't know her instantly like her.
- Is very articulate and conversational, yet can modulate her speech and tone to personalize it to the person with whom she is speaking.
- Can approach people on a *peer-to-peer* basis when appropriate.
- Has a clear, pleasing, yet energetic telephone speaking voice.
- Can be very compelling and persuasive in making a case for what she believes in.
- Has experience in sales or a natural aptitude for it.
- Has some professional fundraising knowledge and skills and a culturally acquired sense of philanthropy.
- Is a self-confident self-starter and is not shy, especially about asking for a gift.
- Has the ability to accept rejection after rejection without its affecting her morale or performance.
- Is self-analytical, creative, and willing to experiment to find the right formula—the magic key to unlock each prospect's philanthropy.
- Is competitive with a healthy ego and good sense of self.
- Is quick and resourceful in answering questions and dealing with objections—thinks well on her feet.
- Is a very good listener and can ask very good questions.
- Is gently persistent, yet never aggressive.

And on top of all of that, she is personable, reliable, and a joy to work with and be around.

Well, at least you can dream that such a person exists! And if you ever find her, just give her the keys to your office and take a vacation yourself!

But other than the ''working for free'' part, to be a good fundraiser, in whatever format, whether face to face or on the telephone, you'll need a least some of these qualities listed above. It's just you need *fewer* of them to be successful with a *prescribed* script format, a few more in a looser call outline or soft script format, and even more to be a great fundraiser with a call guide—or the chief executive in charge of your overall development program.

Summary

So, what kind of script should I use: A, B, or C . . . or somewhere in between?

If you've been responsible for producing these kinds of materials for telephone fundraisers yourself, you may have your own style and your own biases. One of the unfortunate realities of the telephone fundraising profession (I refuse to call it an "industry") is that there has been so little collaboration by nonprofit entities and the professionals in the field who make their living in companies providing telephone fundraising services.

Unlike the direct mail field where fundraising letter writers publish successful letters and proudly share with their colleagues what worked and what didn't, telephone fundraisers have a much more proprietary view of their work. Whether it's a discomfort to make public the messy details of "how the sausage is made" or whether they seek to not divulge their secrets, you will not find very much out there in the way of published telephone fundraising scripts, materials, and call outlines.

True, unless you are considering the "hard script" that is delivered verbatim by a telephone fundraiser, the other two vehicles, the "call guide" and the "call outline," can only approximate the actual content of the phone call, since so much of it relies on the fundraisers putting facts and questions into their own words. And considering that dialogue is involved, who knows what individual prospects are going to say, call to call? You can't very well publish that.

So, the vehicle you choose to assist your telephone fundraisers will depend on a number of things, the main variables include the kind of folks you have making calls for you, the nature of the prospects and the prospect segments you are going to phone, and your budget and organizational objectives.

Do I have an opinion and a bias? You bet.

3

Overview of an Effective Call Process

Every effective phone call is a process that hopefully leads from a ringing phone, through a discussion with the prospect, to an outcome: either a pledge of support or a refusal.

How far the telephone fundraiser gets from that moment when that ringing phone is answered to the point where the prospect has made a decision, either a yes or a no, depends on the effectiveness of the fundraiser in *controlling* the call and *leading* the prospect to a decision, hopefully a positive one.

A good call guide or a script is merely an aid to help the fundraiser achieve that measure of control and should ideally provide the structure or framework enabling a fundraiser to proceed from Point A, when someone answers the phone, to Point Z, where hopefully a pledge of support is secured.

At a minimum, a good script will follow one of the following processes, depending if you're pursuing a two-ask or a three-ask strategy (see Figures 3.1 and 3.2).

Step 1: Identify *the* Prospect

If you are calling a list of the organization's constituents, you will most likely be trying to reach a specific person, and that person will be the decision maker in choosing to make a pledge of support.

If the decision maker, say, Mr. Smith, does not immediately answer the phone, the fundraiser may have to work in getting through various screens in order to reach the decision maker. A "screen" is defined as a gatekeeper who has the power to decide whether to facilitate the fundraiser's desired contact with the prospect or to deny it. In fact, this stage of the call can constitute a kind of negotiation itself as the fundraiser must persuade the screener that the prospect will want to receive the call.

So, the fundraiser must sound professional and engaging, identifying himself as closely possible with the institution that Mr. Smith is part of, be

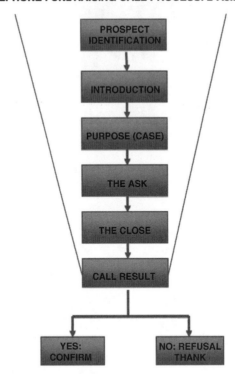

Figure 3.1   Call Process Chart A.

credible and at the same time, be gently persistent, even assumptive in attempt.

In some cases, the affiliation of a single prospect on your list may in fact represent a household affiliation or commitment to your cause or organization. For example, you may be soliciting a wife who shares a subscription to the theater with her husband, and both may have an equal affiliation and interest with your cause. Also, it may be that you are soliciting a household that has a family membership. In these cases, two or possibly more parties may be equal candidates for the fundraising appeal, although usually you will find that one of a pair has more interest or decision-making ability in the matter than the other.

Frequently, your interlocutor will help you out and place you with the correct party. For example:

Oh, you'll want to speak to my husband. He's the one who takes care of these things! John, can you come to the phone? It's XYZ Organization on the line!

Let me turn you over to my wife. She's the one with real passion for the arts! Honey, telephone for you!

You know, I think you should speak to my wife. She just got back from the regional conference on Sudden Climate Change, and I know she'll want to speak with you.

TELEPHONE FUNDRAISING CALL PROCESS: 3-Ask Format

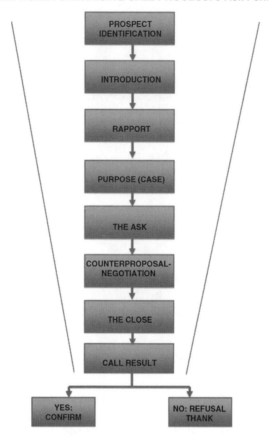

Figure 3.2   Call Process Chart B.

Of course, if you are "cold calling" a list of nonaffiliated prospects, then the axiom "APWD" (any prospect will do) may apply. In this case almost anyone in the household who answers the phone my be a candidate for the solicitation, so long as in the course of discussion he or she can be identified as sharing a concern for your cause and having sufficient ability to make a philanthropic contribution.

Step 2: Introduce and Identify Yourself

Once you have the prospect on the line, you need to introduce yourself, and it's best to do so by your name. At this juncture, the prospect, often unconsciously, will begin to develop a mental image of you and try to determine who you are. As has been mentioned, the telephone can be a very personal medium: person to person.

If the prospect does not know you and is not expecting your call, it's best to introduce yourself with your first and last name. After all, in a face-to-face business meeting or professional setting, when you shake hands, you would normally use your full name:

Hello, I'm Alice Jones. Pleased to meet you!

In a personal setting, Alice would extend a warm and firm handshake and, with a genuine smile, look Mr. Smith in the eye. While that's not possible in the telephone medium, you have to make your voice and tone do the "smiling" for you.

If you were to use only your first name in an introduction, it could seem too casual, even unprofessional, and consequently make you seem un-important—maybe merely a telephone solicitor! For example:

Hello, Mr. Smith. This is Alice.

"Alice who?" the prospect may be thinking. Alice must not have enough self-esteem to offer her last name, Mr. Smith may be thinking, or she may even be trying to hide something!

Conversely, using only your last name with a title like "Mr." or "Ms." can make you seem impersonal, perhaps even a little bit officious:

Hello, Mr. Smith. This is Miss Prescott calling.

Kind of sounds like your kid's school principal calling to say little Johnny cut class!

After you have introduced yourself, identifying who you are is key to completing the mental image Mr. Smith will make. The general rule: Be honest and factual, but try to identify yourself as closely with the institution you are raising money for as you are able.

Perhaps you're the Director of Development:

Mr. Smith, this is Alice Jones. I'm the Director of Development here at XYZ Organization . . .

Maybe you work for the Director of Development:

Mr. Smith, this is Alice Jones. Brad Snyder, the Director, asked me to give you a call . . .

Perhaps you're a fellow subscriber and volunteer:

Mr. Smith, I'm a fellow subscriber and a volunteer here at XYZ . . .

You could be a fellow alumnus at XYZ College:

Mr. Smith, I'm a fellow XYZ grad, Class of 1984 . . .

Perhaps you ardently support the mission of the organization:

Mr. Smith, I'm a fellow advocate for the environment . . .

Perhaps you are a paid solicitor who:

Mr. Smith, I work in the Development Department here at XYZ Organization . . .
Or
Mr. Smith, I'm working on behalf of XYZ Organization . . .

The higher in importance and stature you can legitimately present yourself, the more credible you will seem to Mr. Smith, and the more likely he is to take you and the call seriously and grant you the time to plead your case and ask for a contribution.

Perhaps the latitude you have in presenting yourself is affected by certain disclosures that are required under various state solicitation laws. If you are a hired solicitor and are calling into a state that requires a canned "disclosure," there may be constraints in how you must introduce yourself.

Step 3: Build Rapport

Including "Rapport" as a delineated stage of a call process may be controversial to some professional telephone fundraisers, but no one can deny its importance at least as a feature in an effective telephone fundraising call.

At the minimum, effective telephone fundraisers should sound positive and engaging, the kind of people that Mr. Smith would want to talk to. Furthermore, even if you are using a canned script that solicitors are expected to read word for word, good fundraisers should be trained to respond to unscripted questions and to be sensitive to a prospect's tone and demeanor.

That said, the most effective telephone calls from a statistical standpoint are calls that are interactive, where the unique quality of the telephone medium allowing two-way communication is exploited, and the telephone fundraiser poses questions to the prospect and answers questions posed by the prospect.

It is valuable to note that after the Introduction and Identification stage, virtually any question that is posed by a prospect shows an involvement in the conversation and an interest in the institution, a condition that can be developed by a skilled fundraiser into a pledge of support. Prospects' questions are "buy" signals.

How can telephone fundraisers develop rapport without it seeming an insincere "tactic" by a solicitor? In the vast majority of telephone solicitations, there is some prior relationship of the prospect with the organization.

Perhaps Mr. Smith is a past donor. Well, why not sincerely thank him for his past support and explain how much the organization appreciates it. There is a general rule than you cannot thank donors enough for their support, and a human thanks is so much more effective than a written letter and a receipt.

If Mr. Smith is not a donor, perhaps he is a member who attends performances, functions, or events sponsored by the organization. Why not talk about those things? Talk to Mr. Smith about what *he* likes about the organization, its activities, its positive impact on the community. That will reinforce his affiliation with the organization and why he is a part of it.

Perhaps Mr. Smith is an alumnus of an educational institution. In this case Mr. Smith has a long-term professional and often a social connection with his alma mater. Why not talk about that?

However, even if Mr. Smith is neither a donor, member, nor otherwise can be identified as an active constituent, Mr. Smith may share the work, values, initiatives and programs sponsored by your organization. Identify the things that you have in common, and a skilled fundraiser in the course of a conversation may be able to build a constituent from the "phone-up."

Using the telephone to build rapport is a constituent, donor-centered activity. Your organization and your solicitors may want what *you* want: the prospect's money. You may have your "pitch" that explains how badly you need it. Unless you take into account the prospect's interests, wants, and desires, and unless you make the prospect feel valued, you will not be as successful in your fundraising as you could be.

Step 4: Explain the Purpose of Your Call—Making the Case

Once you have set the table by finding a viable prospect, elicited his or her permission to engage in a conversation, and have developed at least enough rapport that the prospect has not hung up on you or otherwise prematurely sought to terminate the conversation, it's incumbent on the fundraiser to make a case for Mr. Smith's support. In some cases, making the case can be facilitated by sending the prospect a precall letter that explains the objectives of your fundraising campaign and prepares him or her to receive a phone call "from a representative" of your organization.

Making a case in a telephone call is very different than making a written grant proposal to a foundation, writing a solicitation letter or e-mail to a donor, or meeting with a donor face to face.

Grants and letters and e-mails fall into the realm of one-way written communication, and each has its own unique set of principles. A meeting arranged with a prospective donor is usually by appointment, with time set aside specifically understood to be a discussion about the organization and its needs. Conversations in this medium can range from a few minutes to more than an hour.

However, a telephone call, even if it's been preannounced by a letter or postcard, catches a prospect at a time when he or she is doing something else: He is interrupted and often distracted. Good fundraisers, no matter how skilled, are limited by the very nature of the medium in the amount of *time* they will be granted by the prospect. That is why it's important for telephone fundraisers to be concise, compelling, and succinct in making a case. A couple of powerful sentences, the CliffsNotes version of your organization's case statement: That is what is necessary here.

Step 5: Ask, Ask, Ask—The Process of Negotiation

The next stage of a call is what good fundraisers are born to do: ask for a prospect's support.

An effective ask involves making a specific, credible, and tangible proposal to the prospect, much as one would make a written proposal for a grant.

We're talking about a specific number, not:

Mr. Smith, can you give a little something? Please?

The proposal that you make to Mr. Smith should be high enough to "raise his sights" and perhaps get him thinking about an amount higher than he would otherwise consider. However, the amount of the ask should not be so high relative to Mr. Smith's ability to give, and in consideration of his relationship to the institution, that it would appear insincere or ludicrous.

First Proposal: The Sight Raise

An appropriate "sight raise" proposal should take into consideration a number of factors: Mr. Smith's prior record of giving, if any, to the organization; what level of affiliation or interest he may have with your mission; and his ability to make a philanthropic contribution.

Absent detailed donor constituent records or specific donor research provided by a third-party service, assessing a prospect's giving potential on the fly is one of the most challenging and difficult tasks for the telephone fundraiser.

Negotiation: Working with the Prospect to Find a Level of Gift

Congratulations, "game on"! We have entered the realm of "negotiation" where good fundraisers ask (make verbal proposals for funding) and try to find a gift level that Mr. Smith is both able and willing to make to the organization. The word "negotiation" can imply an adversarial relationship, but in the context of a telephone fundraising call, think of it as working together with the prospect to find that level of giving that is "right."

Once a fundraiser has put a proposal "on the table," so to speak, the prospect will either accept the proposal or reject it, oftentimes making an objection that must be dealt with before the fundraiser has license to make a counterproposal.

It is imperative that a good fundraiser *listen* carefully to Mr. Smith's response, not only to uncover potential objections and respond to them, but also to gain *clues* about the degree of Mr. Smith's affiliation with the organization, his general philanthropic willingness to support, and most important, the extent of his ability to make a philanthropic gift.

Counterproposal(s)

After listening to Mr. Smith's response, good fundraisers must formulate a counterproposal for a lesser amount.

Here there is some debate among professionals in the fundraising community. Many feel that *two* proposals are all that a fundraiser can practically offer in the telephone medium, and the second proposal should be the "closing" proposal. These kinds of calls represent the majority of telephone solicitations in practice today.

Others feel very strongly that *three* proposals are optimal, and the *second* ask should be a strategic positioning in a planned negotiating strategy, one that is higher than the fundraiser may believe the prospect can or will give, but nonetheless takes into account the general response and tone of Mr. Smith's reaction to the first proposal.

Regardless of whether it's one, two, or three, the final ask is the "closing ask."

The optimal closing ask should result in an optimal gift level for Mr. Smith. Through your persuasive demeanor, having made a compelling case for your organization, having lent a sense of urgency to give, and yes, being as persistent as good manners will allow, you have found that level of giving that is the highest Mr. Smith is both able and willing to give.

Step 6: The Result of a Negotiation—Yes or No?

After a negotiation, there will be a result: Either Mr. Smith will agree to make a pledge of support or he will not.

Pledges

A "yes" response is defined as a *pledge*—an agreement for Mr. Smith to support the organization with a specified amount of money. It is very important for telephone fundraisers to accurately confirm and reinforce the salient terms of the pledge, as well as Mr. Smith's address information for a response follow-up.

Sometimes pledges can be collected on the fly with the fundraiser receiving credit card information from the prospect that can be processed immediately.

Otherwise, a follow-up component must be employed, either a follow-up e-mail with a link for Mr. Smith to process his credit card through the organization's web site, or more usually, a direct mail follow-up with a response device (return envelope) for Mr. Smith to return his gift.

If the fundraiser is calling a list of recent donors, those who have given in the last year or so, then one can reasonably expect more "yeses" than "nos." If the fundraiser is calling into a list of intermittent, lapsed, or even long-lapsed donors, "nos" may outnumber the "yeses."

Refusals

But most certainly, if the fundraiser is calling a list of prospects who have never given to the organization, and/or who have a more tenuous affiliation (if any) with your organization, the preponderance of responses will be "nos."

This category of result is known as a *refusal.* How good fundraisers handle refusals is also very important for the long-term fundraising viability of the organization's fundraising efforts. Presumably, the list you're calling are constituents in some fashion, people who have demonstrated some affiliation or interest in your cause.

The last thing you want to accomplish in your telephone fundraising efforts is to "poison the well"—and leave such a bad taste in Mr. Smith's mouth (or ear, as it were) that he will not even want to speak with you at all in your next solicitation effort. Even if Mr. Smith refuses to support you this time around, he should be hanging up with a positive feeling about your organization, its mission, its efforts—even the good faith effort to solicit him!

Unspecified Pledges

What about this category of result . . . isn't it a *pledge*? Savvy managers statistically classify this result with the refusals. So many fundraisers, having a difficult time closing a gift, will try to classify prospects who say:

Mr. Smith: *Let me think about it. Can you send something out? I'll take a look at it.*
Fundraiser: *Sure, Mr. Smith, I'll send out an unspecified form and you can send something back when you're ready. Is your address still 1313 Dreary Lane . . . ?*

Sorry, folks, but these are *refusals.* Why? Because they are not *pledges!* A true, bona fide "unspecified" pledge is indeed a *pledge:* a promise to make a contribution, but the prospect is unwilling or unable to specify an amount.

Summary

There are a number of metaphors to describe an effective call process. One is to picture a large funnel: wide at the top, into which you dump prospects.

During the call process, prospects move through the narrowing funnel from the general "Intro and Hello" through the statement of a compelling "Purpose," then narrowing further, on through a persistent "Negotiation." The funnel is the call process and helps keep the fundraiser in control of the call.

At the bottom of the funnel, finally, a call result is achieved. If the fundraiser has followed the stages and moved the prospect gradually through the funnel, has been compelling, has listened well, and has negotiated effectively, then an optimal number of pledges at an optimal average amount is achieved.

Another metaphor is to picture a large distillation vat, with a fire built at the bottom (this may make some feel a bit queasy, unless you are picturing your least favorite prospects). Prospects are dumped into the vat. Near the top of the vat, those who are most valuable rise above the rest and are drawn out from the vat higher up (after a little bit of "cooking"). These are the valuable donors who say yes to the first ask.

Cooking a little longer, farther down in the vat, a few more prospects are drawn out through the second ask: more in number but smaller gift amounts than those above.

Finally, cooking the most, after having applied the most heat, down at the bottom of the vat at the stage of the third ask, or the close, there is a final distillation. The remaining prospects are distilled into those few remaining who will give, that is, make a pledge support to your organization. The remaining prospects are drawn off into the refusal vat. But it's important to consider that these are not "wasted" prospects . . . they can be recycled for future solicitation.

There are other metaphors to describe an effective telephone fundraising process, like panning for gold, fishing, or even dental work. But I'll stop here.

CHAPTER 4

Identification of the Prospect and Introducing Yourself

Picking up the phone, dialing it, and finding a prospective donor is a bit more complex a process than can appear at first blush. Who is your prospect? Will any prospect do? What happens if someone other than the prospect answers the phone and is reluctant or unwilling to put you through to the prospect? How do you honestly and candidly introduce yourself in a way that provides you the credibility to gain access to the prospect's home? Many questions and lots of nuances!

Job 1: Finding the Right Prospect

Prospecting sounds simple enough. You have a record, at a minimum the name and phone number of a prospective donor. Perhaps you have other data as well, a giving history and some notes on the affiliation of the prospect with your organization, like his or her year of graduation. Let's assume that you're calling for "ABC College" where the prospect, "Mr. Alonzo Smith," is an alumnus from the class of 1978. You dial the phone, it begins to ring, your heart begins to race, and then:

Figure 4.1   Stage 1—Identity

Ring, Ring, Ring! Click. A male voice answers the phone.
You: *Hello, Mr. Smith?*
Mr. Smith: *Yes?*
You: *Hi, Mr. Smith, this is Alice Jones from ABC College. We wanted to touch base and let you know about exciting things happening here and also about the Annual Fund . . .*

and a discussion may occur, sometimes for several minutes, until the caller comes to a point of discovery.

Smith: *Oh, "Mr. Smith." It must be my* dad *you want to speak to . . . He's the one who went to ABC College . . . I hope to go there next year myself!*
You: *Is your dad home?*
The Son: *Sorry, he's out of town.*

So, you may have had a delightful time speaking to Mr. Smith's son, but unfortunately he's not likely to be a prospect for the institution you're raising money for—at least not this year. This brings to memory Lily Tomlin's old "Operator" skit: "Hello? Is this the party to whom I am speaking?" We can only hope! Indeed, I've audited scores of calls where an engaging, loquacious fundraiser will chatter on in the most delightful way, only some minutes later to discover he has not identified the correct prospect!

When you call a telephone number, one of two things can happen: (1) either a human being will answer the phone or (2) not. And if someone does, that person either *is* or *isn't* the prospect. There are no other alternatives. Job 1 of every good fundraiser is to find the *correct* prospect. Unless you do, you cannot succeed. Of course, if you're not doing renewal donor fundraising, and if you're calling into a list of nonaffiliated non-donors, where any prospect will do (APWD), it may be less important to speak to a specific individual, so long as the person you speak to is a decision maker capable of making a gift. But this is more the exception than the rule in using the telephone as a targeted medium of communication.

What can you do to ensure getting through to the correct prospect? Ask for the prospect simply and directly:

Fundraiser: *Hello, may I speak to Alonzo Smith?*

with a friendly, cheerful, confident tone that is neither a question nor a command, rather a statement that is a simple request.

Or use a more complete introduction, such as:

Fundraiser: *Hello, this is Alice Jones. I'm a student at ABC University. May I speak with Mr. Alonzo Smith?*

At each stage of the call, one must be aware of the "Principle of Parsimony" in telephone communication, saying only the minimum, without appearing deceptive, in order to achieve your objective.

Fundraiser: *Hello, may I speak to Alonzo Smith?*
Other Party: *Just a moment, I'll get him.*

This is invariably the outcome of the simple request. At the next level it could be:

Other Party: *May I ask who is calling?*
Fundraiser: *This is Alice Jones. Is Mr. Smith available?*

Again, consider the principle of parsimony, saying the minimum necessary, and maintaining control of the call by posing a question of the interlocutor.
This will invariably result in:

Other Party: *This is Alonzo Smith.*
or
Other Party: *Just a moment, I'll get him.*

I have heard, countless times, telephone fundraisers take a detached, even officious tone:

Fundraiser: *This is Miss Andrews with ABC College. May I speak with Mr. Alonzo Smith, please?*

This violates a number of fundraising rules, not just "the principle of parsimony." Remember, the telephone, like a personal visit, should be a *personal* medium. Taking on a title for yourself at the outset, either with the person who answers the phone or later with the prospect, and then addressing the prospect more formally than is necessary detracts from creating a warm, personal relationship. Consider that the prospect has, at the minimum, some regard for your organization, if not respect, esteem, or even affection and love. Build on the relationship at the outset of a call!

Screens

Prospect Not Home or Unavailable   At its most benign, a *screen* involves a person answering the phone who is *not* the party you wish to reach. The relationship of that person to the prospect lies on a continuum of "No Relationship at All," that is, a wrong number, to "Very Close Relationship." It could be the baby sitter, a visiting relative, a child, or the prospect's spouse. If your interlocutor has a relationship with the prospect, and the prospect is

Telephone Fundraising Rule

THE PRINCIPLE OF PARSIMONY

Say the minimum to achieve the objective. Extraneous babble is the enemy of efficiency and effectiveness. Unlike a personal visit, when you make an interruptive telephone call, a clock is ticking.

not home or unavailable to speak, it's the job of the fundraiser to find a time to call back to reach the prospect directly:

Fundraiser: *Hello, may I speak with Mr. Smith?*
Prospect: *He's not here right now.*
Fundraiser: *What's a better time to reach Mr. Smith . . . later this evening, or would tomorrow be better?*

Note: Making a forced choice, offering specific options to the screening party rather than the open-ended "When can I reach Mr. Smith?", and controlling the call through questions can help you get through screens.

How many times have I heard a fundraiser, upon being informed that the prospect is not home, quickly utter something to the effect of "thanks anyway" or simply "goodbye" and then hang up. This borders on rudeness and leaves lingering questions in the mind of the screening party. Courtesy and professionalism require following up and raising the stature of the call in the mind of the screening party for what it is truly: a warm, professional reaching out by the institution through the medium of the telephone into the home of the prospect. This helps lay the foundation for the next attempt to reach the prospect.

Telephone Fundraising Rule

CONTROL THE CALL WITH QUESTIONS

Don't filibuster! Maintaining control of a fundraising call is critical to your success, and you control the call by asking questions, not by monopolizing what should be a two-way conversation!

Active Screening   In many instances, the person who answers the phone will act as a screen to protect the prospect from telephone solicitors, in other words, from people like you! In these instances, you have to persuade the *screening party* that there is a prior connection, an affiliation of the prospect with your organization, and that Mr. Smith, the prospect, will *want* to receive the call. This task may be as simple as this:

Screening Party: *May I ask who is calling?*
Fundraiser: *This is Alice Jones. Is Mr. Smith available?*
Screening Party: *What is this about?*
Fundraiser: *I'm with ABC University, Mr. Smith's alma mater, and I want to bring him up to date on things that are happening here. Is he available?*
Screening Party: *Just a moment, I'll get him.* or
This is Mr. Smith. (Note: Sometimes the prospect screens for himself or herself!)

Occasionally, the screening party, rather than acting as a mere screen door, acts more like a quadruple-bolted steel vault door and will actively challenge the telephone fundraiser on any number of grounds: "Exactly why are you calling?"; "What is this about?"; "Is this a telephone solicitation?"; "Who are you?"; and "Are you a paid solicitor?" Talk about the third degree!

In such instances, it's up to your organization to set up guidelines on how actively you should "push" through that screen door. In *no* instance is it acceptable to mislead or provide false information to the screening party: *We need to speak to Smith so he can claim our $50,000 prize!!!* No. No. No.

The standard rule is to provide the screening party information that will establish a legitimate business and personal connection of that prospect with the institution and to prove to the prospect that you should be granted access. Furthermore, if the telephone fundraiser's credentials are challenged by the screening party, it is up to you to provide those legitimate credentials in as truthful and compelling a way as possible.

Examples
One of the reasons I'm calling to let him know about (the next alumni homecoming event/the next concert in his series) to see what he thinks about our ABC lobbying initiative and how he might be able to help.

I wanted to let him know about (some activity, event of interest) . . . and because he has supported ABC in the past, also speak to him about the Annual Fund.
I'm a student in the Class of 2011. I'm a subscriber as well, and a volunteer. I'm working for the Development Office.
. . . and then to follow with the question: *When will be a good time to speak to Mr. Smith—this evening, or would tomorrow be better?*

Answering Machines/Voice Mail A significant number of attempts to call the prospect will result in your reaching a recorded message, either an answering machine or voice mail. If you're calling from a large telemarketing center that uses a predictive dialing system that can recognize and screen out answering machine messages, this won't be an issue. However, for the vast majority of student and volunteer efforts, or smaller-scale telephone fundraising efforts, this brings the following dilemma: To leave a message or not leave a message . . . *that* is the question!

This has been significantly debated over the years. The benefit of *not* leaving a message is that it allows the fundraiser to move more quickly on to the next prospect rather than wasting time in a nonproductive activity. Also, it eliminates the risk of leaving a clumsy message that might predispose the prospect to not accept a subsequent call.

Arguing *in favor* of leaving a voice message is this: Many people at home use their answering machines to screen out unwanted calls. They may be home, listen to who is calling, and then decide to pick up the phone during the caller's message. If you have good telephone communicators who sound engaging, you may want to train them to leave a brief message, with the hope the prospect will pick up. If you are not bound by the algorithms of your predictive dialing system, you may want to try leaving messages and determine if it statistically increases your contact rates.

Things to Avoid   As we've discussed, there is no excuse for being deceptive or deliberately misleading in order to gain access to the prospect. But there are some gray areas that you should also think about avoiding. Among them is being "overly familiar" with the screening prospect. For example, assume you are calling Mr. William Smith:

Fundraiser: *May I speak to Bill?*
Other Party: *Who is calling?*
Fundraiser: *This is Alice.*

Such a practice borders on deception and is fraught with peril! For starters, William may not even use the nickname "Bill," and always has and always will want to refer to himself as "William." What an awkward way to begin a call, if such is the case. Furthermore, the fundraiser, by only giving her first name, leads the screening party to assume the caller personally knows the prospect, which is an outright deception. Unfortunately, I've audited too many calls where ambitious fundraisers, seeking an "edge," become overly familiar with the screening party and later the prospect. Indeed, this is particularly awkward if the screening party is William Smith's spouse who proceeds to grill poor Alice to determine what her relationship may be with her husband!

Job 2: Introducing Yourself

Great, you've found your prospect and you have him or her on the telephone. It's time to let the prospect know who you are. Sounds simple

Figure 4.2 Stage 2: Introduction

enough but . . . consider the fact that you have just interrupted the prospect from what he or she was doing. He probably does not appreciate the interruption. When the prospect picks up the phone and says "Hello," from your first breath he will consciously make an evaluation of *you*. Based on how you sound, the prospect will draw a mental image of you and begin to answer for himself in quick order a plethora of questions. Who is this person, anyway? Does she have an identifiable accent? Is this person credible? Does she sound professional? Has she clearly articulated a relationship to an organization that I have an interest in? Is this the kind of person, based on her tone and her friendliness, to whom I want to invest my time in speaking?

This is a very critical phase of the call, because at the conclusion of your introduction, the prospective donor will make a decision: Do I speak to this person or do I not (and perhaps even hang up!)? If the prospect lets you in, opens up the door a crack, and perhaps even invites you over the threshold, your chances of achieving a pledge increase dramatically. If the prospect does not let you in, you will find yourself either preemptively refused or negotiating for time to discuss the reasons for your call.

To be successful at this screening phase, there are some general principles to keep in mind:

1. *Tone.* Your tone conveys a lot about how you feel about the organization and its mission. Generally, being warm, professional yet personal, having a positive demeanor, and being upbeat but not to the point of being giddy will help you get to first base. Professional, yes. Officious, no! Remember, if *you* don't sound like you are committed to the cause you're calling for, how can you expect to motivate and inspire the prospect to give? A warm "hello" or sometimes even a casual "hi" is a good way to start.
2. *Name.* Unless you happen know the prospect, it's best to give your first and last name; it's the professional thing to do.

3. *Relationship.* Describe your relationship to the institution as closely as your professional or volunteer relationship will permit.
4. *Person to Person.* Peer-to-peer fundraising is most successful, so if the caller's relationship with the nonprofit organization in any way parallels or overlaps that of the prospect, mention that commonality. Keep in mind that this call is from one person to another, not an "institution" or an "organization." It is you and the prospect.

Example:

Hello, Mr. Smith, this is Alice Jones with ABC College.

But, how many times have I heard the following:

Mr. Smith, this is Ms. Jones with ABC College.

This lends an unnecessary air of formality, more akin to an approach by a bill collector rather than a personal call from, perhaps, the prospect's favorite organization.

I've heard the following approach taken too may times:

Hello, this is ABC College calling.

At the outset, it cedes one of the great advantages a fundraiser has with the telephone medium: It's *personal.* Nothing could be more impersonal than to adopt the vestments of an institution, and not the living, breathing human being you are. People raise money from people much more effectively than an institution can.

At the other end of the scale consider the following:

Hi, Mr. Smith, this is Alice calling from ABC College!

Isn't this warm and personal? While this might seem to be appropriate for a young caller of student age calling a recent graduate, or perhaps even an older alumnus, the general effect of giving only your first name may lead the prospect to consider you to be of limited importance and perhaps not worth speaking seriously to. I have even heard prospects sound somewhat suspicious of a caller who is unwilling to divulge his or her full name up front. What is this person hiding? Exactly who is this person?

There are many ways of describing your relationship with the organization you're calling for. Here are some examples on a continuum of less personal to most personal.

Examples

I'm Alice Jones and I'm:
  . . . calling on behalf of (name of institution)

. . . working with (name of institution)
. . . working for (name of institution)
. . . with (name of institution)
. . . volunteering on behalf of (name of institution)

And if you have a legitimate relationship with the organization you're representing, use it!

This is Alice Jones and:
. . . I'm a volunteer for (name of institution)
. . . I'm a student working with the (name of office) at (name of institution)
. . . I'm an alumna from the class of 2002 and I'm calling for (organization)
. . . I'm a fellow subscriber to (name of organization)
. . . I'm a fellow (music lover, art lover)

What you are saying, in effect, is I'm like you, I'm with you, I believe in the same things, we care about and value similar things. Indeed, this is the first step to building rapport with the prospect, further cultivating a relationship of the prospect with the organization. The closer you can be identified with the organization you're representing, or reinforcing a personal relationship with the prospect, the better!

Unfortunately, some state charitable solicitation regulations require third-party paid solicitors to stipulate they are "paid solicitors" early in a call, even describing the percentage of funds raised that are "commission" to the soliciting organization. I have nothing to say about this other than ouch. What a tough way to begin a call!

Some other approaches I've heard, with pluses and minuses:

Hello Mr. Smith, this is Alice Jones with ABC Art Museum. Thank you for taking my call.

While I grant you that you can't thank constituents enough, the above has the risk of putting the caller at the outset of a call on an unequal plane with the prospect. While it is true that the prospect does not owe a telephone audience with the caller, why not try being somewhat assumptive? Why shouldn't the prospect want to speak to you, converse about an organization that he or she has a relationship with, or whose mission and goals he or she might likely share?

Or, consider the following:

"Hello, Mr. Smith, this is Alice Jones with ABC Organization. I'm so happy we finally got you on the phone!

Ouch.

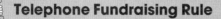

Telephone Fundraising Rule

Identify yourself as closely with the organization you represent as you truthfully can. It will increase your stature in the mind of the prospect and increase your credibility.

Questions, Questions, Questions

After the fundraiser has introduced him- or herself, how many times have I heard:

How are you this evening?

And, how many times have I heard from the objects of telemarketing calls the following:

I hate it when they ask, "How are you?" You know it's a telemarketing call, and of course they really don't care how you are.

This brings to mind another sacrosanct "Telephone Fundraising Rule."

Telephone Fundraising Rule

Asking questions of a prospect is good and lays the foundation for two-way communication. Just make sure you're reasonably sure what the answer is going to be before you ask!

This reminds me of the many answers I've heard brought forth by the poor, innocent fundraiser's query:

Prospect: *I'm feeling very poorly right now. Is this a telephone solicitation?*
or
Prospect: *I couldn't be better. Goodbye.* Click . . . hung up.

Asking Permission to Speak?

After the caller has introduced him- or herself, should the fundraiser ask:

May I speak with you about [name of organization]?

About this there are two schools of thought. One is that the caller should simply plunge into the context of the call, assumptively moving ahead to the purpose of the call. After all, what happens if the prospect in response says:

No, you may not [speak with me].

. . . an awkward position to put oneself in at the beginning of a call!

Another school of thought is that asking permission to speak is a necessary courtesy; unless it is offered to the prospect, it amounts to "sticking one's foot in the door" and entering uninvited into the prospect's home, metaphorically speaking. Keep in mind that the medium of the telephone is very much an "interruptive" medium. Your phone call was not timed for the convenience and availability of the prospect. You do not know if the prospect has just emerged from the shower, whether the baby is stirring in the other room, or what plethora of other circumstances may exist that will ultimately curtail your efforts to fundraise.

By asking permission to speak, and receiving an affirmative answer, you have gained a platform upon which to help build your organization's relationship with the prospect, make the case for organization, and ask for support.

So, which is right: asking permission to speak or not?

The answer: *It depends.* Specifically, it depends to a large degree on the constituency you are soliciting and the strength of any prior relationships you have with it. If you're calling a group of prospects that have been heavily solicited by you in the past, and those solicitations have been less professional, or if your organization has a tenuous relationship with the prospects to begin with, you may want to statistically evaluate how often your callers are told "No, I won't speak with you," and you may want to dispense with the courtesy and plunge ahead with the call.

However, if you have established a prior relationship with the prospect, or if the prospect has a prior connection with your organization that you wish to build on—an alumnus, a subscriber, a prior donor, for example—why not extend the courtesy? If you find that now is NOT a good time to speak with the prospect, then as a first step toward the eventual "negotiation" you wish to establish, negotiate for the necessary *time* to do so. Yes, it may involve calling back later in the evening or another day. But once you have gained the "permission of the platform," you are in effect being invited into the person's home for a short period of time, a much better foundation upon which to ask for funds!

As a kind of middle ground, try:

Caller: *I'd like to speak with you a moment about (name organization), if that's okay . . .*

. . . and then allow a very slight pause to allow the prospective donor to object before moving ahead to the context of the call.

As phrased above, it's not a question, but a presumptive statement that extends the "permission" courtesy. Using the pronoun "I "personalizes the approach, "speak with you" implies a conversation that is less threatening, not a hard solicitation, and a the use of a temporal expression like "a moment" or "a couple of minutes" or "a bit" will inform the prospect you are asking for at least some of his or her time, not an entire evening. The prospect's silence is an implied invitation to enter his or her home and provides a very solid foundation to continue the call.

But what happens if the prospect objects? What if now is not a good time to speak with him or her?

Fundraiser: *Mr. Smith, I'd like to speak with you a few moments about XYZ University, if that's okay . . .*

Mr. Smith: *To tell you the truth, now is not a good time. I'm (rushing out the door/the baby is awake/we're having dinner/and so forth).*

Fundraiser: *When is a better time—later this evening, or would tomorrow evening be better?*

This gives the prospect a *forced choice* for an appointment call back.

In spite of the prospect's declared shortage of time, he or she may ask:

Mr. Smith: *What is this about?* or *Why are you calling?*

In such cases, the caller can accept the above as an implied invitation to continue the call and slide into the next stage, whether it is an attempt to develop rapport or explain the purpose of the call directly.

Summary

These days, simply finding anyone to answer the telephone—that is, a live, breathing human being as opposed to an answering machine or voice mail— can involve multiple dials. In the "olden" days of telephone fundraising, you used to be able to find the correct party from a prospect list of affiliated constituents in three or four attempts. These days with both passive and active screening of calls, and the shift and blending from landline telephony to wireless, you might call an individual prospect a dozen times before you can get him or her on the line. This is simply the nature of the environment and one that has increased costs. Some organizations and call centers have attempted to combat this fact through technology, with automated electronic dialing and sophisticated predictive dialing systems, increasing dials per caller hour. Others simply set a limit on the number of times they will attempt to reach a given prospect. That limit may be as few as four or five attempts to as many as eight—depending the budgetary limitations of the telephone program and the potential value of a list segment.

Regardless of the technology you employ, once you do have a live voice on the line, it's important that you put your best foot forward. There is little room for error in how you present yourself to the person who answers that phone. And if that person is the prospect you're looking for, how you sound and what you initially say will determine whether you are granted access to move ahead with your call. How you sound and what you say at this stage is the equivalent of how you're dressed, what you look like, the sincerity in your eyes, and the firmness of your handshake—if this were a personal meeting, face to face.

Rapport—Developing a Relationship

It's a sad commentary on the state of fundraising that what many fundraisers consider a sacrosanct responsibility, that of *cultivating* a prospect, is completely ignored in the telephone communication medium.

Many years ago in preparing for a Certified Fund Raising Executive (CFRE) exam, I was exposed to the basic formula for successful fundraising: ICAT, the acronym for the essential stages of the fundraising process:

1. Identify
2. Cultivate
3. Ask
4. Thank

Development officers around the country are spending millions of dollars to identify prospects who either have a relationship with their organization or may wish to have one. Many countless staff hours are spent over many years to cultivate the identified relationships of prospects with their institution, to induce prospects to feel valued by their institutions and then to give generously as a consequence. Cultivation can come personally through meetings, events, or less personally through direct mail, printed material, and now the Internet. Also, the "Ask" and the "Thank" functions are now accomplished through a variety of media from a personal visit to direct mail to the Internet.

But when it comes to the medium of the telephone, eyes seem to glaze over and professional development folk see its value and effectiveness in only one of the major functions: the ask.

Indeed, some professional development folks consider the medium of the telephone almost a form of punishment for their most recalcitrant prospects. I'll never forget many years ago meeting a frustrated Annual Fund person with a large body of prospects who had not responded to several years of direct mail appeals. "We're going to telemarket 'em," she said with some zeal, as if they at long last were going to get what they deserve!

I understand the reasons why many development professionals do not look at the telephone medium as an opportunity to further cultivate their constituents:

- It may require more highly trained and skilled communicators, thus putting pressure on recruitment and training efforts.
- It is difficult or impossible to script cultivation.
- Rapport building involves *two-way* conversation that can lead to a loss of "control" of the call and a premature end to it.
- Attempts to engage a prospect in conversation can appear insincere to the prospect and may backfire.
- Building rapport through asking questions takes extra time, and time = cost in the telephone medium, leading to lower telemarketing "income per hour."
- Many don't believe there is a payback for the investment (through higher pledge rates or average gifts).
- Those responsible for a telephone fundraising effort may believe that their prospects are sophisticated enough with the telephone solicitation to know what's up and not expect to be schmoozed by a lowly telemarketer.

Perhaps the most cogent argument from those above is that cultivation takes *time*, and time is money and can increase the costs of a solicitation effort. Better to get to the business at hand, and ask, ask, ask!

Second to this argument is the one that development professionals may feel that any efforts by telephone fundraisers to cultivate prospects over the phone will seem insincere and therefore counterproductive. Look, they may argue, prospects are savvy, many have been telemarketed by their organizations before, and prospects are sophisticated enough to "endure" the process like holding their nose to make the medicine go down.

But there are plenty of reasons to take some time on the telephone with your prospects, or at least those who have an established connection with your organization. To use the telephone medium merely as a *one-way* solicitation tool, a way to target captive prospects, hitting them with a verbal message and then soliciting them (the Ask), cedes one of the greatest advantages inherent in the medium: *It affords two-way communication.* Neither a letter nor an e-mail can answer a prospect's questions or concerns, deal with an objection, elicit immediate feedback, or provide information to alter your appeal to meet his or her unique situation. That can only be accomplished through a personal visit or a telephone call.

Using the telephone call as an opportunity to engage prospects can help reestablish long-existing ties between them and your organization, or be an important first step in establishing relationships where there are grounds to do so. It can help personalize the contact—and help establish the caller as both credible and caring—a much more secure foundation to make an ensuing solicitation. And by being both credible and caring, you can establish an atmosphere of goodwill near the beginning of the call.

Of course, a telephone fundraiser in the course of a 30-second solicitation or even 2- or 3-minute phone call cannot compensate for years of institutional neglect in the long-term cultivation of constituents through other means. However, even modestly skilled and adequately trained telephone communicators can at least develop some rapport with prospective donors, a short-term relationship that can reflect positively upon the institution and its cause.

So, how is it possible to do all of that at the outset of a short phone call? First, if you at all can, *give something to the prospect.* How so?

Put the Prospect at Ease

First, a telephone caller can give the prospect courtesy, sensitivity. In this sense, the process of building rapport begins the second the prospect says "Hello." Remember, you've just interrupted the prospect. Yes, a letter may have been sent out with the intention of preparing the prospect for your call. But at the moment you call a prospect in her home, the prospect was doing something else: reading a book, watching television, eating dinner, working on a house renovation project, catching up on paperwork, helping her daughter with her homework, putting the kids to bed, rushing out the door to a community meeting, or maybe rushing off to the airport to catch a flight.

You have just interrupted her.

That's why many feel it's a good idea to lend the prospect the courtesy of asking for their time, that is, asking "permission to speak" mentioned in the previous chapter. It can be a first and solid step to building rapport. If you consider your phone campaign nothing more than a telemarketing effort to get through the list, without thought of how your subsequent calls to solicit funds will be received, be it the third call or the thirteenth, then plunge forward and get what you can now. If, however, you view this telephone call as an opportunity to build a relationship, to complement your organization's strategy to cultivate donors for the long term, have your telephone communicators approach the contact with some sensitivity and be ready to *listen.*

Impossible to script, however, is a caller's telephone tone and demeanor, and although this book is about "scripting," let me offer a couple of thoughts. Tone and demeanor are the first things the prospective donor will pick up on. In the telephone medium, the prospect cannot *see* you, he or she can only *hear* you. The prospect will want to speak to a representative of your organization, ideally one he or she is already affiliated with in some way if the caller sounds warm, calm, confident, upbeat, and well-spoken. I won't go into detail about all of the characteristics of voice and speech patterns that assist telephone solicitors in being successful. However, if your caller sounds tired at the outset (it may be his twelfth call of the night), uninterested, uninvolved, merely going through the motions, he is unlikely to get through the front door.

Conversely, if the solicitor sounds overly excited, speaks so fast that the prospect has a difficult time understanding him, perhaps is upbeat to the point of being giddy or unprofessional, that can have a deleterious effect on the call as well.

Good callers are empathetic as well and are good listeners. They can pick up on the prospect's mood and demeanor and can tailor their approach to the prospect. The best callers are able to project genuine warmth and seek to put the prospect at ease after they have interrupted them. For example, assume at the outset of a call that the prospect is obviously elderly, and perhaps a little hard of hearing. Good callers may speak up a little louder to enable the prospect to hear them better and perhaps speak a little more slowly and clearly. That's being sensitive and empathetic. Conversely, the prospect might pick up the phone in a breathless rush, but nonetheless, grant the "permission to speak" request I've earlier mentioned. In these cases, the caller might endeavor to get the prospect to slow down a little, by *not* accelerating his own speech patterns and rushing ahead. These sensitive early stages of the call are in a sense playing for time.

Give Thanks When Due

So many times have I been called by organizations that I've contributed to either through membership or to the annual fund, or both, but the caller has never even bothered to thank me for what I have done in the past! If you have prior donors or members in your database, surely you can provide that data to your callers:

Alice Jones (caller): *First of all, Mr. Smith, I want to thank you for your past support of XYZ organization. I see that you contributed $100 last year, and we are truly grateful!*

Mr. Smith: *Sure, no problem. We were happy to do it.*

What if the prospect is a long-lapsed donor or had given only a negligible sum?

Alice Jones (caller): *First of all, Mr. Smith, I see that you've supported XYZ organization in the past, and we're truly grateful to you.*

Even if the prospect were to take the opportunity to respond to Alice by saying:

Mr. Smith: *Well, I can't give anything this year!*

. . . which rarely happens after being genuinely thanked for prior generosity, the caller can easily continue the call by moving to another rapport-building question rather than being lured prematurely into a negotiation. I've audited many situations where the nonprofit organization shows Mr. Smith as having contributed $X, but when thanked, he has no recollection of ever having done so. Rather than creating an awkward situation, the prospect is invariably flattered by the reminder and the recognition of his past generosity.

You may even be able to tell the prospect the good his gift has done. Perhaps it was used to build the new pavilion, provide a scholarship to someone deserving, enable the engagement of a guest artist, or help fund an education or lobbying campaign for the cause he believes in. Donors want to know that what they have done in the past has made a positive difference and was not money merely poured into a bottomless hole. Let them know their gifts have purpose and meaning. And what a great foundation that is upon which to later solicit a renewal!

Other examples of thanking a prospect:

I want to thank you for your patronage. I see you are a (subscriber/member) to XYZ!
I want to thank you for your volunteer work. It's meant a lot to us!

Or, being more specific:

I want to thank you for your help with last month's hunger drive. We all did a great job, don't you think?

Build on Your Existing Relationship

Too frequently, there may be nothing to thank a prospect for in terms of their prior relationship or philanthropy acts. In cases like this, examine your database to find facts about the prospect you know to be true, like his year of graduation, what kind of membership he has, what night his subscription falls on, how long he may have been part of your organization, what he may have listed as an interest or area of concern. Then, confirm that information with the prospect:

Mr. Smith, I see you studied biology here at XYZ. Is that right?
Mr. Smith, I see you graduated in 1978. Is that right?
Mr. Smith, I see you're a subscriber to the Tuesday night series. Is that right?
Mr. Smith, I see you've been a member since the late 1990s. Is that right?
Mr. Smith, I see you subscribe to our environmental update alerts. Is that right?

Telephone Fundraising Rule

You can never thank prospects enough—moreover, it's a great way to begin a call. And when thanking them, be as specific as you can.

Closed-Ended Questions

Asking a closed-ended, yes-no question like those above has a number of effects that lay a foundation for a stronger call.

First, it helps give the caller *legitimacy* as a representative of the institution she is representing. The information or specific facts she is asking to confirm are generally known only to a few people, most specifically bona fide representatives of the institution and the prospect and his family. The prospect can conclude at the outset the call is legitimate.

Telephone Fundraising Rule

Address the prospect by his or her name and use it frequently, but not so conspicuously as to appear insincere. Using the prospect's name helps to personalize the call and lays the foundation for dialogue.

Second, by asking a *closed-ended* question, but asking one to which you know the prospect will answer "yes," helps lay the groundwork for future "yeses" in the call—most specifically a "yes" to a request for pledge support that is coming a bit later! Admittedly, this is a well-established trade technique for sales, not just fundraising. But if it works, why not use it?

Third, it helps *buy time* at a critical early stage in the call. The prospect, having just been interrupted moments ago, will be somewhat uncomfortable, and may be thinking of ways to curtail the call, knowing or believing that a solicitation is coming. A "yes" response to a question briefly distracts from this notion, and helps lengthen the call by precious seconds to enable the caller to move ahead.

Think for a moment of door-to-door sales as a metaphor of your telephone solicitation. You've knocked on the door, the prospect has opened it a crack, and now you'd at least like to be invited to the foyer for a brief chat!

Telephone Fundraising Rule

Avoid the "Imperial 'WE'" when trying to build rapport. Refer to yourself as "I"—it helps personalize the call, creates a basis for two-way communication, and elevates you, the caller, higher in importance and stature in the eyes of the prospect (or at least his ears).

Of course, you want to avoid asking a number of closed-ended questions in rapid-fire succession, even though you know all the answers are "yes," lest it seem like an interrogation!

"I see you're a grad from the year 1984, is that right" "I also see you studied business, right? And that you were a member of Phi Kappa So, and you live in Lowell, Maryland, 242 Brant Lane, right? . . . Okay, hands up against the wall, spread 'em wide. You must be the Mr. Smith we're looking for!"

Open-Ended Questions

Better, a closed-ended question can lead to a good *open-ended* question as a follow-up. Based on the answers to questions like those above:

What did you go on to do after graduation, Mr. Smith?
When was the last time you had a chance to visit campus?
What's been your favorite performance so far in your series?
How have you been enjoying the plays this season, Mr. Smith?
What do you think about our environmental update alert program?
How was your experience with our orthopedic department?

I've seen savvy, articulate fundraisers, sensing the prospect's interests, ask other open-ended questions that help foster the "relationship" (between prospect and the caller/institution).

How did you feel when we won the championship—how about those Huskies, eh?
What do you think of our stance in favor of the new legislation?
So, you really enjoyed the Monet exhibit, that's wonderful. Who are some of your other favorite Impressionists?

Ask the prospect what he thinks, how he feels, questions that have him reflect *positively* on his experience with your organization. These questions can focus him on how he *values* your organization and its work. In a sense, asking him questions is *giving* something to him: the knowledge that his thoughts, opinions, likes, even dislikes, are valued by the institution.

Telephone Fundraising Rule

Ask closed-ended questions that you are assured of getting a "yes" response to. Ask open-ended questions that begin with "what," "how," and even sometimes "where" or "why" to get the prospect to open up and facilitate two-way communication.

Frequently, a prospect will lower any defensive mechanisms he may have raised at the outset of a call and may want to open his floodgates of opinion and dialogue. When this happens, metaphorically speaking, the caller has just been invited from the foyer to sit for a bit with the prospect in the parlor. When this happens, the chances for a gift increase exponentially.

When a prospect wants to register a comment or opinion, a mechanism should be present for the telephone fundraisers to pass those comments along. I've seen hundreds of comments written from telephone fundraisers that are of value to the institution:

- Loves the new president.
- Hates the new president.
- Thinks the new web site is great.
- Thinks the orchestra plays too much modern music.
- Likes the storybook ballets best.
- Thinks the orthopedics department is terrific and wants to thank Dr. Jones especially.
- Love the nurses, thinks they're cute.
- Thinks the school places too much emphasis on athletics.
- Thinks more money should be devoted to women's sports.
- Wants the head coach fired.

And when a telephone fundraiser, after listening to the comments and request of the prospect (explicit or implied) to pass them on, says:

Thanks so much for that feedback, Mr. Smith. I'll be sure to pass it along to the Development Office (or appropriate area).

. . . the prospect feels satisfied that he is valued, that what he has said is important and will be registered.

And, how many times I have been thanked by development officers who eagerly read these unsolicited comments and opinions, and who gain greater insight into the interests, hopes, cares, and sometimes fears of their constituents. Perhaps not as valuable as the total dollars raised, or the statistics of the night's performance in terms of pledge rate and average gifts, but very valuable information nonetheless!

A great way to conclude the part of the call devoted to cultivation or building rapport and segue into the next section of the call is to once again *give* the prospect something. But other than offering thanks for past patronage or philanthropic acts, what else can you give? Here it's up to the invention and creativity of your organization to deliver something.

One way is to provide some information the prospect may find valuable:

I wanted to let you know that we're going to launch a new television advertising campaign to save endangered species. You'll want to be on the lookout for that!

I wanted to let you know we've added some great things to our web site that I know you'll want to check out . . .

The schedule for the free summer concerts has just come out for July. I know you won't want to miss them . . .

We're going to open the new arachnid pavilion in September, and knowing how much you love spiders . . .

Information can be valuable to the prospect, and the cost to you of providing it (while getting some good PR in) is negligible.

Another effective technique, when possible, is to invite the prospects to some specific occasion or event that you may have already planned.

I wanted to invite you back for alumni weekend. It's the first weekend in October—we'd love to see you!

Let me invite you to our members' appreciation party coming up February 3rd, at the Museum.

There's a pre-concert cocktail party next Saturday, all our subscribers are invited—we'd love to see you!

The new exhibit opens June 3rd—we'd love to see you!

Our executive director of political operations is doing an online text question-and-answer session next Thursday at 8 PM. You can access it off the front page of our web site. It should be really interesting and will give you a chance to let him know what you think!

Is there such as thing as too much rapport? Regrettably, I've heard too many calls with telephone fundraisers who are extraordinarily adept at creating rapport, engaging the prospects in conversation, enjoy doing that, and go on doing it for several minutes. Some of them have the gift of gab and are born PR people. But they never seem to get to the most important part of the call . . . the "asking for support" part!

Rapport can be a good thing, but in such cases it's "too much of a good thing."

The telephone medium grants you finite time. You may have a chance to ask two, perhaps three questions of the prospect, with brief controlled follow-ups in an effort to develop rapport. Your efforts should yield two-way conversation lasting around 20 seconds, but seldom more than 60. It's all the time you have, but it should be enough.

Listening for Clues

If you are successful in establishing a rapport with the prospect and putting him at ease, you may be the beneficiary of information that will help you evaluate the prospect as a potential donor. For example, you may be able to get a rough estimate of the prospect's age either by information you have been provided from the organization's database such as a year of graduation or by the sound of the prospect's voice.

There may be obvious things that you hear, like a baby crying in the background, the type of music you overhear from the stereo, or the prospect's offhand reference to his or her husband or wife.

As a product of your efforts to build rapport, the prospect may even offer some explicit information about himself that can be a valuable clues. Some examples:

We really enjoy living in Manhattan.
I work really long hours as a litigation attorney. You were lucky to catch me at home.
My husband will be back soon from his dealership.
I just put the kids to bed.
I do a lot of traveling and missed that performance.
We spend summers in Nantucket and can't attend the summer events.
I usually work the day shift.
The family membership works out great for us. We have five kids!
I also support the World Wildlife Federation. I really like the work they do, too.
My wife recently died, and I'll probably be moving in with my daughter's family.
Thanks to Dr. Jones, I was able to get back to work right away!

Good fundraisers will try to develop a mental image of their prospect and look for subtle clues that will help them determine two things: the prospect's ability and willingness to give.

Consciously or unconsciously, the prospect will be doing the same thing with the caller: developing a mental image of who she is. If the prospect can hear dozens of other voices in the background—a din of noise—he can reasonably conclude the caller is sitting in a call center.

Summary

There is a long-term and a short-term objective to developing rapport with a prospect.

At the moment of your call, you want to put the prospect at ease and overcome any "moods of the moment" that distract the prospect from speaking with YOU. You want to prove your credibility and believability as a bona fide representative of the institution you are raising money for. You want to reinforce the existing ties of the prospect with his or her organization. If there are no prior ties, and it truly is a cold call, you want to discover or uncover the prospect's sympathies with the mission of your organization. And importantly, you will want to listen for subtle clues that can uncover what the prospect's giving potential may be.

In the long term, hopefully you will consider your telephone calls as one component of a donor cultivation strategy: to make the prospects feel that they are valued members of the extended community of your organization, its mission and beliefs.

The Purpose of the Call

N ow you've identified the prospect, briefly built a rapport to the extent that he or she is not yet ready to hang up on you, and hopefully established a connection between his or her interests and the organization you're representing. Now what?

As every good development officer knows, whether in a capital campaign or an annual giving effort, you've got to make the *case*, baby. But first, you have to make a transition from the more lighthearted relationship building to something more serious, your *case*.

The Segue to the Purpose Section of the Call

Moving between sections of an effective telephone fundraising call presents some challenges, and moving from rapport to the purpose is one of the most critical as well. Needless to say, the following sequence is somewhat awkward:

Figure 6.1   Stage 4—Purpose

Rapport:

I'm happy to hear you've been enjoying the alumni newsletter!

Purpose:

Mr. Smith, right now, we're building a library that can accommodate thousands more volumes that our students need access to, and we need your help to complete that project!

Talk about moving from one topic to another at lightning speed. The above, somewhat abbreviated example, while accomplishing a function, doesn't quite flow effortlessly in the syntax of a two-way conversation. Much better is to set up the purpose with the rapport like:

Rapport:

Mr. Smith, I'm calling for a couple of reasons, but first I wanted to thank you for your past support. It's helped us do X and Y—which is terrific, I'm sure you'll agree! I see you get the alumni association newsletter. How have you been enjoying it? [Response] That's terrific!

Purpose:

Mr. Smith, you've probably heard that XYZ right now is in the middle of a capital campaign. I'm also calling to let you we're nearing the final stage . . . the construction of a new library that will be state of the art, one of the best in the region, which is terrific, I'm sure you'll agree!

The Four Cs of Effective Case Making

In the above example, rapport and purpose are knitted together, beginning with "I'm calling for a couple of reasons"—first to thank and build upon a past or current relationship, and second, later in the call, to make a case statement for individual funding.

Whether you're soliciting a past donor or trying to make a new one, you must present a reason for them to give that is:

1. Credible
2. Convincing
3. Compelling
4. Concise

We call it the four Cs of effective case making in telephone fundraising.

Credible

The reason you give for the prospect's support must have the ring of truth and authenticity. Yes, your development officers must always be creative in finding hot buttons that will excite and motivate your constituents. But just make sure that your creativity does not get in the way of the facts!

Convincing

Your oral case statement should be based on a foundation of logical soundness, so that the prospect, upon being presented with the facts, might be seen to be nodding her head in agreement.

Compelling

The purpose or case statement of the call should have a call to action and a sense of urgency that will motivate that prospect to give, one that lays a compelling foundation for the ask.

Concise

And now for the fun part: In the telephone medium you have about 15 to 20 seconds to do this! Take any longer and you can lose the attention of your prospect. The last thing you want to happen is for her to back away from you, literally and figuratively, at this critical stage of the call! Think of the analogy of fishing. During the introduction and rapport phases, you got the prospect to nibble, and now we want a bite . . . or at least a buy-in to your cause.

Exactly how you accomplish this in the telephone medium, with its constraints on time and attention, and the very limited bandwidth you have to play with can spell success or failure of the call.

Far too many development officers who have had loads of experience in writing solicitation letters mistakenly borrow the same jargon of the written letter and try to transpose it to the telephone medium. Long will I remember the development officer of a major educational institution who insisted on our solicitors delivering a canned speech, something like the following:

Institutional excellence can only be achieved through the broad-based participation of alumni through XYZ's Annual Fund. The Annual Fund provides that critical margin of excellence that separates truly great universities from those who merely excel. If XYZ is going to maintain its preeminent position among our peer institutions, it is imperative that each alumnus and alumna make a commitment to provide those extra resources that help define greatness, and solidify our position for years to come . . . et cetera, et cetera, ad nauseum.

Rather than long-winded speeches from the podium, think of the purpose as your best elevator pitch, one that can be executed compellingly between the third and fifth floors!

Other Challenges

There are other critical differences you should consider in crafting an effective purpose case statement in your telephone presentation, ones that delineate the peculiarities of the telephone medium in contrast with the media of written or personal face-to-face speech.

Poor Quality of Land-Line Voice Transmission

Over 160 years since the invention of what many people consider to be an infernal instrument, the quality of analog voice transmission over twisted copper wiring is still severely wanting—far, far from CD digital quality sound. Also, consider that fact that your prospect may be using a wireless handset of modest quality, prone to background electronic interference.

Cellular Telephone Issues

In the age of digital cellular voice transmission the barriers between land lines and mobile phone numbers is beginning to blur. Indeed, many have given up land lines altogether, relying only on their cell phones for voice communication. Not long ago, the thought of soliciting someone on her cell phone was an anathema, using the prospect's valuable cell minutes adding injury to insult. However, with the reduction of price for mobile phones and cell plans, the cell phone has become an "always on" ubiquitous channel for voice communication. No doubt, many of the telephone numbers you have in your database are cellular. But soliciting over a cell line has its own unique set of challenges.

Digital cellular quality is variable and often unreliable. One can think back to the famous Sprint commercial of the 1990s, the video of the pin dropping next to a telephone, "so clear you can hear a pin drop!" Not! While I have been impressed more recently with voice quality transmission of VOIP (Voice Over Internet Protocol), it will be some years before its usage is as ubiquitous as, or begins to converge with, fixed point land-line and mobile cellular usage.

Background Distractions

Even with the best direct-wired home handset devices, some concentration is necessary to follow your prospect's words and voice pattern, and that may even further be complicated by other aural background distractions, be it the TV blaring at home, extraneous conversations carried on elsewhere in the room, or at the solicitor's end, the background din of dozens of solicitors in your call center. This is a limitation that works both ways, as the solicitor may strain to pick up subtle verbal clues of the prospect's reactions to your pitch. The distractions of the prospect on her cell phone can be particularly daunting, particularly if she happens to be driving, biking, or even walking down the street.

The bottom line when crafting an effective purpose is to consider these limitations of medium in which you are working. Three-dollar multisyllabic words, complex extended sentence structures, and extensive elaboration on a topic . . . leave that to the realm of the letter and brochure writers. Such will not translate nor transmit well in the electronic medium. To be an effective writer of a case statement in the telephone medium, think:

- The four Cs mentioned above, plus:
- Natural speech patterns (of spoken, not written English, or native tongue of constituency)
- Syntax, usage, and vocabulary in sync with your audience or constituency
- Conversational tone (leaving open the opportunity for dialogue or to answer questions)
- Personal (keeping in mind the prospect's interests, involvement, passions to your cause—it's not the reason YOU want her to give, but why SHE wants to give)

Time

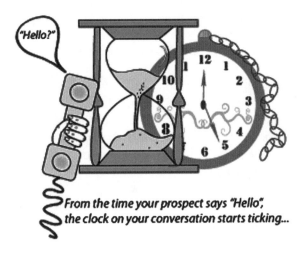

From the time your prospect says "Hello",
the clock on your conversation starts ticking...

Why do you have so little time to make your case? As we've mentioned before, the telephone is an *interruptive* medium. The prospect was engaged in some activity at the moment of your call, and you have taken her out of that space and asked her to enter another. Furthermore, the prospect you have persuaded to spend the last minute or so on the phone with you, no matter how successful you may have been in building rapport (that short-term relationship that hopefully will carry you into the negotiation phase) will not sit still (or stand) for a long-winded speech. She wants to get back to doing whatever it was she was doing in the moments just before your call, be it finishing her evening meal, cleaning the kitchen, finishing that next chapter of the exciting book *Effective Telephone Fundraising*.

Also, ideally you already have invested some critical moments in developing rapport with the prospect, doing some positive PR for your organization that will parlay itself into being permitted additional *time* with the prospect, time that can be invested in making a cogent case, but leave plenty of room for the "ask" and time to answer any questions the prospect may have or to rebut any potential objections.

Brevity Is the Essence of Wit—and Effectiveness

So, exactly how concise can a purpose telephone case statement be and still be effective? At its essence, the purpose can be boiled down to one word: HELP! Mr. Smith, XYZ more than ever needs your help!

Over the years, I've seen some off-the-track fundraisers do exactly that, boil their purpose down to that one word: "Mr. Smith, another reason for my call is to yell 'Help!'"—a succinct and genuine call for help, the candor of which can elicit a chuckle of humor from the prospect, followed by the necessary elaboration from the solicitor.

In another instance, I observed one solicitor, going to the extreme of candor, begin his purpose thusly: "Another reason I'm calling, Mr. Smith, is to pick your pocket," spoken with a kind of deadpan humor that would invariably elicit a genuine chuckle from the prospect, albeit at times somewhat nervously.

 Telephone Fundraising Rule

Condense your case statement by doing syllable counts—the fewer the syllables, the better, and use monosyllabic action verbs to create a compelling case. Rewrite, craft, and hone your message.

More practically and professionally, however, an effective purpose can be condensed to a sentence or two.

Our institution needs your help, right now, because:

Thousands more will be able to visit the museum thanks to the new exhibit hall—plus we'll be on sound financial footing for years to come!

With the latest round of city budget cuts, we urgently need community support to be able to house and feed thousands of our animals!

Last year we set a new annual giving record, but this year, we want to beat it, and set a new record in alumni participation—you can help make that happen!

Although we set a new record in alumni support last year, we still lag behind some of our peer schools like Havilland and Princeforth—and we don't want to be second to anyone!

Although we have one of the state's best cancer treatment programs, we urgently need the funding to complete the late-stage care unit that can vault our hospital to among the best in the nation, but more important, we'll save thousands more lives!

With additional funding, we can increase our environmental educational programs to the schools here in our community and make our city among the greenest in the country!

Bottom line, we need your support to help save the planet from catastrophe!

Telephone Fundraising Rule

Use "tie down" questions in the purpose case statement—questions that invariably elicit a "yes" response by the prospect. This helps keep the call interactive, engender two-way communication, and create buy-in to the cause.

The Purpose: Case Statement Strategies

Some of the above mini-case statements are positive and some negative in tone, which poses the question: What's my best telephone strategy, positive or negative?

Positive Strategies

These are the most preferred, year-in and year-out strategies, effective not only for annual giving, but essential in capital campaigns. Here it's necessary to look inward and forward at the same time, to emphasize what is positive about your organization, how it's meeting the challenges inherent in your organizational mission head-on, how it's providing solutions to problems, and building a base for a better tomorrow—one that the prospect is part of, and has complete buy-in to. "Hop on the bandwagon," you might say.

Bottom line, your constituents want to be part of a winning team, not a losing one. Your success is their success, and they should feel good about it.

This is an appeal, not only to their sense of equity, social conscience, and willingness to do the right thing—it's an appeal to their ego and sense of self-worth!

Educational Institution (We're Okay, You're Okay)

Mr. Smith, I'm also calling to let you know that US News and World Report *just ranked XYZ in the top tier liberal arts colleges in our region . . . which is good news, I'm sure you'll agree! (Response) So, Mr. Smith, your XYZ diploma means more than ever, but if we're going to stay on top, we need every alum to support the Annual Fund this year!*

Athletic Program Foundation (Join the Team!)

Mr. Smith, as you know, last year the team was 11 and 1—almost a perfect season, and that was just terrific, wasn't it? (Response) But Mr. Smith, if we're going for 12 and 0 and finally beat ABC next year in the finals, we need every former athlete, such as yourself, to contribute to the "Victory Fund"—you know, the funds for athlete assistance, equipment, and training to help put our program over the top!

Community Advocacy Organization (Feel Good about Us, and Yourself)

Last year, your gift helped move over 300 homeless from temporary shelters into permanent housing, along with counseling and training that can help them become happy, productive citizens, with dignity and self-respect—that's something we can all be proud of, don't you think? (Response) But with the economic pressures we're facing, this year, demand for our services will be even greater, and that's why we need your renewed support of the "Advocacy Fund."

Museum (For the Kids)

This year's Monet exhibit brought in thousands of new visitors to the museum, including nearly 3,000 area school kids, many of whom had never visited us before, isn't that terrific?! (Response) Mr. Smith, as you know, making special exhibits free to school kids is very costly—well beyond the regular membership fees—and that's why we need your support for the museum's "Education Fund" to help instill a love of art in our young people.

Performing Arts Organization (Keep Good Things Goin')

Mr. Smith, you probably know that tickets and subscriptions account for only about a third of the cost of our plays; the rest must come from grants and contributions from people who love the theater, such as yourself. That's why your renewed support of the Annual Fund is so important!

Capital Campaign (Be a Part of Something Lasting, Short of Immortality)

Mr. Smith, as you know, we're considered one of the top organizations in the country, but we're looking ahead to strengthen our already fine reputation—and that's why building this new state-of-the-art facility is so important—to improve our services for years to come!

The bottom line of all of these vignettes: Things are going well, but things can go better with your help. Share in our success. We are a winner. You are, too. Let's win together! The only downside to this kind of approach is that the prospect has so many competing demands on limited resources, is there sufficient urgency to move her into the pledge column? Is that bandwagon sufficiently attractive that she'll want to make the effort to hop up on it? For the "Good News" approach to work, the elevator pitch must be sufficiently upbeat and compelling and delivered by the fundraiser with such commitment and enthusiasm that the prospect is pulled up onto the wagon by your outstretched hand. Be irresistible.

Telephone Fundraising Rule

Use the words "I" and "we" to identify yourself as part of the "team" in creating a compelling case. Avoid phrases such as "They need the funds to build their new gallery." Be personal and personable.

But, there is the dark side to consider, too.

Negative Strategies

You are asking the prospect to join you in fighting some external threat, preventing consequences that are unwanted, unacceptable, painful, chilling, and catastrophic. Without Mr. Smith's support, right now, this year, during this call, bad things are going to happen. Don't let it happen! Don't let the enemy win! Give now!

Educational Institution (External Funding Cuts)
Mr. Smith, I'm also calling to ask you if you've heard about the massive state budget cuts for XYZ this year . . . [Response] Well, these cuts are so drastic, we'll have to lay off staff, even faculty—cuts we can't accept in a great school. But your gift to the Alumni Fund can help right now—and show your confidence in what we think is a great school. I hope you agree!

Arts Organization (Internal Budget Crisis: Bad News—Good News)
Mr. Smith, you've heard the news about the Ballet's budget problems, right? [Response] Well, the bad news—it's a real crisis—a one-million-dollar deficit. But the good

news—we can get through the year without canceling a single performance if every patron gives to the Emergency Fund!

Political Advocacy Organization (You versus Them)

Mr. Smith, I assume you've been hearing about the lies and distortions about the ABC legislation. [Response] Well, they are well funded through special interests, and have millions to spend, but we need fight back right now, and take to the airwaves in a truth campaign—but that takes money, and the support of every well-informed person who cares about this, like you do.

Disaster Relief Organization (Master of Disaster)

Mr. Smith, you've probably seen the horrific scenes on the news—this week's tsunami killed over 30,000 people, but even worse, nearly 10 million people are homeless and lack food, medical care, and basic sanitary needs—an unbelievable disaster, I'm sure you agree. [Response] Mr. Smith, we must raise over $50 million now if we're going to save millions of lives—and we need your help today . . .

A well-crafted negative campaign can be very compelling and can achieve increased participation and average gifts in a time of crisis. But please know that, ultimately, donors will want to support and be a part of a winning team, not a losing one. At some point, psychologically, emotionally, and practically, your negative well is going to run dry. Save this strategy for a real crisis, not a contrived one.

Telephone Fundraising Rule

Avoid long-winded speeches—for every sentence or statement of fact, inject at least one interactive question, or "tie-down" that seeks the prospect's buy-in and agreement to the premise.

Precall Letters: Yes and No!

There are many advocates of sending prospects a precall letter that not only informs the prospect he or she will be receiving a call asking for a contribution, but also explaining the scope and objectives of the fundraising campaign. The rationale for sending precall letters is to explain the objectives and purpose of the fundraising campaign and announce that a representative of the nonprofit organization will soon be making a call—the letter does not specifically make the ask but may provide guidelines for the prospect to think about in making a gift.

A precall letter also has the intent of legitimizing the solicitor, so that the call does not come in cold—the prospect presumes its legitimacy. Furthermore, crafty letter writers assume their letter will do the heavy lifting in explaining the often complex objectives of the fundraising campaign in a detail that simply cannot be accomplished in a 3- or 4-minute phone call. This frees the solicitor to simply make the ask.

So, it makes sense to send precall letters, right? Perhaps.

There are a number of downsides in going to the trouble of adding a precall direct mail component to your telephone fundraising campaign.

Expense

First of all, sending individual, word-processed personalized letters adds expense to the campaign, with first-class postage as much as $1.25 to $3.00 per piece, depending on the degree of personalization, length of the letter, and complexity of the mailing. The bottom line cost of this component must be justified in either increased income of the campaign through its effectiveness or decreased costs of the telephone solicitation phase. Some campaigns try to cut the cost by sending a nonpersonalized bulk mailing, perhaps even a postcard. But as conventional wisdom goes, the less the degree of personalization, the less the effectiveness.

Complexity

Adding a direct mail component, coordinated with a follow-up telephone phase can add a fair amount of complexity to a telephone campaign. Ideally, first-class mailings are timed to be received a few days before the phone call so that the recipient has the time to digest and reflect on the contents and prepare for the impending phone call. Staging mailings to achieve maximum timed effectiveness requires a great deal of administrative oversight, because the pace of the calling may fall short or exceed the pace of the mailings leading to phone calls and are consequently too early or too late.

Once It's Gone, It's Gone

Adding a creative mail component can lock you into a case statement strategy. Once you have the objectives and goals of your campaign decided, your letter writer must come up with the creative strategy to make that case statement speak to your constituents. With letters this is a one-size-fits-all strategy, and once decided, it's difficult to change course, or even tweak or fine-tune. Logically, the telephone call is tied to that strategy, so once you've mailed, you are somewhat locked in. What if it's the wrong strategy or there is a segment of your list, a subconstituency that requires a different direction? You're locked in. One of the great advantages of the telephone medium is that messages and strategies can be tweaked, fine-tuned, and changed on the fly based on auditing, feedback, and performance results. That flexibility can be compromised if you're joined at the hip with a precall letter strategy.

Do They Read it?

Prospects have gotten savvy to even the most skilled efforts at letter personalization.

Back in the olden days of early processing, the technology was awe inspiring. In the early 1980s data came into our word-processing shop at the lightning rate of 300 baud. Names and addresses were sorted to create word-processed letters on a massive ink-jet printer (these things looked like they weighed a ton), with what appeared to personally typed inside addresses on stationary somewhat smaller than standard business size, and the obligatory "Dear Mr. Smith" in the salutation line. Signatures were offset printed, in blue or black. Individual envelopes were printed, as opposed to using impersonal labels, and with luck, the personalized letters were matched by hand with the correct envelopes, and then mailed with a real first-class postage stamp. There was a lot of licking and stuffing going on in those early days!

Early on, most prospects were fooled into believing they were receiving a personal letter, ostensibly from a highly respected member of their community, and would take the time to open and carefully read the missive.

Well, as baud rates and computer processing power increased and the cost of ink-jet printers decreased along with their size, word-processing costs significantly decreased. Everyone began to personalize letters using word processing. These days word-processed letters are so ubiquitous few people think they are getting a personal letter from someone important, even if the letter includes a handwritten message in the margin.

Furthermore, as postage rates have significantly increased, some non-profits have sought to use lower-cost nonprofit rate presort postage, again something that is unlikely to fool a sophisticated public. Furthermore, as the mailing is bulk, effective timing to a phone call is virtually impossible.

Bottom line, many, if not most, of these letters are likely to end up in the circular file and have no positive effect on the results of your phone campaign. Prospects will get your letter in the day's mail, along with a dozen other such items. A quick glance at a standard-size business envelope carrying a nonprofit bulk postage stamp may very well be sorted to the recycling file along with the other pieces of junk mail. Even if the prospect opens the mail, he or she may give only a cursory glance to its contents, devoting only the time necessary to determine that it is an unwanted solicitation letter.

Preparing the Solicitors to Succeed or to Fail?

So, either your prospects will have received and read your letter, or they will have not.

Let's assume that the letter is an effective letter, well crafted, informative, readable, and engaging. It is read and digested by the prospect. The telephone solicitation might go something like this:

Fundraiser: *Mr. Smith, I'm also calling to follow up a letter that Jim Geary (our most famous and highly respected constituent) sent you a few days ago. Did you receive the letter?*

Mr. Smith: *Yes, I did.*

Fundraiser: *Terrific! What did you think about the objectives of our "Campaign for the Eons"?*

Mr. Smith: *I agreed with the objectives and think the organization is headed on the right track with this campaign!*

The above presents a best-case scenario for the intent of a precall letter, or series of letters building public consciousness and awareness of a campaign. The letter was received by the prospect, the letter was read, its contents digested, and the leading question by the solicitor, one that is designed to elicit a positive response by the prospect, received the hoped-for reaction. At this juncture the solicitor is free from explaining the details or the purpose of the campaign and can move directly in to the ask phase of the call.

Now, let's assume the following scenario:

Fundraiser: *Mr. Smith, I'm also calling to follow up a letter that Jim Geary (our most famous and highly respected constituent) sent you a few days ago. Did you receive the letter?*

Mr. Smith: *Yes, I did.*

Fundraiser: *Terrific! What did you think about the objectives of our "Campaign for the Eons"?*

Mr. Smith: *The campaign is okay, as far as it goes, but there is no way I'll be able to give anything.*

At this juncture, a hole has been dug for the solicitor who is left floundering, having a difficult task to develop enough of a base in order to be able to proceed to the ask phase of the call and engage the prospect in some rudimentary negotiation.

Now, let's assume that a letter is sent out and is either *not* received or *not* read by the prospect:

Fundraiser: *Mr. Smith, I'm also calling to follow up a letter that Jim Geary (our most famous and highly respected constituent) sent you a few days ago. Did you receive the letter?*

Mr. Smith: *No, I didn't.*

Fundraiser: *Well, let me take a moment to tell you about our "Campaign for the Eons."*

Mr. Smith: *Can you just send the letter out? I'll take a look at it, and if I'm interested, I'll send something back.*

This scenario presents an even greater challenge for the fundraiser. Not only is he or she under the pressure of explaining the purpose of the campaign in a concise and compelling way, taking a few words to cover what was the content of one or more mailings, but the fundraiser is forced into a difficult position of refusing a prospect or a constituent's request:

Fundraiser: *I'm sorry, it's not possible to resend the information. Let me take just a moment to tell you about the Campaign.*

. . . or disingenuously stating:

Fundraiser: *Basically it was just a note to let you know I'd be calling about the Campaign for the Eons—just to tell you a bit about it . . .*

Of course, the right thing to do is what the donor or the constituent requested: Resend the information. Not only is this administratively complex, costly, and difficult to do in a coordinated direct mail telephone campaign, but any pretense of the letters being personal is dropped. Furthermore, there is no assurance that Mr. Smith is being genuine in requesting the information to carefully consider his participation in the "Campaign for the Eons" and is not merely trying to get a solicitor off of his phone. The costly remailing and follow-up phone call is more likely than not to come up short.

Of course, there is always the exception to the rule. The fundraiser may have spent a considerable amount of time with the prospect, may have determined that the prospect has the capacity to give substantially, and that there is genuine interest in the organization and its mission—a diamond in the rough. These are the exceptions you have to decide upon in a coordinated mail-phone campaign.

So based on the scenarios presented above, precall letters, or even less costly postcards, aren't worth the hassle, right?

Well, it depends. Perhaps you are targeting a group of highly affiliated prospects who take interest in what you doing, follow your activities closely, and read what you mail them. In these cases, it makes sense to mail—there's a high probability they will read it, so that nonreceipt of the mail is usually a nonissue.

Furthermore, for capital campaigns that cover multiple years and are complex in scope, and for which you are seeking a capital-sized commitment, the general publicity surrounding the campaign and your organization's efforts to build general awareness and buy-in among your constituents may augur for a mail component. Constituents will want to know the details far beyond your callers' ability to explain it in 25 seconds. But, if you're concerned that nonreceipt of mail can become an obstacle for fundraisers, you can still mail precall letters, but not center the phone call on them:

Fundraiser: *Mr. Smith, you've probably read about (or have heard about) the Campaign for the Eons—we're really excited about this because we'll be able to add both a new auditorium and a library to our campus, which is sorely needed, I'm sure you agree!* [Response and Discussion]

Another option is to test a precall mail to a portion of your database against a cold call. If you can show better statistical performance in the mailed segment, more than covering its cost, then go for it!

Telephone Fundraising Rule

If the prospect has questions about the fundraising effort, or any questions at all about the organization and its welfare, take the time to answer them and engage the prospect. Questions from the prospect = a "buy signal" that will translate to a pledge of support!

Summary

Sometimes you don't even have to make an effective case for your organization. Repeat givers who are accustomed to an annual giving appeal may simply be persuaded to give due to the immediacy of the call. Were it so that all constituents could be so effectively trained!

The vast majority of your database or your extended constituency is likely to consist of nondonors or lapsed donors that will need to be persuaded to make a gift to your institution. So the more concise and compelling you can state your case, crafting an effective purpose for your call, the more that will translate into increased pledge rates and average gifts.

CHAPTER 7

The Ask!

Just to review the process and how far you've come, first you identified the prospect you wanted to speak to, gained an audience with him or her, and hopefully developed some degree of rapport. Then, after he or she is reflecting positively on you and your organization, you made a compelling case for the prospect to contribute his or her hard-earned dollars.

Now what? Well, "follow the yellow brick road" to the next, most essential if not inevitable stage of a fundraising call: the ask. You might not find yourself in the Land of Oz with a benevolent Wizard ready to whisk you back to Kansas, or better, write a huge check five seconds after you say "Hello." With persistence, skill, and a little luck, your first ask may take you to the next stage of the phone call, the negotiation, or the close and keep you in the game of creating a new donor or renewing an old one.

Figure 7.1   Stage 5—The Ask

The Weak-Kneed—Need Not Apply

As I've mentioned before, some telephone fundraisers are born to do this: ask prospective donors to give money. These naturals have the instincts and persistence to be successful, and the thought of asking a donor to give a substantial gift is second nature to them.

Others, more meek and mild, are congenitally disinclined to be so assertive as to ask for a specific contribution, a reticence rooted in meekness, acute sensitivity, a false sense of empathy for the prospect, and perhaps even a lack of self-esteem. Psycho-babble aside, one of the challenges of a scriptwriter is to make it easy, if not imperative, for telephone fundraisers to perform the most fundamental task of their job description: ask for money.

Part of your success with new fundraising staff lies in your preparation and training prior to their ever taking up a script.

Some fundraising staff may not know what philanthropy is about, and may not even know the meaning of the word, having grown up in households where their parents never gave to charities or volunteered their time to benefit a local charity. These recruits may pose the greatest challenge to training, to get them believing that is not only appropriate but imperative for charities to solicit prospects.

Others will have grown up in households where charity was a regular feature: donating time to the local church or homeless center, tithing, giving to one's school or college, giving to the local museum, or supporting a political or social cause they fervently believe in.

Regardless, it is useful background training to explain to new fundraisers that the vast majority of dollars given to nonprofits do not come from corporations, foundations, or other institutional funders, but instead come from *people*—individuals like Jane Doe and Mr. Smith, without whose support charities and the good work they do would not survive.

And further, it's very useful to explain that *people* are most likely to give to other *people*—like the caller who is representing the nonprofit organization—and that's why *her* call, person to person, is so very important. Indeed, if you're the one in charge of a telephone fundraising program, perhaps you feel it's a *responsibility* for people to give, to the extent that they are able, to support worthy causes, particularly causes they believe in, or organizations of which they are a constituent and from which they may have benefited. If such is your cultural value, then share it with your staff.

Setting aside for the moment the "big" philanthropic picture, how do you get your staff to believe it's okay to ask a prospect for a contribution of a *specific dollar amount* as opposed to the:

Uh, Mr. Smith, uh, can you give a little something this year, I mean, uh, whatever you can do—uh, we'll appreciate it . . .

If the caller doesn't believe that what he is doing is not only appropriate, but right, that may be reflected in his voice, and that lack of conviction can be sensed by the prospect—not a firm foundation to enter into a negotiation.

The Concept of a "Proposal"

One way of explaining the ask process to your staff is to draw a parallel to charities that get funding from institutions, like corporations and foundations.

You can assure your staff that the job of a development professional is *not* simply to open the mail and see what checks may have arrived that day. In the case of corporations and foundations, fundraisers go to considerable pains to develop a written "proposal" that makes the case for funding and requests funding *for a specific dollar amount.* Furthermore, the funding the development professional requests is usually a multiple of what they think the foundation will actually give them. In other words, you aim to ask high.

So, what you're asking a telephone fundraiser to do is essentially the same thing: Make a proposal, a *verbal* proposal to a prospective donor, and to ask high.

Make It Personal

Another training tactic, particularly if you're calling in to a database of prospects that are identified *constituents* of the organization in some way or another, is to explain to your staff the desire of the nonprofit to contact prospective donors *personally,* one on one. Many donors or prospects may never have had the opportunity to *personally* speak to a representative of the organization they support. And many have never given or have never increased their giving because they were never *asked* to do so. The immediacy and intimacy of a personal contact they will make is actually a service to the donor. Give the donor the opportunity to give—it's your responsibility!

Regardless how you do it, you must get the buy-in of your fundraising staff. No matter what kind of script, or how explicit the text in making the ask, it must be done so with *conviction* by the fundraiser.

There have been a number of maxims or platitudes in the fundraising arena to explain the importance of this concept:

If you don't ask, you won't get.
Ask and you shall receive.
You need to step up to the plate if you're going to hit the ball.
If you don't ask, the answer is always "no."

But fundraisers who can't ask for money can't fundraise. They become, to paraphrase an old comedy show "former fundraisers, defunct, expired, demised, ceased to be, fundraisers no more, in a word—*ex-fundraisers!*"

Strategies for the First "Ask"

Strategy 1: The Sight Raise

This strategy is used in either annual or capital campaigns, for either non-donors, donor upgrade campaigns, or membership campaigns. The theory here is "shoot high . . . you can always come down."

Furthermore, it is a strategy that works far better in medium like a personal visit or a telephone call than in direct mail or online. In those media, you can initially suggest a substantial gift, and then through back-and-forth, find a lower gift that works.

But in the written media, all of the options must be laid out for the prospect to consider:

Please, we'd like you to consider giving as much as $1,000 this year to our Millennium Campaign. Even $500 or $250 will have substantial impact. But whatever you give, $100, $50, or even $35, it will go a long way . . . etc., etc.

Indeed, there may even be a blank space for Mr. Smith to fill in his own number, if he doesn't like any of the options. You can't present them one at a time, having him focus on one to the exclusion of others. But, in the telephone medium, you can lay out your proposals, one at a time, engaging in dialogue with Mr. Smith about each.

One key to using the sight raise strategy effectively is to find a number, a proposed level of giving, that is most definitely a reach for the prospect, but is not completely unrealistic for a large percentage of the constituents you are targeting, relative to their ability to give. Indeed, it is a level that a few of your constituents *will* give, if asked.

If you ask well beyond the ability of the group to give, for example, you suggest to each prospect the figure of $1 million, the proposal will seem ludicrous, unbelievable, and can undermine the credibility of the caller at a crucial stage of the call. So, before you pursue this strategy and bandy about a huge number, you should know at least something about your constituents before you ask.

For example, let's say you are a college or university that is calling non-donors for an annual fund. You're a good school, and most of your graduates go on to rewarding careers. You may decide to divide your database on the following basis:

Years Since Graduation	First Ask Target
15+ years	$1,000
6–14 years	$ 500
1–5 years	$ 250

Or let's say you are a social service organization with several thousand donors. You may do an analysis of your database, and find a healthy average gift, nearly $70, with a number of gifts of $250 and a several gifts of $500 helping pull the average up. Perhaps many of these donors are ready for an upgrade proposal to the $1,000 level.

Objectives of the Sight Raise   Remember, the objective of the sight raise is not to ask what you think you're going to get. Your purpose is the following:

Raise the Prospect's Sights   Asking for a relatively hefty gift induces the prospect to think in financial terms substantially above what he or she would have thought given his or her own discretion. Perhaps Mr. Smith, who was a 1971 grad from the Business School, on his own may have been happy to quickly write a check out for $25 to his alma mater, XYZ University, if you were to ask him:

Mr. Smith, can you give anything to XYZ this year?

But XYZ is asking him to consider a level far above that, on the logical assumption he has a career, is well along into it, and may have at least some philanthropic potential. Perhaps $1,000 is an appropriate starting point, or $500. It may be that Mr. Smith, having never given before, will want to make up for some lost time!

Provide Room to Negotiate Down   By beginning at a level that is arguably ambitious if not stratospheric—it leaves the telephone fundraiser plenty of room to come back to earth, to a level that is more feasible for Mr. Smith to give, based on the fundraiser's perception of his giving potential. If you began the solicitation at a $50 level or less, where do you have left to go in a negotiation? Down to $25? Or, perhaps, $10. Or less?

The simple fact of the matter is that your average gift will be a function of where you begin a negotiation, and telephone fundraising programs cannot sustain themselves with $15 average gifts!

Uncover Clues   You are making a first proposal to Mr. Smith. One of two things will happen as a result. Either he will accept the proposal, and will say "yes," or he will not. And if he says "no," invariably it will be accompanied by some reaction on his part that may range from silence to hearty laughter or a simple explanation that he can't or won't give that amount.

When Mr. Smith declines your proposal (we won't use the word *refuses*), he may provide you with a wealth of information that will give you a clearer picture of what his giving potential is. Or he may be quiet, taciturn even, and you may have to ask some follow-up questions to help get a better read of where he is coming from. This is information that you will need to formulate a credible counterproposal—or go right to a "close."

Yes!   One important reason to make proposals for "sight-raised" amounts is that some of your constituents, right off the bat, are going to say "YES!"

It is one of the miracles of the medium that has always continued to astonish me—that a constituent whose giving potential was unknown, who never showed tremendous affinity or affiliation to the nonprofit, is professionally and warmly approached on the telephone and instantly says "yes" to your first proposal. I grant you, it doesn't happen a lot, but when it does, it is cause for excitement and celebration in a phone room, does wonders for the day's stats, and really helps your overall average gift.

Moreover, it helps everyone "believe." New fundraisers will look over at the cause for commotion, the fundraiser being congratulated, and the large gift posted for all to see, and say to themselves, "Hey, this actually works!"

Articulating the Sight Raise   What are some effective ways to phrase a sight raise? Obviously you don't want to express it in such a way that we are *expecting* Mr. Smith to give a huge sum of money or that we feel he *owes* it to the organization or is morally obligated to give.

Rather, because we usually *don't* know what Mr. Smith's ability to give is, think of the sight-raise as a way of giving Mr. Smith the *opportunity* to support substantially by making this personal call—indeed, some *are* able to give large sums and maybe Mr. Smith can give, too.

There are a variety of ways to nuance a sight raise.

Example: School Annual Fund

Fundraiser: *Mr. Smith, to keep XYZ a great school, a few alumni have been able to make substantial gifts to the annual fund this year, some as much as $1,000—is that something you could consider as well?*

Example: Giving Levels, Recognition

Fundraiser: *Mr. Smith, some of our friends have been able to join one of our most prestigious donor groups, the Benefactors. Is this something you could do with a gift of $1,000?*

Example: Annual Fund, Giving Levels with Benefits

Fundraiser: *Mr. Smith, some of our members are joining a special group of our most loyal supporters, the "ABC Friends Society." To say thanks, we'll send you free tickets to the Donor Appreciation Dinner, along with the Friends Special newsletter—how do you feel about doing this with a gift of $1,000?*

Example: Action Fund, Advocacy Campaign

Fundraiser: *Mr. Smith, to make our voice heard, we really need to you join this campaign. A few folks we've spoken to this evening of been able to give $1,000—how do you feel about making this kind of commitment to our cause?*

Some Guidelines for Phrasing an Effective "Ask"
Get to the Point   The "ask" is not a time for an extensive speech. You've already expended a fair number of compelling syllables in the purpose section of the call; now is the time to ask. Loquaciousness does not equate to persuasiveness:

Mr. Smith, it's really important that everyone give this year because it will provide the resources we need to keep XYZ a first-rate organization, and we really need as many of our constituents to participate, so we can show broad-based support, and set a positive example for everyone else. So, what do you think about giving $500 to this year's Annual Fund? . . . We'd really appreciate it!

Look, you've already laid the groundwork in the purpose section of the call for *reasons* to give. By talking, talking, and talking some more, you're apt to have Mr. Smith drumming his fingers on the table, just at the point where you want to keep him listening intently. He knows you've set him up for the ask at this point. It's in both of your interests to get to it.

Telephone Fundraising Rule

Use the two-breath measure for an effective ask. If a fundraiser can't make the proposal in a single—or at most a couple of breaths—shorten your text!

Summarize Benefits Let's say you're dealing with an annual or capital giving campaign where there are donor recognition levels with benefits, or you're soliciting for a membership campaign where there may be some extensive benefits for "joining" at a specific level. (See the Appendix, Section A for some sample donor recognition and membership levels.)

One of the challenges of a scriptwriter is how best to capsulate the benefits so that they will accomplish their objective: to interest a prospect in joining at a specific level. Consider the following example:

Mr. Smith, a few of our friends are joining at the Benefactor level for $500. As a Benefactor, you and your family will receive the monthly e-newsletter that will keep you up to date about all of the events going on here, four free tickets to the members-only party next October, the ABC calendar, which I know you will enjoy, a ticket to the Benefactors' dinner next April and recognition in our annual report—and I almost forgot, you also get the ABC coffee mug with the motto "Let's Drink to ABC!" on the front! (Pause) Oh, and I need to mention that $405 of the $500 is tax deductible! (Long pause) Uh, what do you think?

That was a long breath full. But, depending on Mr. Smith's "mood of the moment" he probably found the long list, orally delivered, a tedious exercise, with the fundraiser reeling off the benefits in a kind of aural blur. And, even if Mr. Smith was listening intently, and was visualizing each benefit as the fundraiser presented it, consider the following eventuality:

Mr. Smith: *That's pretty interesting, but I can't afford that much.*

Fundraiser: *Oh, I understand, Mr. Smith. Well, let me suggest the Sustainers with a gift of $250. At this level we'll send you two tickets to the members-only party next October—that's two fewer than the Benefactors, but you'd still get the ABC calendar, recognition in the annual report, and of course, the ABC coffee mug so you can still drink to us every morning! It's just that you won't be invited to the Benefactors' dinner (trust me, the food isn't that good), but it's only $250 and $212 of that is tax deductible! So, how do you feel about that?*

Mr. Smith: *Uh, what did you say your name was?*

Fundraiser: *Elaine, Mr. Smith—Elaine Peters!*

Mr. Smith: *Well, Elaine, is there anything you could send out to me that explains all the membership levels so I can really understand what I'm getting?*

Elaine Peters: *Uh, well, I'm happy to take the time to explain everything on the phone to you . . . Let me suggest the "Friends Level". . . . etc., etc.*

Which brings me a telephone fundraising rule:

Telephone Fundraising Rule

The telephone is a lousy medium for transmitting detailed information.

We've already discussed much of the background for why the above is true: poor or variable quality of voice transmission, the interruptive quality of the telephone, and the limited attention span of the medium. So, if benefits are going to work *for you* in a telephone call and not *against you*, you've got to present the CliffsNotes version, in simple, clear, and attractive language the prospect can understand and quickly digest:

Fundraiser: *This year, some of our friends are joining the "Benefactors." To say thanks, we'll invite you to the annual Benefactors' Dinner, and some other great benefits including our famous "Let's Drink to ABC!" coffee mug! Mr. Smith, how do you feel about this for a gift of $500?*

The above script is shorter and cleaner. The most important and salient benefit unique to the "Benefactors" level, the Benefactors' Dinner, was mentioned prominently. The fact that other benefits were included was alluded to, but the caller didn't list them in a tedious fashion. And the one benefit that *all* members receive, regardless of giving level, and that you know is immensely popular, the "Let's Drink to ABC!" coffee mug, was prominently featured. In the telephone medium, Mr. Smith should be able to digest that much information.

And consider some of the possible eventualities, given the CliffsNotes benefit presentation:

Elaine Peters: *This year, some of our friends are joining the "Benefactors." To say thanks, we'll invite you the annual Benefactors' Dinner, and some other great benefits including our famous "Let's Drink to ABC!" coffee mug! Mr. Smith, how do you feel about this for a gift of $500?*
Mr. Smith: *As a Benefactor, would I receive anything else?*

What a wonderful "buy" signal that is for a fundraiser! Elaine Peters, our intrepid fundraiser, can then consult her written information and comply with Mr. Smith's request. Here the prospect has opened the door wide for more information; you're not trying to shove what you can through a crack. Give the prospect what he wants!

Or consider the following:

Elaine Peters: *This year, some of our friends are joining the "Benefactors." To say thanks, we'll invite you to the annual Benefactors' Dinner and some other great benefits including our famous "Let's Drink to ABC!" coffee mug! Mr. Smith, how do you feel about this for a gift of $500?*
Mr. Smith: *I'd love to be able to do that this year, but I just can't!*
Elaine Peters: *I understand. Well, Mr. Smith, let me suggest the "Sustainers." Among some other benefits we'll send you two tickets to the annual members-only party, and of course our famous coffee mug . . . and this would be only $250. Is that more comfortable?*
Mr. Smith: *Sounds terrific, but I'd rather have a "Let's Drink to ABC!" beer mug instead.*
Elaine Peters: *Oh, Mr. Smith, you're teasing me!*

The capsulated CliffsNotes version of the sight raise sets up the Cliffs Notes version of a counterproposal—or the "close" if you're pursuing a two-ask negotiating format.

 Telephone Fundraising Rule

Mention only the most salient and attractive benefit that either first becomes included at a given level or is unique at that level. Don't list all the benefits for each level.

Benefits before Dollars It is recommended that you *front load* the *benefits* of your ask, and attach the price tag, or price of admission if you'd prefer, afterwards. Consider one of the scenarios presented earlier:

Mr. Smith, a few of our friends are joining at the Benefactor level for $500. As a Benefactor, you and your family will receive the monthly e-newsletter that will keep you up to date about all of the events going on here, tickets to the members-only party next October, and most important, a ticket to the Benefactors' dinner next April, not to mention our famous coffee mug. Is this something you could do this year?

Not only does the above example have the "listing benefits" problem to a degree, but the "ask" is prominently featured right at the beginning. Once you've dropped the sight-raised figure, Mr. Smith may not hear anything else you have to say. Who knows, he might be in shock at the amount you've suggested.

For the benefits to have a positive effect, it is better to warm him to the sight-raised number by presenting some enticing benefits before you drop the bomb—what it's going to cost him.

This is a standard practice in commercial advertising that is extraordinarily effective. Consider the following advertisement for a famous automobile maker, which I've paraphrased below. The announcer begins with serious intensity:

Enter the world of the new Double ZZ class sedan! Revolutionary engineering, designed to overwhelm and excite your senses, from its plush leather interior and wood grained dash to its dynamic, windswept body, and visionary technology—the pure essence of class. Plus, pure excitement, it will whisk you from 0 to 60 in 4 seconds, yet keep you safe with its revolutionary new "Sensory Assist" technology. The Double ZZ class—you've worked hard to get where you are. You deserve it! Starting at only $55,000 . . . ZZoooom!

Listening to the ad, it sounds so alluring, attractive, and enticing. You want the "Double ZZ" state-of-the-art sedan so bad. You see yourself in the cockpit, the powerful feel of it, you imagine how you will look in it, the thrill and excitement of driving it. Then, you find out how much the "Double ZZ" costs. In spite of everything, you may still want it. But, maybe you have to settle for Single Z model, with the imitation leather instead. It starts at only $35K.

***Mention the Dollars* LAST (*or Near the End*)**   This is the corollary of the third rule mentioned above—try to place the specific dollar ask at the very end of the "ask" or as near to the end as you can. As was mentioned, once the dollar amount is placed on the table, the "cat is out of the bag," so to speak, and what you say *after* is not likely to have an effect on the outcome of the proposal.

For example, consider the following scenario: In the abbreviated, condensed environment of telephone fundraising, every second, every nuance counts. Once you mentioned "the number"—an eventuality that Mr. Smith has been anticipating, perhaps with some apprehension since by now he certainly is aware it's a fundraising phone call, he may not hear anything else you have to say after the words *"five hundred dollars."*

In this way, you're kind of like a pitcher who, having released the baseball after the windup, can do nothing to alter the speed or trajectory of the ball. Once released, the ball will follow whatever path has been given it, its impetus determined according to the laws of physics.

Or, at the risk of wearing out sports metaphors, it's like a bowler who approaches the line and releases the ball. She can see the ball veering off to the gutter instead of the sweet spot for a strike between the number 1 and number 2 pins. She may try to apply whatever "body English" she can, by jumping up and down, or falling to her knees and waving her hand frantically to get the ball to alter its course. All of that is to no avail. It's a gutter ball.

Or, like golf, you drive the ball off the tee—well, you get the idea.

A better proposition for the fundraiser:

Fundraiser: *To help XYZ stay the top nonprofit organization in the world, a few of our friends have been able to join one of our most important donor groups, the Benefactors. Mr. Nichols, how do you feel about giving at this level with a gift of $500?*

For whatever reason, if you just can't finesse the wording of your ask so that "the number" is placed in the last position, and instead falls in the penultimate position, make sure the ask is followed by a question and not a statement.

Take the example of soliciting for an advocacy organization, mentioned previously:

Fundraiser: *Mr. Smith, to make our voice heard, we really need you to join this campaign. A few folks we've spoken to this evening have been able to give $1,000—how do you feel about joining them this year at that level?*

The $1,000 proposition is laid, followed by the ask in the form of a question. This format can work satisfactorily with constituents who have a bit more defined relationship with the organization, like prior donors, or in situations where the callers perceive they are being granted a bit more time by the prospects.

What does *not* work quite as well is the following format:

Fundraiser: *Mr. Smith, to make our voices heard in Washington, we really need you to join our campaign! A few folks we've spoken to this evening have been able to make substantial gifts, some $500, some even as much as $1,000 or more—and if you could do anything like that, we'll count it toward this evening's goal. We'd really be grateful.*

Not only is the phrasing nebulous—"anything like that"—there really is no specific proposal on the table. Instead of an ask, you have the presentation to the prospect of a *concept*—the idea that some people are giving substantially. Can't Mr. Smith join them? Bottom line, this requires too much thinking by the prospect, who you want to focus on a single issue to either accept or reject.

Telephone Fundraising Rule

The "Rule of Specificity": In the telephone medium, prospective donors understand a number better than a concept. Asking for a specific contribution helps you maintain control over a negotiation.

Open-Ended Question versus Yes-No   Some telephone fundraising script writers feel strongly that the ask should be phrased as an open-ended question:

How do you feel about giving $500?
What do you think about giving as much as $1,000 this year?

Using such phrasing has the advantage of eliciting a fuller response by the prospect. After all, one of your objectives with the "sight raise" is to get the prospect to open up and provide clues to his or her giving potential, such as:

Well, I wish I could give that much, but I have two kids in college right now, one at Columbia, the other at Georgetown, so I have to pare back on my contributions for a while longer.
I just can't do anything like that this year. My business is off a bit from last year and I may even have to lay off workers.
I'm sorry, I just can't—my husband works for the state and he was furloughed last week, so making large financial commitments is out of the question.
It's just not possible. We're heavily involved with several local charities, and on top of that, I pledged a large amount of money to my college's capital campaign.

In the first example, the prospect's kids attend expensive, prestigious schools; in another, the prospect clearly owns a business. In the third example, one can conclude there will be a reduction in household disposable income, and in the last, a prospect with substantial wherewithal for philanthropy, but with split loyalties.

So, ideally the prospect will volunteer some clues for the fundraiser to digest, clues that will help determine what level of counterproposal or close is warranted. What counterproposals would you make, based on the information above?

Other fundraising experts feel that phrasing the ask as an open-ended question is a contrivance requiring somewhat unnatural syntax; the prospects will see through it as a tactic and psychologically move themselves away from the negotiating table. They feel the following phrasing is simpler and cleaner:

Mr. Smith, this year can you join us as a Benefactor with a gift of $500?

Absent an objection (a statement indicating the prospect can't or won't give *anything*), the prospect will answer either positively or negatively to the proposition:

I just can't . . .
I'm sorry, I can't do that this year.
I just can't do that much.

It may be possible that the fundraiser picked up on certain clues earlier in the call and can sense from the prospect's tone and telephone demeanor that he or she is somewhat receptive or is not. But absent that, in the situation described above, the fundraiser doesn't have a lot to work with.

He or she can either rush off to make an immediate counterproposal with a best guess for the prospect's giving potential or ask the prospect some follow-up questions to help clarify his giving potential, which are known as *probes*, and then make another ask.

Factors in Setting the Sight Raise   So, in setting your sight raise, how high or how low should you go? Well, that depends on a number of factors.

Age   If you're a school with clearly defined years of graduation, or if you're an organization that has managed to acquire your prospects' birthdays or age, you can proceed under the hypothesis that those in the 25 to 34 age group will be able to give less than the those in the 35 to 49 age group. And that both groups in turn will be able to give less than the people in the 50- to -64 age group, the empty nesters in their prime giving years. And, conversely, the 65+ group of retirees may be somewhat constrained through fixed income considerations. You may wish to set different starting points for different folks.

Address, Zip Code   You may do a zip code analysis and, based on areas and neighborhoods the census has determined are higher income, adjust your sight raise up. Areas that are less affluent, adjust downward.

Electronic Screening   You may have sent your entire database out to one of the fine services that are available to electronically screen your records, so that a giving potential or score is assigned to each prospect. Those prospects that are scored with higher giving potential can be segmented for higher asks, and so on.

Personal Knowledge   There is no substitute for experience. Some development officers have spent years with their organizations, and they just *know* what is appropriate and feasible to ask. Indeed, they may know many of the names on their list and their families firsthand. Here it's entirely appropriate to rely on their judgment as to what is feasible.

Too High or Too Low—How Do You Know?   Once you launch your campaign, how do you know if you've got it right, that is, if you set your sight raise too high or too low?

If you're asking for an amount, like $1,000, and prospective donors are offended rather than flattered, you may have set it too high. The frequency of hang-ups at that point in the call may be higher than you think is appropriate, or feedback from your fundraising staff indicates that rather than $1,000 being a good "opening position," they find it difficult to continue on with the call. Prospects who were warmed through a rapport-building process may suddenly become distant and disengaged. Pledge rates (the percentage of prospects you are contacting who say "yes") are running below what you projected.

Remember, if the prospect's reaction is laughter, it may not be a bad thing. However, if the laughter is another way for the prospect to say, "Are you out of your ever lovin' mind?" and is masking anger, it is. You may want to adjust your sights down a bit.

Conversely, you may find things going splendidly well with your first ask of $250. There are lots of pledges, the pledge rate is far exceeding what you anticipated. Moreover, more than just a couple of your fundraisers are showing the $250 number on their tallies—in fact, you're getting quite a few "hits."

But are you leaving money on the table? If you start at $500 instead of $250, you should still be able to garner those $250s on the second ask. Moreover, you may find that a number of $500 gifts are there for the asking. And who knows, maybe some $1,000 gifts, too!

Strategy 2: Percentage of Income Ask

The *percentage of income* ask is actually another form of a sight raise proposal, only instead of suggesting a specific dollar amount, the fundraiser asks the prospect to consider a commitment *as a percentage of his or her annual income.* This technique is typically used in capital campaigns rather than Annual

Fund solicitations and is indeed a proposal involving a commitment. In capital campaigns, usually a fair amount of research is done to identify those constituents capable of truly substantial gifts out of their capital resources, gifts in the $100K to $1 million range, and above. These "top of the pyramid" prospects are usually slated for personal visits by peers or professional development staff.

The vast majority of the remaining database, prospects lacking substantial capital resources but some having substantial annual incomes, are enabled to participate by devoting a part of their annual incomes to the capital effort *over time*.

It is usually phrased in a manner similar to the following:

Mr. Smith, many of our friends are making a substantial contribution for the period of this campaign, a commitment of 2 percent of their income, each year, over the next five years. How do you feel about doing something like this?

Asking for a gift in this manner obviously solves the dilemma posed by the fixed dollar sight raise, what level do you set? How much money do you specifically ask for? In a database where there may be wide variations in people's income, the percentage of income asks each for substantial amount of money *relative* to his or her own income. It's self-adjusting.

So, an executive or professional who is making $400,000 each year is asked to consider a gift of $8,000 annually, for a total of $40,000 over the period of the campaign. Someone making far less, perhaps $ 90,000, is asked to consider a gift of $1,800 annually, or $9,000 over the five-year period. A schoolteacher making $40,000 is asked to consider $800 a year, or $4,000 over the five years. And so on. In this way it's a variable "ask" proportionate to a key factor in one's giving potential: income.

A number of organizations have had success with this technique. It is most apt for organizations where you find one or more of the following factors at work:

- A high degree of affiliation with the nonprofit organization, a sense of "belonging" like schools, colleges, and fraternal organizations
- Constituencies with a higher cultural sense for philanthropy and where the concept of tithing is not alien
- Prospects who regularly budget a given percentage of their income to philanthropy
- Constituencies that are predominantly affluent

Asking a prospect for a gift in this manner will ideally give the fundraiser plenty of clues as he or she gauges the prospect's reaction to the proposal, evaluates the prospect's giving potential based on feedback, and then is able to formulate a solid and credible counterproposal, based on a *specific dollar amount.*

But there are some drawbacks. Because you're asking for a commitment and not a mere contribution, an amount that is often in addition to and far above a donor's annual gift, it may be so substantial and burdensome that it's concept is most narrowly appropriate for once-in-a-generation capital campaigns.

Furthermore, once in a while organizations' capital campaigns can collide, one into another, so nonprofits can be competing for the same resources. For example, Mr. Smith might be an alumnus of both ABC College and XYZ University. ABC solicits Mr. Smith nine months before XYZ, and when XYZ finally calls, it is out of luck. Mr. Smith has already made his commitment. That's not to say a smaller token annual gift might still be had. But the big bucks are spoken for.

Moreover, from a technique standpoint the percentage of income ask falls prey somewhat to the "Rule of Specificity." Rather than a tangible proposal, you are presenting "Mr. Smith," the prospect, with a concept. You are requiring him to think, to calculate, and to compute. If Mr. Smith already feels strongly about your mission, is highly involved, and has a high degree of affinity, that might not be bad. But prospects like this "Mr. Smith" are often the exception than the rule in most organizations' databases.

Last, your organization may not have earned the right to ask for such a commitment. To ask for something so substantial, hopefully your organization has a superb and compelling case to make and many years of constituent cultivation, such that your call isn't coming out of the blue, or worse, the only time Mr. Smith hears from you is when you want his money. In this case, you better hope Mr. Smith likes you anyway.

Strategy 3: The Incremental Upgrade

Your organizational objectives are not to squeeze every last dollar from your constituents through a sight raise and an extended negotiating process. You may have a list of donors who have been stuck at a given level for several years. Rather than asking each of them for the sun, the moon, and the stars, you may simply just want to bump them up a level:

- The $25 "Donors" increase to $50 "Friends"
- The $50 "Friends" increase to the $100 "Contributors"
- The $100 "Contributors" increase to the $250 "Sustainers"

. . . and so on.

By your calculation, if just one in five of your donors upgrades to the next level, you'll far, far exceed your annual giving target for the year. So, if our intrepid fundraiser, Elaine Peters, is calling our old, reliable Mr. Smith, her ask might go something like this:

Mr. Smith, if we're going to meet our most ambitious goal ever, we need each of our friends to renew and increase their support for the upcoming year. Now last year, I see you generously gave at the Friends level. This year could you increase that just $50 more to the Contributor level? How do you feel about that?

In the example above, a discussion might ensue, so that Elaine explains that would be a total gift of $100. (Note: Some discussion about the proposal with Mr. Smith is a good thing—it extends the process without predictably rushing off to the next proposal, something I'll discuss in more detail in the next chapter.) A little nuance to consider, Elaine is presuming the *renewal* and is asking Mr. Smith only for the incremental *increase*, a relatively small number equal to the previous gift. Ultimately, any ambiguity will be cleared up as Elaine proceeds to the "confirmation" of the pledge.

Or Mr. Smith may decline:

I'm sorry, did you say your name was Elaine? I just can't do that much this year, but I'll be happy to renew my gift from last year.

So, the worst that Elaine will accomplish is a renewal, or she may feel that a modest increase of $10 or $15 may be possible and choose to pursue that course in the counterproposal.

Strategy 4: Everybody on Board

Maybe you're a new organization, without a long-established constituency with an identified affiliation or affinity or dedication to your cause. Or let's say you have an existing constituency with a group of donors, but now you're asking them to support something different from the fund they are normally accustomed giving to—a subordinate cause, a special mission or fund for your organization. In effect, you're building from scratch.

Rather than maximize dollars from a few donors, you want as broad-based participation as you can. You want a lot of donors. You'll build on that later, in future years.

In this case, you may want to propose a smaller, even nominal sum such that it may appeal to a prospect's sense of "impulse philanthropy." A sum like $500, or $250, even $100 may be something that requires discussion and deliberation.

But $50 or $25, or even less—hey, no problem. For example:

Mr. Smith, we need all of our donors to give at least something to the new "Action Alert Fund," and to help get it off the ground, can you help us with a gift of just $75 or even $50?

In the above example, depending on the constituency, you may even wish to start at $100. Regardless, you still have some room to negotiate down—not much, but a little. Remember the objective: high participation, high pledge rates, and usually, covering as much territory as you can in limited time.

Summary

There are as many ways to ask for a contribution as there are fingers and toes, collectively, on your development staff. There is no one *right* way, but there is a way that, taking into account your prospects, will achieve the best results, whether your objectives are for the short term or the long term.

Your job is to *find* it. But whatever you do—*ask!*

CHAPTER 8

Negotiation

After you've found your prospect, gained an audience, stated your case compellingly, then crossed that invisible line into a new region of the call, and you asked for money, now what? It is time to negotiate (see Figure 8.1). For some, the word *negotiation* implies an adversarial struggle with the prospect like the cartoon on the preceding page. Instead, think of this as a process of working with the prospect to find a level of giving that he or she is both willing and able to give.

Wouldn't it be nice if the money just came spilling forth from the receiver of the phone, kind of like a $100,000 slot machine in Vegas when you hit all cherries, the bells ring and the sirens blow, little LED lights are flashing everywhere, and money comes gushing out from the machine like a wildcat oil rig that's just struck oil? "Thar' she blows!" And everyone rushes to stuff the money into his or her pockets.

No such luck—your work as a telephone fundraiser has just begun.

Figure 8.1 Stage 6—Counterproposal

If you're pursuing one of the small upgrade or participation strategies mentioned previously, congratulations, you can skip this chapter and go to the next one called "The Close." That is, you're pursuing a two-ask strategy, a "two and done," "two and out," or what I call, "let's do two, and then skidoo" on to the next prospects. Usually in these instances you have a *lot* more calls to make and don't want to tarry with a single prospect.

But if you're engaged in a capital campaign, are dealing with mid-level prospects or higher, or have a finite constituency from which you absolutely want to maximize results, many telephone fundraisers will ardently make the case for the three-ask strategy.

The Three-Ask Strategy

Why do many professional telephone fundraisers consider "three" the magic number? Why not just two, or four, or five, or six?

One possible reason lies in the realm of consumer sales psychology.

- High price versus low price: "No, X is just too expensive, Y is more affordable, but right now, I'm going to save money and pick Z."
- Three options presented, pick the middle one: "So, there's the green dress, the black dress, and the red dress. Green is 'in' right now, and red is snazzy, but I'll play it safe with black. You can *never* go wrong with black!"
- Too many options are confusing: "Let's see, OxyMiracle-Kleen comes in Small, Medium, Large, Extra-Large, Jumbo, and Super Jumbo, hmm . . . and in Fresh Scent, Luscious Lavender, Clean Cucumber, Likable Lemon, Morning Orange, and Sensible Scentless. Which one, which one?"

In the first example above, all other factors being equal, people will naturally gravitate to the lower or lowest price when presented with two or more options. Hey, they want to save money.

And in the second option in physical and visual media, people often gravitate to the middle option, among three that are presented. You need to present three options to make consumers feel they have the free will of choice, but mix up the options, put red dress in the middle, instead of black one, and the consumer will likely still take the middle choice.

And in the last example, most advertising executives will tell you that offering too many choices becomes confusing to consumers, making it difficult for them to make any decision at all—or worse, deciding to buy something else: "Gee, with OxyMiracle-Kleen, is so hard to make a choice . . . let me take good old reliable, one-size generic Acme-Kleen instead." Indeed, in the case of "Oxy," there are a possible 42 combinations of products to choose from!

This consideration is especially true in the telephone medium, with its unique constraints. For example, I've never seen the following approach particularly successful:

Mr. Smith, we have a wide array of giving opportunities for you to consider. If you don't want to personally endow the new library for $2 million, you can still help by naming a meeting room for only $100,000, or for $50,000 name a classroom, or be listed among the "Union of Concerned Citizens" for just $10,000—or for $5,000 or even $1,000 be listed among the Benevolent Benefactors. Uh, Mr. Smith, does any of that interest you?

I remember, back in the "olden" days of telephone fundraising, it become apparent that the more you asked for money, the more money you raised. Logical, no? In fact, it sounds pretty *fundamental*. That is, fundraisers who asked for gifts of specific dollar amounts more often raised more money than those who didn't, and who were more reticent and less assertive. This led me to include in trainings the following formula:

$$P = f(A)$$

. . . where *P* is the number of pledges a fundraiser receives, and *A* is the number of asks, and *f* indicates "function." *P* does not simply equal *A*, but it is a function of it, along with about a billion other factors.

Well, Einstein this isn't, but it did lead some of the fundraisers to believe, perhaps erroneously, that I knew what I was talking about. I thought the formula might help them be aware of a truth: "In order for ye to receive, ye must ask." To lead them to the fundraising promised land, I even experimented with a script, having them follow step for step a "giving ladder."

First Ask: *Mr. Smith, how do you feel about $1,000?*
Second Ask: *Mr. Smith, is $500 more feasible?*
Third Ask: *Mr. Smith, how about $250, is that more comfortable?*
Fourth Ask: *Mr. Smith, could we include you for just a $100 gift?*
Fifth Ask: *Mr. Smith, can you participate with only $50 this year?*
Sixth Ask: *Mr. Smith, can we count on you to come on board with $50, or even $35?*

Needless to say, the above approach wasn't a stunning success. It was modeled on the theory that the more arrows you shot at the direction of Mr. Smith, sooner or later you were going to get lucky and hit something. That is, Mr. Smith, in response to the barrage of asks, would at last relent and yell, "stop shooting, I give up. I'm coming out with my hands up, holding a $100 bill!"

Call it the $P = f(A)$ on steroids experiment.

The problem was the $f(A)$ part of the equation needed a corollary, and that is a subfunction *O*—for "optimal." In the telephone medium it's not the sheer number of asks you make, it's the *optimal* number, and that number can vary somewhat, prospect to prospect, situation to situation. True believers in the three-ask pattern of negotiation are convinced that on average, that optimal number is or approaches three.

Mr. Smith, we have pledges in 5 flavors today, Magnanimous Macadamia, Benefactor Berry, Very Generous Vanilla, Renew Now Raspberry, and Mint Donor Chip. Which would you prefer?

Other Factors Limiting the Length of a Negotiation and Number of Asks

Time

There are other factors that limit your field of negotiation, and first among these is *time*. Some negotiating frameworks are quite broad, complex, and open-ended, like the negotiation of a treaty among nations. Here discussion can occur among many groups of people through a variety channels over a number of years until there is a resolution. Scores of proposals and counter-proposals can be generated and evaluated by the many parties involved over an extended period of time, years, perhaps or even decades.

Or a negotiation framework can occur in a smaller background, like a labor union negotiating a contract with a city. Here the negotiation can occur over a shorter time period, perhaps months, among designated representatives of the organizations. Multiple proposals and counterproposals can be exchanged and evaluated until agreement is found.

Or you may simply be looking to negotiate the best home equity loan you can with your bank. Here, over a period of several days, there may be some back and forth until you find an appropriate dollar amount for the best possible terms.

In the rarefied atmosphere of the telephone medium, you don't have years, months, days, or hours. You have minutes and seconds to come to a resolution.

First of all, in the telephone medium there's no group to complicate making a decision. This is a one-on-one conversation. Second, your prospect has a finite time limit to deal with the matter you're putting forward: a pledge to your organization. You've interrupted her, and she is anxious to get back to what she was doing before you called.

Moreover, YOU have a finite amount of time as well. You can't spend an hour with Mr. Smith, even though he may be willing. You have too many other prospects to reach, and besides, you have a deadline of your own to meet: You want a *pledge* by the end of this call.

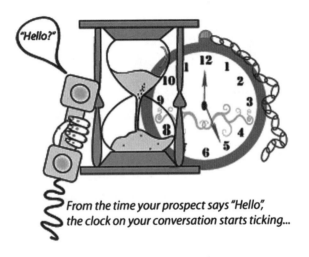

From the time your prospect says "Hello",
the clock on your conversation starts ticking...

So, with that external clock ticking on you both, you have between two minutes and no more than five for you to arrive at some outcome to your call. This will permit time for three or fewer asks, and in the vast majority of your calls, that outcome will either be a pledge or a refusal.

Sequential Nature of Telephone Medium

Negotiating in broader arenas, like diplomatic or corporate environments, often allows the negotiators to communicate through a variety of channels: written, visual, electronic, face to face, and the telephone. With written and visual media, it's easier to present whole ideas and concepts through pictures, graphs, and charts.

We've already discussed the limitations of the telephone medium—it's two-way, one-channel communication—it's *aural,* what both you and Mr. Smith are hearing.

You might like to be able to show Mr. Smith a chart, how alumni participation and giving at rival ABC University surpasses XYZ University, but you can't. Or you might like to show Mr. Smith a photograph of the last benefactor's' party, where the donors are obviously happy and everyone seems to be having a good time. But you can't. You have only your voice to communicate.

So, instead of presenting choices or benefits as part of a broader concept, in the telephone medium you must present them sequentially, one by one, having Mr. Smith focus on each, considering the potential benefits and weighing them against the cost of his philanthropy.

Having to present choices sequentially further limits the number you practically present in a given period of time. By reducing choices to three, it helps the prospect make a choice, with a focus and discussion on each. Simplify, simplify, simplify.

Maintain the "Bubble"

From the moment Mr. Smith has said hello, as a fundraiser you have sought to buy time by being polite, engaging, developing some degree of rapport, and getting him interested in your case. In other words, you have sought to create a temporary bubble around the prospect, for a brief period, insulating him from the distractions in his immediate environment and getting him to focus on you, your message, your cause. He's been interrupted from another task or another activity and really doesn't want to talk to you now.

By presenting alternative levels of giving, that is, making asks, it helps you, the fundraiser, solidify your control of the call. You are having him focus intently on something he is interested in: *his* money. Mr. Smith may initially want to draw away when the subject turns to money. In fact, in the telephone medium, you can even sense when a prospect recoils.

Mr. Smith may have enjoyed chatting with you and responded in agreement about your mission and your cause, but now he is not willing to talk about money. This is going to cost him, and his natural instinct is to draw back and accelerate the call to a conclusion.

Here we have a conflict. Mr. Smith wants to speed up the conversation. You want to slow it down. That's why making a credible counterproposal taking into account Mr. Smith's reaction to your first proposal is key to keeping the bubble from bursting, that is, rushing headlong to a close.

A good fundraiser is sensitive to these issues lying in the background of what at first may appear as a simple conversation between two individuals. By being aware of the overall environment, good fundraisers can gauge how far they can go in a negotiation, even finding ways to extend a call that might be prematurely cut short of a successful negotiation.

First Things First: Setting the Stage for the Counterproposal

A good fundraiser should have a pretty fair understanding of why the first proposal is being rejected. Let's consider Mr. Smith's reactions to first proposals from the previous chapter.

Fundraiser: *Mr. Smith, how do you feel about joining the Benefactors this year with a gift of $1,000?*

Mr. Smith: *Well, I wish I could give that much, but I have two kids in college right now, one at Columbia, the other at Georgetown, so I have to pare back on my contributions for a while longer.*

What does this call tell you about the prospect's giving potential? Does it mean that he has the financial wherewithal to give $500 or $250, since he is potentially footing a tuition bill of $80,000 or more? And what about the statement that "I have to pare back on my contributions"? He's not saying that he doesn't give, just not as much.

I just can't do anything like that this year. My business is off a bit from last year and I may even have to lay off workers.

Parsing this reaction "can't do anything like that this year"—Mr. Smith has just told you he is going to give something. And analyzing the "my business is off a bit" tells you that Mr. Smith is not facing bankruptcy and is in fact solvent enough that he obviously has employees, in some kind of business of undetermined size. Does this tell you that he has the potential to do half of your previous proposal, or even a quarter?

I'm sorry, I just can't—my husband works for the state and he was furloughed last week, so making large financial commitments is out of the question.

Analyzing this reaction, what information can you glean? Potentially we're dealing with a two-income family, or were. One can infer that Mrs. Smith's husband is not a very highly paid executive. But it doesn't give any information about her. Perhaps this is enough information to deduce you don't want to ask for $500 and want to find a level lower.

It's just not possible. We're heavily involved with several local charities, and on top of that, I pledged a large amount of money to my college's capital campaign.

So, parsing this information, one can hear clearly that the prospect is a philanthropist, a caring individual who supports nonprofits in the community, and pledged a "large amount" to a capital campaign. Perhaps $1,000 is a bit much this year—but is $500 out of the question?

Effective Listening Is Key

Whole books have been written on the art of listening. Let me summarize. Please *listen to what the prospect says to you.*

Sounds so simple, but in the telephone medium, with the pressure of making contact after contact and soliciting pledge after pledge, it's so hard for solicitors to stop soliciting for a moment and just to shut up and listen. Which brings me to a very important telephone fundraising rule:

Telephone Fundraising Rule

After you present your first proposal to the prospect, SHUT UP!

How many times have I heard $1,000 laid on the table, and the prospect reacts with a pause, as if he or she is thinking, but the solicitor just can't stay quiet:

Fundraiser: *Mr. Smith, how do you feel about $1,000?*
Mr. Smith: *[Long pause]*
Fundraiser: *I know that's a lot of money. How about $500?*

Ouch! Not only could the long pause be interpreted as Mr. Smith weighing the $1,000 option, but the nervous solicitor reverts to auctioneering. And I *have* heard the following dialog in real fundraising situations more than once:

Fundraiser: *Mr. Smith, how do you feel about $1,000?*
Mr. Smith: *[Long pause]*
Fundraiser: *I know that's a lot of money. How about $500?*
Mr. Smith: *Well, I could do the $1,000, just not until the end of the year.*

It has always been a continuing source of wonderment, how some telephone fundraisers will do their best to talk themselves out of $$$. Bottom line, maybe you don't need a counterproposal at all! In the above example, the prospect has upgraded the solicitor's ask. It doesn't happen often, I grant you, but it does happen sometimes.

Furthermore, all of the examples in this chapter illustrate well the importance of listening carefully to the prospects' responses to your first proposal. If you give Mr. Smith a chance, he will give you the information, the clues you need to provide a credible counterproposal (assuming you need one) that is *credible* in the ears of Mr. Smith.

Whatever counterproposal you make, it should take into account what Mr. Smith has said. And, just as important, it should be clear to Mr. Smith that *you* heard what he has said—that is, you were *listening* to him, and not merely rushing off to make another counterproposal, as if you were reading from a script. Rushing into a second proposal will appear to him that your first proposal was insincere and was merely a tactic.

Telephone Fundraising Rule

Don't rush to the counterproposal after your first proposal: It will appear to the prospect that you're reading from a script—or worse, that you're an auctioneer.

Some of you may remember the old commercial for the American Tobacco Company, where an auctioneer, in rapid staccato speech, auctions lots of the finest tobacco: "forty-fort-forty-five, forty-fort-forty-five, beed-ada-beed-ada-beed-ada-beed—sold American!"

This is the last thing you want to appear as to your prospect. Do I hear a thousand, how 'bout $500, do I hear $250? One hundred dollars, going once, twice, three times—sold to Mr. Smith!

React to What the Prospect Has Said

As a way of not rushing off to a counterproposal and showing the prospect you are listening and not just soliciting, react to what he or she is saying.

Mr. Smith: *I just can't do that much right now.*
Fundraiser: *Mr. Smith, you say you just can't do that much right now? [Pause]*

This is an excellent technique for both showing Mr. Smith that you're listening *and* holding him at the first proposal without rushing willy-nilly to the next. It's as if you're saying, "Help me understand what you're saying, Mr. Smith." This brings to an effective negotiator the possibility of a modest deferral of the gift, or installments, both of which accomplish your desired goals: holding the prospect for a bit at the first proposal and showing you're listening.

How might an effective fundraiser react, show empathy, show that she is listening, and garner even more clues for an effective counterproposal?

Mr. Smith: *Well, I wish I could give that much, but I have two kids in college right now, one at Columbia, the other at Georgetown, so I have to pare back on my contributions for a while longer.*

Fundraiser: *That's wonderful you have kids in college. Georgetown and Columbia, wow, you must be very proud! [Allow prospect time to respond and potentially discuss]*

In the above example, the fundraiser continues to build rapport, further personalizes the relationship, and allows for some time before rushing to the counterproposal.

Mr. Smith: *I just can't do anything like that this year. My business is off a bit from last year and I may even have to lay off workers.*
Fundraiser: *I'm sorry to hear business is off a bit, it's always rough in a downturn . . . may I ask what field are you in? [Allow time for Mr. Smith to react, discuss]*

There's always a risk it might appear that a solicitor is too nosy. But if the solicitor has been effective at building rapport earlier in the call, the above question can seem to be a natural, empathetic follow-up—especially if the prospect has a defined relationship with the organization. The answer to the question can provide a wealth of information for the fundraiser and provide a strong basis for an effective, credible counterproposal.

Mrs. Smith: *I'm sorry, I just can't—my husband works for the state and he was furloughed last week, so making large financial commitments is out of the question.*
Fundraiser: *Oh, Mrs. Smith, I'm so sorry to hear about that! What was he doing for the state? [Discuss] I certainly hope Mr. Smith's chances for a callback are good! [Discuss]*

In any situation where the prospect volunteers bad news, showing empathy will help build a foundation for a counterproposal. In the brief discussion that follows, Mrs. Smith's employment situation may be clarified, so that the prospects for at least some kind of gift, even a renewal of a previous gift, may be solidified.

Mr. Smith: *It's just not possible. We're heavily involved with several local charities, and on top of that, I pledged a large amount of money to my college's capital campaign.*
Fundraiser: *That's wonderful that you are so generous, Mr. Smith! What kind of charities are you supporting in your town? [Discuss]*

In situations like the one above, I have frequently observed rightfully proud donors provide some information, often in detail, that solidify their position as a philanthropist and provide other bits of information that help the fundraiser formulate a credible counterproposal. Moreover, the nature of the "large amount" pledged to the college may come into clearer focus. It would be great to know the amount of the commitment, when it was made, and how long the commitment remains. Tactful and resourceful telephone solicitors are sometimes able to get very clear pictures of the prospect's giving potential through gentle probing.

Telephone Fundraising Rule

Good fundraisers use "probes": tactful follow-up questions that help clarify the giving potential of a prospective donor.

So, even *before* you lay a counterproposal on the table, use this checklist to determine what you have accomplished:

☐ You listened to Mr. Smith's response to the first proposal.
☐ You understood what Mr. Smith had to say.
☐ If Mr. Smith did not articulate a response you understood, you asked him follow-up questions, so that you *do* understand what his position is.
☐ You are sure Mr. Smith thinks that you have listened to him by his reactions.
☐ You have listened to Mr. Smith's reasons for declining the first ask and can formulate a counterproposal, taking into account his particular financial picture.

Articulating the Counterproposal

What's the best way of articulating a counterproposal?

Here's the gist of what you want to say: *Mr. Smith, I understand based on what you've told me [tuition, business downturn, loss of job, competing charities] that the higher amount we discussed isn't feasible, but in light of what you've said, can you please consider a lower amount of [$X]?*

In the first situation a fundraiser may pivot:

Fundraiser: *Mr. Smith, I can understand that $1,000 given your tuition expenses might be out of the question, but this year, how do you feel about a more moderate gift of $250?*

And in the second situation:

Fundraiser: *Mr. Smith, taking into account your current business conditions, this year, how do you feel about a gift of just $500? Is that more feasible?*

And in the third situation:

Fundraiser: *Mrs. Smith, considering what you've told me, could you help us with a much smaller gift this year, of just $100?*

And last:

Fundraiser: *Mr. Smith, in light of all of your generous philanthropy, this year can you include us with a much smaller gift of $500?*

The other rules we discussed for articulating and formatting an effective first proposal still apply for the second ask: personalizing, avoiding long speeches, summarizing benefits, and placing the "number" at the end, or as near the end of the "ask" as possible.

So, how far do you drop your ask? How low do you go on a counter-proposal? Here's the general rule:

Telephone Fundraising Rule

Avoid skipping over more than one step of a giving ladder at a time.

If your giving ladder looks something like the one in the Appendix, Section A, which shows steps of $1,000, $500, $250, $100, $50, and $35, you'd like to go rung to rung and avoid skipping over more than one rung at time. So, if you began your negotiation at $1,000, you'd like your next proposal to be $500 but will go down to $250 if you must. Likewise, if you began your negotiation at $500, you'd ideally like to fall to $250 on your counter-proposal, but will fall to $100 if you have to.

At all costs, you want to avoid the "crashing elevator" syndrome of negotiation, where you start at stratospheric heights, and then, in a blink of an eye, find yourself crashing through the floor of the negotiating ladder:

Fundraiser: *Mr. Smith, how do you feel about $1,000 this year?*
Mr. Smith: *No, I can't do that.*
Fundraiser: *Well, then, Mr. Smith, can you at least give a little something, maybe just $50, or $35?*

As many of you know, this example is all too common, particularly with inexperienced fundraisers who have not developed their "chops." In the above situation, there is no place left for the negotiator to fall; our fundraiser may be backed into a situation of "Gee, Mr. Smith, how much money can I give to *you?*" Such "falling elevator" negotiations are unlikely to lead to any pledge at all, leaving the fundraiser only with "the shaft."

There may be situations from the prospect's response where it could be crystal clear to the fundraiser how much the prospect is able to give:

Fundraiser: *Mr. Smith, how do you feel about $1,000?*

Mr. Smith: *I really can't do anything beyond a token gift this year, perhaps nothing at all. I just lost a fortune in the stock market, my wife died last week, this morning I was diagnosed with an inoperable brain tumor, and my dog, Sparkie, was hit by a car and is in intensive care at the vet's.*

While the above may be a bit of an exaggerated, overstated, melodramatic situation, a resourceful fundraiser in difficult financial situations can still position a counterproposal using an installment device:

Fundraiser: *[Discussion of Mr. Smith's tragic situation] Mr. Smith, in light of your circumstances, could you give just $50 to our campaign now, and perhaps another $50 in six months? It would be terrific if you could do that.*

Which brings us to the final "rule" of this chapter:

Telephone Fundraising Rule

Effective counterproposals shouldn't be based on what a fundraiser believes a prospect is *going* to give, but based on the most you think a prospect *could give*, if he or she were willing to make a modest sacrifice.

The positioning of a counterproposal in telephone fundraising is a *tactical device* designed to hold the negotiation higher than it would otherwise fall to, and thereby maximize the prospect's ultimate gift. In many cases, the mere insertion of a counterproposal will salvage a smaller gift at the lowest levels.

Imagine the following situation, where our imaginary Mr. Smith is really being imaginarily candid:

Fundraiser: *Mr. Smith, how do you feel about a much smaller gift of just $100?*

Mr. Smith: *Well, you know, I could do that if I really wanted to, but I just don't want to do that amount. It's too much for me right now, this year. I've got payments on my new Audi, I want to go to Barbados in January, I want to renew my seats at the 50-yard line for the Chargers, I want to get my wife a piece of jewelry for her birthday, and I want the 50-inch flat screen LCD, 1080p, with a surround sound system in my new home theater . . . etc., etc.*

It's not that Mr. Smith *can't;* it's that he *won't.*

The counterproposal is the point in the call where the nonprofit's chorus of needs battle the prospect's chorus of unfulfilled desires, often with predictable cacophony the result. It's at the close where you hope the dissonance is resolved harmonically to a pledge.

Articulating Benefits in the Counterproposal

Again, all of the "rules" mentioned in the previous chapter regarding the effective presentation of benefits in either donor recognition or membership campaigns remain in effect. Don't list! Highlight only the salient benefit(s) at that level, and avoid long-winded expositions! For example:

Mr. Smith: *I'm sorry, I just can't do the Benefactor level.*

Fundraiser: *Mr. Smith, based on what you've said, let me recommend the Sustainers. At this level, among other benefits, we'll send you two tickets to the annual members-only party, and of course, our famous "Let's Drink to ABC!" coffee mug. Is this more comfortable for just $250?*

Upgrading Previous Donors in the Counterproposal

Basically, there are two strategies to pursue in formulating an effective counterproposal for prior donors:

1. Negotiating down from your sight-raised first proposal
2. Negotiating up a level or two from their prior gift

In the first strategy, you may be dealing with prior donors of a modest amount of $100 or less. You may have thanked them for the prior giving, without acknowledging the specific amount, and then proceeded to offer a substantial sight raise at a level of $1,000 or $500. Here it makes sense to follow the "not skip over more than one rung of the giving ladder at a time" rule of negotiating.

Fundraiser: *Mr. Smith, I can understand this year $1,000 might be out of the question, but tonight we're hoping to add just five more donors at the $250 level. How do you feel about doing that much for XYZ?*

Here, if the donor's prior gift was $50, the fundraiser is well positioned for a close at the $100 level—a still substantial increase.

In the second strategy, the donor may have given a not inconsequential $100 gift in the prior year. Here, you might acknowledge that prior generosity, yet go for the substantial upgrade:

Fundraiser: *Mr. Smith, you're currently a member of the Donor group with a gift of $100—but it would be terrific, just great if you could increase this year to the Sustainers. We need 25 more if we're to reach our goal. Can you join this group with $250?*

Here the fundraiser is well positioned not merely for a renewal of the $100 gift, but an incremental upgrade of $25 or $50 more—perhaps not the full level upgrade, but still a nice increase!

Increase the Urgency as the Call Proceeds

One final word about *negotiation* and then we're off to the close. Despite your having made an excellent case for giving to your organization in the purpose section of the call, now you're talking about money, and in the prospect's mind, Mr. Smith, he will have plenty of reasons why he doesn't want to give (not really that he can't) or that he doesn't want to give more.

Sometimes it is useful to segue from the first proposal to the second by adding a sense of urgency that emphasizes your stated purpose, much like getting some top spin for your next pitch:

Disaster Relief Fund:

Fundraiser: *Mr. Smith, I can understand from what you've said that a really large gift is out of the question, but if we're to make our goal and to save the planet from impending disaster, we need everyone to support the Disaster Fund this year.*

School or University Annual Fund:

Fundraiser: *Mr. Smith, if we're to keep XYZ a really top school, we need the support of every alum in this campaign, and go for 100 percent participation!*

General Fundraising Campaign:

Fundraiser: *Mr. Smith, I understand joining the Sustainers might be out of the question, but if we're going to make this evening's fundraising goal, we need everyone's support—we have only $2,000 to go to put us over the top!*

Membership Campaign:

Fundraiser: *Mr. Smith, from what you've said, I can understand the Benefactors level is out of the question, but this year to meet our budget, we need at least 25 new Sustainers!*

Annual Giving Program for Subscribers to an Arts Organization

Fundraiser: *Mr. Smith, I understand that a large gift might be out of the question, but you probably know that subscriptions and tickets cover only about half of annual expenses for the performances, the other half comes from contributions. That's why your support in this program is so important!*

Then following the above segue that increases a sense of urgency, comes the ask:

Fundraiser: *So, Mr. Smith, in light of what you've said, how do you feel about a smaller gift of just $X?*

What kind of transitory segue you can devise to increase urgency in a phone call is up to the creativity of the scriptwriter and the facts inherent in your particular situation. Obviously, you can't make stuff up: "Mr. Smith, if you don't pledge tonight, we're going out of business tomorrow!" But whatever you are able to come up with, all the rules regarding effective telephone speech still apply: Keep it short, pithy sentences, action verbs, and no long-winded speeches!

Matching Gifts

One of the most effective devices for increasing the sense of urgency, and turning the tide with prospects who have only a moderate interest in giving or increasing their support, is positioning the *matching gift* as a segue to a counter-proposal—that is, for organizations that are lucky enough to have a match!

Fundraiser: *Mr. Smith, I can understand a gift that large might be out of the question, but let me share some exciting news. The XYZ Foundation has awarded us a $50,000 challenge grant that will match any gift you make tonight, dollar for dollar, so this is a terrific opportunity. I'm sure you agree . . .*

 . . . and then proceed to the counterproposal. You might even use a tie-down question in the middle:

Fundraiser: *But let me share some exciting news. We've been awarded a $50,000 challenge grant from the XYZ Foundation . . . isn't that terrific? [Response] Mr. Smith, it will match any gift you make tonight, dollar for dollar . . . and so* on.

With such a great "sales point"—such good news, why not "lead" with a matching gift, right in the purpose of the call? For a couple of reasons.

First, adding the existence of a matching gift to an already verbose purpose where you are presenting the urgent needs of your organization will lengthen the ask, provide too much information for the prospect to digest, and dilute the effectiveness of the matching grant. At the risk of an inappropriate metaphor, by leading with a "match," you shoot all your "bullets" right at the beginning, without saving any ammunition for later.

Second, positioning the match *after* the first proposal has been rejected can energize a call that has been momentarily deflated, with excitement and energy. And once you have the match positioned right after the first ask, there's nothing to prevent you from wielding it again, at the most critical stage of the call: the close.

Summary

Adding a counterproposal—a second ask—in a three-ask negotiating strategy adds a substantial amount of complexity to an overall fundraising phone call.

First, it is very difficult to hard script a three-ask strategy without it appearing to the prospect that it is indeed a very scripted solicitation, and that can significantly dilute its effectiveness. Second, it relies on the fundraiser's listening skills, intuition, and sensitivity in asking the kind of follow-up questions that are appropriate based on prospects' responses, and then to intelligently choose an appropriate level of contribution to ask for in the counterproposal.

All of this can significantly complicate fundraiser training issues and/or require the recruitment of a calling staff that has better-than-average communication skills. It is one thing to hire people to read a script. It's quite another to ask them to be fundraisers.

Finally, with the three-ask strategy comes a paradox: The fundraiser gives up some control in order to gain control. Sounds very "Zen," doesn't it?

The Close

T he close is the stage of a call that all good fundraisers live for: the point where you reach agreement with the prospect for a pledge of support, a "Yes, I'll give."

But getting successfully through this point from the previous stage of the call, whether preceded by a "first ask" or a "negotiation" involving intermediate amounts, can present the greatest challenge to a fundraiser (see Figure 9.1).

Ideally, you've worked your way down from the heights, suggesting a level of giving to Mr. Smith that wasn't outrageous, but would have represented a catch. If your prospect, Mr. Smith, declined your invitation to support, you need to come to the ultimate compromise, a level of giving that he is both *able* and *willing* to give to your organization.

Figure 9.1   Stage 7—The Close

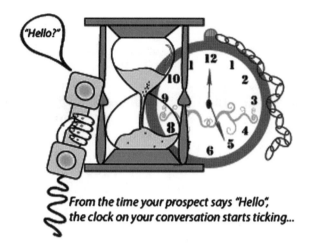

*From the time your prospect says "Hello",
the clock on your conversation starts ticking...*

As we have discussed in a previous chapter, the telephone medium has its own unique limitations in terms of the amount of time a prospect will grant you to complete your mission. Like sands through the hourglass, your time is about out.

The bubble you sought to blow around your prospect, Mr. Smith, to temporarily insulate him from the environmental distractions and activity that he was involved in prior to your call is stretching thin and is in danger of bursting.

Yes, you have done a great job in being articulate, informative, energetic, and compelling in presenting your mission, empathetic to Mr. Smith's particular needs and situation regarding his ability to give. You've presented him with an initial first proposal and possibly a counterproposal. You've listened to him and made an assessment of his ability to give, along with his willingness to do so.

But now he's begun to draw away from you. He may not be ready to give, not right now, not at this time. He's been barraged with requests, demands, and other solicitations. You might be the first or the fourth call he has received this evening.

It's time to come down the giving ladder and find that level that he *can* give, and you need to be at your most intense (see the sample giving ladder in the Appendix, Section A).

It may be that Mr. Smith is somewhat reluctant to commit to a contribution. He may be a nondonor or a long-lapsed donor, or he may feel that he has already done enough for your organization this year. At this stage of the call, it might be necessary to remind him of the most salient aspect of your purpose—your capsule case statement, or some other compelling reason to give that will make it harder for Mr. Smith to refuse.

The Final "Spin" of Urgency—an Optional Strategy

It may be that you know Mr. Smith is already primed and is ready to agree on an amount. (Remember the "Principle of Parsimony"—saying only the minimum amount necessary to get you efficiently to your goal.) If so, you can skip on, right to the close, and lay your bottom line number on the table.

But Mr. Smith might need a little nudge to pull him from the "no" column to the "yes" column. You're seeking that final hot button, the "compelling key" to unlock Mr. Smith's philanthropic instincts. Because this is your last pitch, you'd better make it good! The sense of it is: "Mr. Smith, I realize I've asked you for a lot of money earlier in this call, but we really, really, really need you to give as much as you can, or at least *something*, to participate in this campaign because. . . . "

Segue Strategy 1: The Matching Challenge Grant

Perhaps you're among the lucky nonprofit organizations to possess the valuable tool of a matching challenge grant.

If you are pursuing a two-ask strategy, you can present the matching challenge grant for the first time, much in the same way as in Chapter 7.

Mr. Smith, I can understand a large gift is out of the question, but let me share some exciting news, the XYZ Foundation has awarded us a $50,000 challenge grant that will match any gift you make tonight, dollar for dollar—so this is a terrific opportunity! I'm sure you agree!

Conversely, if you're pursuing a three-ask strategy, with your final ask preceded by a "negotiation," and you have a matching challenge, you can go right back to the well. Professional fundraisers know that challenge grants can be used in ways such that they are the "gifts that keep on giving"—one of the most compelling reasons for potential prospects to give, or to at least participate in a fundraising campaign.

Mr. Smith, I understand that [previous amount] isn't possible this year, but with our the XYZ Challenge Grant, anything you give tonight will be matched dollar for dollar. It would be shame if we didn't earn all of the grant monies this year. I'm sure you agree!

Or, rather than in the negative, you can couch it in the positive:

Mr. Smith, I understand what you've said, but please be aware that any amount you give tonight will still be counted toward the XYZ Challenge, which is a terrific opportunity. I'm sure you agree!

By phrasing your script in the above manner, you not only remind Mr. Smith about the challenge, but you are stating a fact that is urgent, that any gift tonight will be matched. That's not to say that they won't be matching gifts tomorrow, but narrowing the focus to now creates a further sense of urgency. And last, by, inserting the close-ended tie-down "I'm sure you agree" in such a way that Mr. Smith can't say "no" is a good way to precede the final ask.

Perhaps you are dealing with a prior donor, and the challenge grant applies only to the portion the donor increases a gift from the prior year.

> *Mr. Smith, we're hoping every donor will renew and increase his gift, even a bit. The XYZ Challenge Grant will match whatever increased gift you make tonight, dollar for dollar—a terrific opportunity, I'm sure you agree!*

The fundraiser can seek to propose a specific dollar amount that is the incremental *increase* over the donor's previous gift, a technique explained later in this chapter.

Segue Strategy 2: Last Chance to Jump on the Bandwagon

If you've presented in your purpose section's mini–case statement one of the positive strategies—"building a better tomorrow," "part of a winning team," "be part of our success," "feel good about us and you"—here's the prospect's last chance to jump on the bandwagon. To mix transportation metaphors, the "train is pulling out of the station!"

School Annual Giving Program
Mr. Smith, to keep XYZ a great school, please help us achieve our goal of 50 percent alumni participation in this year's Annual Fund—we can't do it without you!
Or
Mr. Smith, we need just five more pledges from your class (Class of 1982) to make our goal!

Theater/Performing Arts Organization
Mr. Smith, to keep ticket prices affordable for everyone, we need each subscriber to at least participate in our Annual Fund!

General Phonathon/Fundraising Effort
Mr. Smith, we still need 20 more donors if we're going to make this evening's goal of [x] . . . we want you to be one of them!

Advocacy Organization
Mr. Smith, your gift this evening can ensure that we'll be able to keep up our good work. We need you to join us this evening!

Specific Goal
Mr. Smith, tonight's goal is $2,000—and I can see by the board we're just $900 short . . . We really need your help right now to put us over the top!

Specific Program

Mr. Smith, any gift you make this evening will help ensure we'll keep our "Toys for Good Boys" program making a real difference in our community!

Recognition

Mr. Smith, if you give this evening, we can place you on the "Honor Roll of Friends." . . . Mr. Smith, I'd really like to add your name right now!

Institutional Funding

Mr. Smith, your participation is really important this year . . . You see, corporations and foundations ask how many of our friends in the community are supporting us before they commit anything.

Sense of Self-Worth

Mr. Smith, we'll appreciate any gift you make this evening, and I just know that if you come on board, you'll feel good yourself about helping this important cause.

It's up to your creativity and the specifics of your organization and its fundraising program to find that compelling key that will impact Mr. Smith. Again, all of the rules that have been mentioned before apply: short, pithy sentences; action language; no long-winded speeches!

Segue Strategy 3: Last Chance to Avert Disaster

Your organization may be unfortunate enough to be dealing with a real crisis, an external threat, or some funding issues that are potentially catastrophic. If this is the case, in your purpose section of the call, you may have pursued a mini–case statement with a "bad news" strategy. Here's your last chance to remind Mr. Smith of the consequence of his *not* giving!

Recalling the educational institution from a previous chapter that was experiencing state budget cuts:

Mr. Smith, I'm also calling to ask you if you've heard about the massive state budget cuts for XYZ this year. . . . [Response] Well, these cuts are so drastic, we'll have to lay off staff, even faculty—cuts we can't accept in a great school. But your gift to the Alumni Fund can help right now—and show your confidence in what we think is a great school. I hope you agree!

Your "bad news" segue might follow as follows:

Mr. Smith, like I said, we're really under the gun, the budget cuts are set to begin October 14ʰ, and if we're going to avoid faculty and staff layoffs, we urgently need every one of our alumni to step up with a pledge tonight!

Recalling the ballet arts organization from a previous chapter with a budget crisis:

Mr. Smith, you've heard the news about the ballet's budget problems, right? [Response] Well, the bad news—it's a real crisis—a $1 million deficit. But the good news, we can get through the year without canceling a single performance if every patron gives to the Emergency Fund!

Your "bad news" segue might follow as follows:

Mr. Smith, it would be a shame if we had to cancel a single performance this year, I'm sure you agree! But with your help tonight, you can help keep us dancing!

Recalling the political advocacy organization from a previous chapter pursuing the "You versus Them" strategy:

Mr. Smith, I assume you've been hearing about the lies and distortions about the ABC legislation. [Response] Well, they are well funded through special interests and have millions to spend, but we need to fight back right now and take to the airwaves in a Truth campaign—but that takes money, and the support of every well-informed person who cares about this, like you do.

Your "bad news" segue might follow as follows:

Mr. Smith, please don't let the special interests win! We're up against a lot, but with your help tonight, we'll be able to fight back now!

Recalling the disaster relief organization in a previous chapter dealing with a natural disaster:

Mr. Smith, you've probably seen the horrific scenes on the news—this week's tsunami killed over 30,000 people, but even worse, nearly 10 million people are homeless and lack food, medical care, and basic sanitary needs—an unbelievable disaster, I'm sure you agree. [Response] Mr. Smith, we must raise over $50 million dollars now if we're going to save millions of lives—and we need your help today!

Your "bad news" segue might follow as follows:

Mr. Smith, every gift in the campaign is important and can literally spell the difference between life and death for thousands who are waiting for help!

Increasing the Sense of Urgency—Slow Down

If the overall call process can be thought of as a funnel, in the beginning wide at the top, then narrowing through the purpose section of the call, and narrowing yet further through your specific dollar asks in a negotiation and culminating to a point in the close, the sense of urgency and its amplification go in the reverse direction, like an inverted funnel or a megaphone.

The beginning of the call is amicable, personable, and general in nature as the fundraiser identifies the prospect, introduces himself or herself, and attempts to develop some rapport. But then, things get more urgent, a sense of energy increases in the purpose, and the intensity reaches a peak at the final close.

The wording, tautness of speech, use of action verbs, and the discussion of consequences, good or bad, predominate. Moreover, good fundraisers use their voices to convey a sense of earnestness and belief in the cause. While the prospects are more interested in speeding things up to a conclusion, better fundraisers will often slow down a bit, emphasizing words and articulating clearly. This helps them control the call. Weaker fundraisers, fearing loss of control, will often speed up, to match pace with the prospect, speaking faster than they were at the beginning, hoping to get out everything they have to say before Mr. Smith hangs up.

 Telephone Fundraising Rule

Avoid speeding up your speech patterns to match pace with a hurried prospect.

Beyond controlling their speech patterns, even slowing down a little bit, I've observed some of the most successful fundraisers gesticulating, making a variety of expressive hand motions to further emphasize what they are saying.

A good fundraiser may be sitting at a desk, having had an, up until this point, unsuccessful negotiation with the prospect. But nearing the final ask, he will gesture with one or both hands, expressively extending his palms to emphasize a point, or pointing out an important issue with his index finger—all invisible to Mr. Smith, who is at the other end of a phone line perhaps a thousand miles away. At a key point in the call, the fundraiser may even rise from his desk to his feet to gain that bit of psychic energy that Mr. Smith may not be able to see but can somehow feel. And then, somehow, what had been an obvious "no" turns into a "yes."

I confess, I don't know how it works. If I did, I would bottle it up and sell it, after guzzling a few bottles myself. But for many fundraisers it does work, leading me to the conclusion that there is indeed a metaphysical dimension to the medium.

 Telephone Fundraising Rule

Prospects can sense your commitment to your cause—and they respect it.

Decisions, Decisions: How Low to Go

Before the fundraiser begins articulating the final ask, he or she will need to decide: How low do I go? By this time you should have a pretty fair assessment of how much Mr. Smith might be willing to part with.

The Two-Ask Strategy

If you've pursued the two-ask strategy of fundraising, chances are, this will bring you to the bottom of the giving ladder (see Figure 3.1 on page 44).

If you had been dealing with prior donors, your first ask may have simply been a level above the prior gift. That is, if it's a donor who last gave in the $25 to $50 range you're dealing with, then your first ask might have been in the $100 range.

Positioning yourself in this way, it brings you down the ladder to straight renewal. Obviously, you don't want to fall *below* the prior gift and downgrade your donors! If the prior donors were three figures or more, then your first ask probably was the donor group level immediately above the prior gift, again positioning yourself for straight renewal.

If you're dealing with a group of nondonors, constituents who are affiliated in some way with your organization, but have never given, it's likely you're pursuing a strategy to maximize participation, rather than combing carefully through the list to find a few golden nuggets with beginning asks of $1,000 or more. In this case, your first ask may be something in the $100 range, leaving your second proposal in a range at the bottom of the giving ladder.

Bottom line, in the two-ask strategy of fundraising, you're more than likely going to find yourself at the bottom of the giving ladder with non-donors or seeking a straight renewal for prior donors. This simplifies things immensely, is not very demanding of your fundraisers, and fits the constrictions of the hard script more easily.

Three-Ask Strategy

However, if you're pursuing the three-ask strategy, with a negotiation your final drop may present you with a decision. If you will recall the general rule of negotiation—that you try to *not* skip over more than one level of the giving ladder at time to avoid the "falling elevator" syndrome that will take you crashing through the floor to a refusal—you may have the two, or possibly three amounts to choose from.

Let's say your giving ladder is:

$1,000
500
250

100

50

35

Moreover, let's assume you began your fundraising proposal in the stratospheric heights of $1,000, and the prospect did not react by having a heart attack.

Consequently, you decided a counterproposal of $500 would not be inappropriate, which puts you in a position for a close for as much as $250. Assume further that the prospect's response was less than enthusiastic at the $500 counterproposal—you even sense by the reaction that you might lose the prospect altogether. The question of the moment: Can I fall to the $100, or perhaps only $50 or $35 to salvage something?

These are the last-minute decisions that have to be made on the fly by the resourceful fundraiser. If the fundraiser guesses wrong, and asks too high on the close, she risks having to wield a *fourth* ask. As we've discussed in some detail earlier, four proposals in the context of the interruptive medium of telephone communication with finite time and clock ticking may only serve to tick off the prospect.

Mr. Smith may be asking himself, "What? You didn't hear me? I can't do that much!" That's why *listening* to the prospect's reaction at the counter-proposal is just as critical as it was to his reaction at the first proposal.

Consider the following hypothetical responses of our prospect, Mr. Smith, to a second ask of $250:

I just can't do quite that much this time around.

No, even that number is out of the question this year.

In light of all of my other philanthropic commitments, giving substantially is completely out of the question.

No, no, no, I just can't! Look, I can do something, just send me out an envelope and I'll send something back.

I don't think I'll be able to help you out much this year.

I'm sorry my kids' tuition is killing me! I don't think I'll be able to help you for a while longer.

Ha, ha, ha! I'm sorry; you must have the wrong Mr. Smith!

Based on the nuance of these responses, how low do you go? If the fundraiser falls to just $50, could she be leaving $50 on the table that she might otherwise have had, if she had asked for $100? Making correct decisions like these, one right after another, significantly impacts the overall average gift of your campaign, not to mention your bottom line.

Please note, I have never, ever seen successful telephone fundraising efforts where amounts below $25 were ever included in a "giving ladder," nor where fundraisers were coached or even permitted to ask for amounts below that number. Doing so will lower the overall sights of your campaign and will result in such a low average gift that even with the modestly higher pledge rates associated with broad participation, your bottom line dollars overall will not be enough to cover your expenses.

If you are dealing with a group of raw, unaffiliated prospects, I understand your objective may be to build a group of supporters from the ground up, and you might be willing to take a loss on your fundraising program. But if your prospect list is comprised of *constituents*, individuals who are affiliated with your organization in some way or another, asking for increments of $10 or $15 can have the effect of training your fundraisers to ask for low amounts and conditioning your constituents to not have a lot of expectations placed on them—ever.

That's why in telephone programs we say we aren't after "donations." Rather, we seek "contributions," "gifts," and "commitments"—amounts of money that represent a modest sacrifice on the part of the contributor, or potentially, significant philanthropy at significant sacrifice. These are the numbers that truly add up.

Articulating the Close

At this point, you've said everything there is to say. So has your prospect. It's now time for the final "ask." If you've employed a segue to precede your ask like those mentioned earlier in this chapter, you need do nothing more than cleanly and clearly lay the number on the table. The sense of the ask is this:

> So, Mr. Smith, I've heard everything you've had to say about your ability to give, and I have a fair assessment of your willingness to give to our organization, and conversely, you've heard the strong, even urgent case we've presented why you should give, as generously as you can. In light of our needs and your ability, can we count on you for at least a contribution of $X?

Use short sentences, clean and powerful verbs, monosyllabic words, the final dollar request positioned at the end, or as near to it as possible. Some examples:

Nondonors, General

> So, Mr. Smith, can we count on you for a gift of just $50?
> In light of what you've said, can you join us this year with only $35?
> Mr. Smith, I understand what you've said, but this program is so critical to our future, can we count on you for a gift of $100?
> Mr. Smith, in light of what you've said, it would be just terrific if you pledged only $50 tonight!

Nondonors: Donor Recognition Levels and Benefits

Mr. Smith, we'd be very grateful if we could include you in the Donor group with a gift of $125!

Mr. Smith, our most popular donor group is the Friends . . . Can't we include your name among them tonight with a gift of only $50?

Mr. Smith, based on what you've said, the Family Membership will work best for you—of course, you and your family will still have unlimited visits to the Museum, and we'll provide six free guest passes to bring friends any time you want . . . all for just $125!

To make your ask very compelling and assumptive, employ strong phraseology in your final ask:

include you
include you tonight
count on you
at least participate
give just $X
give an amount of just $X
give only $X now
have you join us

Prior Donors

At the minimum, you'd like to be able to at least *renew* the last previous gift of a donor, and ideally you'd like an upgrade. To this end you may have pursued one of several negotiating strategies.

It could be that you were dealing with a prior donor of such a small amount, perhaps $15 or $10, that you pretty much considered her as a nondonor and used a standard sight-raise strategy with a beginning amount of $250 or $500, then may have fallen to $125 on counterproposal. This would position you for a potential gift in the $50 or $75 range, or barring that and based on how positive or negative the prospect's reaction, perhaps $50 or $35.

Or, if you were pursuing the two-ask strategy and began with an ask in the $100 range, you are now ready to fall to the base level, *without any reference to the prospect's prior gift*, since it was so low.

Mr. Smith, we thank you for your generous support last year, but this year, can we count on you to join our Friends group with just $35?

It may be that you are dealing with a prior gift in the $100 to $250 range, and began your negotiation with a suggestion of a substantial increase, in the $1,000 range, and worked your way down, through a counterproposal in the $500 or $250 range, and are ready to focus on the prior gift as a way to "bump" the prospect up.

Mr. Smith, I see that last year you were a member of the Donors with a gift of $125 . . . This year can we count on you to join the next level up . . . the Sustainers for $250? It would be terrific if you would do that!"

. . . and if there were recognition benefits involved:

Mr. Smith, I see that last year you were a member of the Donors with a gift of $125. This year can we count on you to join the Sustainers and come to the annual donor appreciation party in December—for a gift of $250?

Moreover, considering the fact that most donor recognition groups are in ranges:

Benefactors:	$500–999
Sustainers:	$250–499
Donors:	$100–249
Friends	$ 50–99

. . . going for a modest, incremental increase:

Mr. Smith, I see last year you were a member of our Donors group, but if we're going to make our goal this evening, can we count on you to renew your last gift of $100, and add just $25 to it? That's feasible, isn't it?

Or you may be dealing with the smaller donors in the $25 to $99 range and are looking to increase them a full level, perhaps to the base level of a donor recognition program:

Mr. Smith, this year can you join the Friends, and we'll add your name to honor roll of donors—by adding just $25 to your last years' gift—making it an even $50 . . . can we count on you to do that?

Or, if you've already mentioned the specific amount of gift the donor had made in the previous year:

Mr. Smith, can we count on you to renew your gift from last year, and add just $25 to it? $25 dollars!

The above is an effective technique, without being deceptive, because it focuses the prospect on the increment and not the total. Of course, the total amount is clarified in the next stage of the call, the confirmation.

Lapsed Donors: Best Strategies for Closing

The above examples all reference "last year's gift." What about donors who have given sporadically or have given only once to your organization? And what if the previous gift wasn't last year, but maybe two, three, or more years ago, or in other words "long lapsed"?

I have audited numerous calls where a donor's record had shown a $35 or $50 prior gift, perhaps four years before, and when thanked for their previous gift, the prospect says:

Mr. Smith: *You mean I've donated to your organization before?*
Fundraiser: *Uh, yes . . . at least that's what our records show, Mr. Smith.*

. . . not exactly the smoothest beginning to establishing a long relationship.

Indeed, the prospect may suspect he's being bamboozled with false information. Sometimes it's just an honest error on the part of an organization, a case of data entry perhaps. Or sometimes organization will classify an item as a gift to the annual fund when in reality it was something else completely. I recall the case of a large university having $24 book return fees never claimed by graduating students, so trying to find a place to park the money, they simply threw it into their annual fund. (Well, that's one way to get your participation rates up!)

The question here is whether to treat long-lapsed donors as never givers, and rather than trying to close on a renewal of a previous gift, simply negotiate down to the best number possible. Which method will produce better results will vary from organization to organization, and from list to list.

At the other end of the scale, you may have more than a handful of $250, $500, or even $1,000 donors that had given four or five years before, sometimes even longer. These kinds of donors should be treated somewhat gingerly. There is a reason why they didn't keep giving. Perhaps it was a one-shot gift at a gala, perhaps one of a couple has passed away, or it may be they have a significant complaint about your organization that was not resolved.

If at all possible, these kinds of prospects should be segmented from a more general list, with well-trained fundraisers ready to deal with a variety of situations. Regardless, if you could manage to renew just a fraction of these midlevel donors, it can be a significant boost to your phone program.

Other Techniques in the Close

There are a few other considerations that can affect your close and significantly improve your chances of success.

The Forced Choice   This is a well-known favorite that just keeps working and working. Basically, it focuses the prospect's attention on two numbers: A and B, and not on "Do I give or do I not?" It is an effective technique for practically all of the "closing" situations previously described, *except* for membership campaigns, where there are fixed levels of membership, not giving ranges.

For example, for nondonors, a forced choice at the end of a negotiating process makes for a very compelling close:

Mr. Smith, since this is such an important program, can we count on you for a gift of just $50 or $35? Which is more comfortable?

Mr. Smith, we really, really need you to come on board tonight for just $100 or $120. Which works better for you?

Mr. Smith, I understand what you've said, but this program is critical if we're going to overcome our opposition, so can we at least count on you for $75, or even $50?

Mr. Smith, in light of what you've said, it would be just terrific if you pledged only $50 tonight, or at least $35. Which is more comfortable?

And the forced choice works well, even when donor recognition levels are involved:

Mr. Smith, we'd be very grateful if we could include you in the Donors group with a gift of $100 or $125. Which works better for you this year?

Mr. Smith, our most popular donor group is the Friends. Can't we include your name among them tonight with a gift of only $50 or $75?

Or sometimes the forced choice works in a more assumptive and assertive context:

So, Mr. Smith, based on what you've said, let's get you in this year as a Sustainer or a Benefactor for $250 or $500. Which works better for you?

Of course, the forced choice can also work very well with prior donors when you're seeking an upgrade:

Mr. Smith, we thank you for your generous support last year, but this year, can we count on you to join our Friends group with just $35 or $50? Which is more comfortable? (for a prior donor of negligible amount)

Mr. Smith, I see that last year you were a member of the Donors with a gift of $125. This year can we count on you to join the next level up, the Sustainers, for $250 or $300? Which works better for you?

Mr. Smith, I see that last year you were a member of the Donors with a gift of $125. This year can we count on you to join the Sustainers and come to the annual donor appreciation party in December, for a gift of $250 or $300? Which do you want to do?

Mr. Smith, I see that last year you were a member of our Donors group. If we're going to make our goal this evening, can we count on you to renew your last gift of $100, and add just $25 or $35 to it? Which is better for you?

Mr. Smith, this year can you join the Friends, and we'll add your name to honor roll of donors, by adding just $25 or $35 to your gift last year? Which works better?

Mr. Smith, can we count on you to renew your $250 gift from last and add just $50 or $100 to it? $50 or $100 dollars?

When you're dealing with prior donors of a specific amount, the forced choice increase temporarily deflects their attention from the total amount they gave before and focuses them on a smaller increment of increase—one figure or another. With the prospect's assent, the total is added up immediately in the confirmation phase of the call.

Telephone Fundraising Rule

The "forced choice" is one of the most effective tools in the telephone fundraiser's bag of techniques. Save it for the end when you really need it.

Percentage Increment Increase   I'm not the biggest fan of this technique, but it can occasionally work in either a two-ask or three-ask format. It is usually preceded by a segue that presents the proposition to the prospect. Let's take the case of our wonderful prospect, Mr. Smith, who had last given $100:

Mr. Smith, we'll be able to make our goal this year if every one of our friends increases his gift just 10 or 20 percent over last year!

And then the close:

So, in light of this, can you add just $10 or $20 to last year's gift—that would be $110 or $120? Which works better for you?

. . . or, in a non–forced choice format, with a different kind of tie-down:

So, in light of this, can you renew last year's gift, and add just $10 to it? Would that be fair?

. . . or even stronger:

. . . that would be fair, wouldn't it?
. . . that would be reasonable, wouldn't it?
. . . isn't that doable!?
. . . why, of course it's fair, reasonable, and doable!

In this case, or all of the others above, note the absence of the question mark at the end of the final ask. While it is true, you're asking Mr. Smith a question:

Can we count on you for a gift of just $50 or $35?

. . . it is very important that the fundraisers do not couch the close meekly, with an upward, weak, lilting, pretty-please interrogatory in a Minnie Mouse voice. The close should be strong and assumptive . . . try using an exclamation in your scripts as kind of a cue to urge your fundraisers to be strong, bold, and successful!

 Telephone Fundraising Rule

A strong ``!'' works better than a weak ``?'' in the final close. Note: This is also true in life.

The "Bounce" Question: What do you do if the prospect, at any stage of the call, seeks to short-circuit your solicitation and offers you a "number?"

Fundraiser: *Mr. Smith, I'd like to speak with you a few moments about . . .*
Mr. Smith: (interrupting) *. . . look, what did I give last year?*
Fundraiser: *Mr. Smith, you gave a hundred dollars.*
Mr. Smith: *Just send me out a form for $100.*

Answer: You negotiate!

Fundraiser: *Mr. Smith, that's terrific, we really appreciate that, but if we're going to make our goal this evening, can you:*
. . . add just $25 or $35 to your gift this year? It would be terrific if you do that!

or

. . . join the Donor level this year for just $50 more? We will be very grateful for your added support!
or
. . . renew that gift now, and perhaps do the same amount in another six months?

In a certain percentage of calls, as many as one-third, either with a prior donor or a nondonor, this technique will result in a higher gift than the prospect would otherwise have given. Employing this technique can modestly increase your overall average gift performance.

Some folks may think this may be overly pushy, but I have never heard a prospect back out of his or her gift after being presented with a good reason to increase it. On the contrary, prospects will respect your assertiveness on behalf of your important cause, a modest assertiveness that falls well short of audacity.

The worst that is likely to happen:

Mr. Smith: *No, thanks, let's just keep it at $100 this year.*

Which brings us to the final fundraising rule of this chapter and all that came before it:

Telephone Fundraising Rule

Nothing ventured, nothing gained.

Summary

The close is the make-or-break stage of the call. You may have made some mistakes earlier in the call. Perhaps your tone was tentative, or you found it somewhat awkward to get Mr. Smith on the line. Maybe you mangled some words in the purpose section of the call and didn't make as compelling and effective a case as you might have.

But it's the close that separates the really good fundraisers from the average and not so good. If you can excel at the close, in spite of everything else, you will be a successful telephone fundraiser and will garner lots and lots of pledges for your organization.

Your sincerity and your sense of conviction will carry over to the prospect. Couple that with the sense of credible urgency you impart and you can and will sway the Mr. Smiths of the world to open their hearts and their pocketbooks to your cause.

The Result

Now we've come to the end, waiting for Mr. Smith's response to our last proposal, our close (see Figure 10.1). You've given it your best effort, and you've made the best case possible. You've been assertive, direct, and compelling in presenting proposals to elicit his generous philanthropy. But from your perspective, there can be only *two* possible outcomes: "yes" or "no."

What Is a Pledge?

A "yes" is called a *pledge*.

Regrettably, at this juncture, the money doesn't come spilling out of the phone, like you've hit the jackpot in Las Vegas, although you wish it might be true. I'll admit, it would be fun to observe in a phone room—a telephone fundraiser "hitting" and then the red lights flash, the bells ring, and the sirens wail, as the cash starts gushing forth from the telephone, the eager phone room manager frantically grasping for each $100 bill spilling out to place in his "pledge bucket." What wouldn't that do for morale?

Figure 10.1   Stage 8—Results

In reality, a pledge is really nothing more than a verbal promise to give a specified amount of money to your organization. You must still collect it. So, your job isn't over just yet!

For most purposes a telephone pledge can be defined according to the following rule:

 Telephone Fundraising Rule

A pledge is a verbal promise by a prospective donor to pay a specified amount of money to your organization, on a predetermined basis, on or by a specified date or dates.

Let's examine each element in some detail.

The Verbal Promise

A promise is a good-faith commitment to do something, short of a contract. Many would argue that an oral telephone pledge is a binding, legal commitment. From a practical standpoint, however, organizations must rely on the character and goodwill of their donors to follow through.

I've heard numerous occasions where a prospect has made a good-faith commitment to give a substantial amount of money, perhaps $500, sometimes promising that gift on an annual basis over a period of years, as in a capital campaign. With some concern the prospect may ask:

What happens if something happens and I can't pay? What if I lose my job, or get hit by a bus? Am I still obligated? Will my heirs be obligated?

In the vast majority of cases, organizations don't want to lower the hammer on small and midlevel donors who have made promises in good faith, and then through unfortunate circumstances are unable to pay. A simple e-mail or letter from the donor to the organization canceling or restructuring the terms of a commitment is usually sufficient to satisfy the parties.

As someone who *has* been hit by a bus, I know that "stuff happens," and with the approbation of my clients, I would usually instruct our fundraisers to handle prospect questions like the ones above in the following manner:

Mr. Smith, we're looking for a good-faith commitment tonight, what you believe is doable right now. If something happens and you find you're not able to pay, XYZ organization isn't going to send the pledge police out to your house to collect!

These kinds of situations are fairly rare, usually represent gifts that are in the $500 to $1,000 or more range annually, and affect situations where the prospect is beginning to butt up against the limits of his or her giving potential.

That said, a verbal pledge can subsequently be solidified and made more formal, closer to a contractual commitment by having the pledger subsequently sign a pledge card or letter of intent. But for the vast majority of under-$1,000 gifts that are typically solicited in a telephone program, this is usually neither desired nor necessary.

The Specified Pledge

Pledges are made for specific amounts of money: $500. $1,000. $50. $35. There should be no ambiguity or confusion.

Occasionally in capital campaigns, the pledge may be made in stock or other financial instruments, the value of which translates to a specified amount of money. $3,000. $45,000. And so on.

The following expressions by a prospect are *not* "promises to pay a specified amount of money":

Yeah, I think I can do that.
Well, I think I can do something like that.
It's probably about right.
Yeah, I can do something in that range.
I'll do the best I can with that amount.
Send me out the pledge card for that amount, and we'll do the best we can.

In these cases, the fundraiser has failed in the close to find that level of gift about which there should be no uncertainty. The fundraiser is in the unfortunate position of shoring up the pledge by negotiating further down:

Mr. Smith, it's important we know the minimum amount you're certain you can do tonight!

. . . and perhaps reinforcing the sense of urgency:

. . . so we can add it to our goal this evening!
. . . so we know how far we have to go to meet our budget!
. . . so we can immediately apply it to the challenge grant!

. . . and then renegotiating down to find the level of gift about which Mr. Smith is absolutely, positively certain.

. . . Mr. Smith, would the minimum tonight be $100 or $125?
. . . Mr. Smith would the minimum tonight be only $50 or $75?
. . . and so on, basically "reclosing" the close.

The Method of Payment

Exactly *how* you want Mr. Smith to make his pledge should be clear to him, and he should agree. Will he be paying by personal check? Perhaps the check will be coming from his business or company, or even his family foundation.

How will he get that check to you? In a few rare cases, it may be that he'll want to drop it by your office directly. Otherwise, he may wish to mail it to you, preferably in a return envelope you mail out to him, so he can enclose his check to ensure that it will be directed to the right fund account and be properly applied.

Perhaps you would prefer that Mr. Smith pay immediately by credit card. If so, you will need to ask him for his credit card information. Perhaps he will not be comfortable in giving you that information over the telephone, which is understandable. The issue of credit card information security is widely acknowledged, as is the broader issue of identity theft. No matter how carefully you screen telephone fundraisers, asking them to immediately perform a "collection function" creates another layer of management oversight and control of your telephone program: security.

The upside is, 95 percent of the time, once you have the credit card *information*, you have *payment*, and it eliminates one layer of the collection process—the return mail function.

With the advent of the Internet, getting the credit card collection data you need could be easily accomplished with a follow-up e-mail, if you have the technology. If Mr. Smith says "yes" to a $100 pledge, but doesn't want to give you his credit card over the phone, you might send him a "thank you" e-mail for the gift, along with a link that would forward him to a secure site, so he could enter his credit card payment in safety, security, and confidence.

But if the method of payment is to be check, with your sending out a reply envelope, you better make sure the address you have on file for Mr. Smith is the correct one! That is, you better recite Mr. Smith's address to him and make any necessary corrections.

Regardless, all of these details need to be worked out with prospects who say "yes!"

The Specified Payment Date(s)

By soliciting Mr. Smith and eliciting a pledge, one would assume your organization would like to receive the funds as soon as possible. While, technically, pledges can make your financial reports look good, it's the *cash* in your account that really impacts your mission. Without the cash to spend, your organization can't accomplish or do all of the good things you're supposed be doing.

So, rather than leaving it up to Mr. Smith to return his check anytime he wants, you have yet one more thing to negotiate: payment date or payment dates (if the pledge involves installments).

I've heard many instances of fundraisers leaving the payment situation all too unclear:

Mr. Smith, I'll send you out a pledge card for the $100, along with a return envelope. Thanks so much! Goodbye!

These kinds of pledges are less collectible: They provide no *temporal* basis upon which to collect the pledge or send reminders if necessary.

Perhaps not quite so open-ended is the following situation:

Mr. Smith, I'll send you out a pledge card for the $100, along with a return envelope. Can you get that back to us as soon as you can?

"As soon as [Mr. Smith] can" may mean anything. Next week. Next month. Next year. Next millennium. Next Interstadial Warming Period of the next Ice Age, and so on. Leaving a detail like this so open-ended invites inevitable procrastination on the part of the prospect.

And leaving it up to the prospect is usually never a good idea:

Mr. Smith, when do you think you can get that $100 pledge back to us?

Or, consider the following:

Mr. Smith, I'll send you out a pledge card for the $100, along with a return envelope. Can you get your check back to us by the end of our fiscal year that ends June 30?

If you're making this call on June 15, that's not bad. If you're making the call in January, however, you're giving the prospect way too much leeway. Which brings me to one of the most important "rules":

 Telephone Fundraising Rule

There is an inverse relationship between the length of deferral of a telephone pledge and its collectability.

While the above rule might be true for all kinds of pledges in fundraising through every medium, it's *especially* true for the telephone medium. And this brings me to another rule:

Telephone Fundraising Rule

It's not easy to get prospects to pledge. And—it's not easy to get prospects to pay.

With the above rules in mind, it's important that *you* take control. If Mr. Smith declines to pay his pledge immediately by credit card, it's best to suggest to him the date when *you* would like to receive his check, most optimally by return mail:

Mr. Smith, I'll send you out a pledge card for the $100, along with a return envelope right away. Can you get your check back to us in two weeks? That would be October 15—is that comfortable?

If that isn't comfortable, then the payment date becomes yet another topic for negotiation:

Mr. Smith: *Can't I get it to you by the end of the month, when I take care of all of my bills?*

Fundraiser: *That's no problem, Mr. Smith, I'll mark this for payment by October 31 for you!*

What if the prospect has made a commitment involving installments? Well, that can complicate things quite a bit:

Mr. Smith, thanks for your pledge of $100! I'll send you out a confirmation and pledge card for your first installment of $50 right away. Can you get that back to us by October 15? [Discuss] And for the second $50 in two months, say December 15, is that comfortable? [Discuss]

If the pledge is for a capital campaign commitment over a period of several years, perhaps as many as five, things can get really complicated:

Mr. Smith, thanks so much for your pledge of $1,000—$50 quarterly over the next five years. I'll send you a confirmation and a reply envelope for your first $50. Can you get that back to us by October 15? [Discuss] And then we'll send out reminders every three months, on the 1st of January, then April, July, and the 1st of October, over the five years, if that's comfortable.

Like I said, installments can get complicated. Clearly written follow-up confirmations with clearly delineated payment schedules are very important. Remember the ''Telephone Fundraising Rule'' from an earlier chapter:

Telephone Fundraising Rule

The telephone is a lousy medium for transmitting detailed information.

Pledges: The Confirmation

Keeping in mind all of these critical elements to make sure a pledge is indeed a pledge and, moreover, one that it is *collectible*, most effective scripts contain a section called "Confirmation" or "Pledge Confirmation" that seeks to remove any ambiguity whatsoever.

This is a section of the script or call outline that is very much a *script*, with more formalized language that is better recited verbatim by the fundraiser. Leaving anything out in the confirmation can compromise the integrity of the pledge, and hence its collectability.

The fact that its language may be a bit more formal and less conversational than what has previously transpired is a further signal to the prospect, now the pledger, that this is a promise not to be taken lightly. An effective format for confirming a $100 pledge that touches on all four points raised earlier is:

> *Mr. Smith, thanks so much for your $100 pledge, it's just terrific! I'll send a confirmation for the $100 and a reply envelope. Should I send that to 1313 Dreary Lane, North Central City, South Dakota, 70201? [Prospect's response] Terrific, and can you get your check back to us in two weeks, by October 15? [Prospect's response, negotiate payment date if necessary]. Great, Mr. Smith, thanks again for your $100 gift, and have a great evening!*

Here, all of the salient issues are dealt with cleanly and concisely. There are some other guidelines to observe in an effective confirmation.

Repetition of the Pledge Amount

Most fundraising professionals recommend repeating the pledge amount a minimum of *three* times in the course of the confirmation. This reinforces the amount of the gift in Mr. Smith's mind and leaves little ambiguity of the pledge amount. More than a few times, I've heard mistaken amounts or wishful thinking cleared up at this point in a phone call:

> *No, I said $15, not $50!*
> *No, I said I would* try *to do $100. I can't commit to a date!*
> *You know, I don't want to extend myself more than I should, on second thought let's just make that $500 instead of the $1,000, I'm sure I can do that!*

. . . and conversely, I've heard pledgers take the fundraiser in the *opposite* direction:

> *I'll tell you what, Elaine, let's make it $1,000 instead of $500. You've done a great job! You're a really good fundraiser. I could use someone like you in my sales department!*

Hey, it doesn't happen a lot, but it *does* happen!

Thank, Thank, Thank, and Thank Some More

Both in your tone and your words, keep thanking the prospect. There is a general fundraising rule that you cannot thank prospects enough. At this point in the call, you may have gone through a lengthy negotiation to work out an amount that was the maximum possible for Mr. Smith. He may not be excited at having been persuaded to give, or give more than he might have had in mind. You've imposed and interrupted him and have taken his time.

Thanks!
Thanks so much!
We can't thank you enough!
We're very grateful for your support!
This is just terrific!

These and other accolades of appreciation will be valued by the prospect and increase the chances for collecting the pledge.

While at this stage of the call, it may not be the best place for fundraisers to be creative, genuine gratitude can sometimes bring a smile to the face of a pledger:

Mr. Smith, you're just super!

Continuing to Address the Prospect by Name

Even if the wording of a confirmation may be a bit more formal or scripted, that shouldn't prevent you from addressing prospects by name. It continues to keep the call personal, and the prospect, Mr. Smith, will understand that it is *his* commitment and that your gratitude is directed to *him*.

Other Issues

The Credit Card Ask

If you're an organization that has the capability of accepting credit cards and want to use your telephone fundraising staff to try to immediately collect the pledges they solicit, then you'll have to include the "Credit Card Ask" in the confirmation:

Mr. Smith, thanks so much for your $100 pledge, it's just terrific! For your convenience, should we put that on Visa or Mastercard? [Prospect's response]

If "yes" to credit card:

Mr. Smith, that will be [Confirm name of card]
And the card number is [Take card number, repeat to prospect]
    And the name as it exactly appears on the card is [Take card name]

Thanks again for your $100 gift, which we'll process tomorrow. It should appear on your next statement. We'll send a thank-you for your gift to [Confirm prospect's address].

If "no" to credit card:

Okay then, Mr. Smith, I'll send a confirmation for the $100 and a reply envelope. Should I send that to 1313 Dreary Lane, North Central City, South Dakota, 70201? [Prospect's response] Terrific, and can you get your check back to us in two weeks, by October 15? [Prospect's response, negotiate payment date if necessary]. Great, Mr. Smith, thanks again for your $100 gift, and have a great evening!

Or you can be a little more assertive in the "credit card close:"

Mr. Smith, thanks so much for your $100 pledge, it's just terrific! For your convenience, should we put that on Visa or Mastercard?

If prospect says "no":

Mr. Smith, putting your gift on credit card now helps XYZ Organization put your gift to work right away, so can you help us out in that way?

If Mr. Smith still doesn't want to put his gift on his credit card, then you can proceed with the confirmation in the conventional way, confirming his address and payment terms.

One further note about credit card closes is worth noting: phraseological nuances that may not be so apparent at first in effective closing. Back in the "olden" days of telephone fundraising when our company was first accepting credit cards for our clients' campaigns, one of our fundraisers who had extensive commercial telemarketing experience critiqued my scripted "credit card close," which went something like this:

So, Mr. Smith, can we put that pledge on credit card tonight? We can accept American Express, Mastercard, or Visa!

No, no, Jim would say, make it a forced choice:

Should we put that on Visa or Master . . .

What about Amex? Well, nine times out of ten, he said, they'd have one or the other of the two cards, and if they didn't or preferred Amex, the prospect would usually say:

Prospect: *Uh, can I use American Express?*
Fundraiser: *Of course, may I have the number?*

In Jim's further critique, he advised that you begin with the word *Visa* which has a rising, interrogatory inflection, ending with the *Master*, which is downward, declarative, and affirming. A spirited debate ensued, with my countering that the constituents we're dealing with probably don't use the abbreviation "Master," and instead used the full expression *Mastercard*. So, we compromised; he continued to use *Master* while everyone else followed script and used *Mastercard*. It worked.

Confirming Other Information with the Prospect

It may be that you want to confirm other aspects of the prospect's record or collect other data during this phase of the call. There is a danger in loading up the confirmation with too much extraneous stuff and further detaining Mr. Smith who, by this time, is ready to get off the phone. But there is one aspect of data that is very much worth your while to collect, update, and confirm: the prospect's e-mail address.

It's true today that e-mail addresses don't change as frequently as they did five or six years ago. But whenever possible, you should do what you can to open up and facilitate this new channel of communication between you and your constituents.

If you don't have an e-mail address for your prospect, now is as good as any time to collect it. And if you have the capability of sending pledge confirmations and links for secure credit card payment, you are killing more than one bird with a single stone. E-mail may be less personal than a visit either in person or by phone, but it is a lot faster and cheaper.

Pledge Cards, Reply Envelopes, and Thank-You Letters

The kind of pledge card, pledge form, reply envelope, and thank-you note or letter you use to follow up a pledge confirmation is a function of many things too numerous to list. However, keep in mind the following:

Mail Confirmations Quickly   If you can process confirmations immediately, record, batch, and process the same day or evening, and get them to the post office before the midnight pickup, that's optimal! In these cases, some of the pledge confirmations will be received by prospects the next day—and in the case of first-class mail, no more than four or five days after you mail them out. Which brings me to a fundraising rule:

Telephone Fundraising Rule

Collectability of a pledge is in inverse relationship to the length of time it takes to mail out the confirmation.

If you wait two days, three days, or more, the chances of your collecting the pledge decrease. Never mail it, never collect. Add to that the vagaries and uncertainties of postal mail delivery, and you have a situation where you're no longer in control. Oral pledges have a psychological expiration date. Mail fast, keep them fresh.

Of course, if you have an Internet-capable state-of-the-art phone center, and your phone fundraisers have the capability of generating a personal e-mail follow-up the moment after Mr. Smith makes the pledge, along with a hyperlink to enable his payment, so much the better. He may have the confirmation in his Inbox before you hang up the phone. But the caveats concerning e-mail mentioned in Chapter 1 still bear consideration.

Make Confirmations as Personal as You Can   The pledge confirmation is not merely a bill; it should also be a thank you. Remember the standard rule of fundraising: You can never, ever thank prospects enough. So, along with the pledge form, payment device, and reply envelope, it's nice to include a thank-you note that has some degree of personalization.

At one extreme is the handwritten note, or at least handwritten comments in the margin of a form letter, thanking the prospect, and having him or her recollect the conversation and the pledge promise that was made. Of course, this is very costly in terms of personnel time and mailing coordination. This may not be a significant issue if you're dealing with volunteer fundraisers who would probably rather write than talk. However, if you're dealing with paid telephone fundraising staff, production and cost are key considerations: You have a *lot* of calls to make.

The next best thing is a word-processed confirmation, perhaps a letter, that at the minimum uses the prospect's name in the salutation line, and the pledge amount and payment terms in the body of the letter. Any further personalization increases the costs and the risks of error, but it's nice if you can do it and exercise a little bit of creativity, even though it may drive your IT staff a little nuts.

Make It Easy for the Prospect to Pay   Your payment device—that is, the pledge card, form, or reply envelope—should be tested and idiot-proof. This is the extreme opposite of most state and local income tax forms that have you mail to "Address A" Part B, Form II, but to "Address B" Part C, Form IV, unless you are declaring exemptions, in which case . . . well, you get the idea. If you are hoping for pledgers to honor their commitment, please make it easy for them. They are going to get your follow-up mail, along with a dozen or two other pieces of mail, many of them bills, and your mailing is but one of many.

Mr. Smith should recognize at a glance your mailing from the envelope as separate from other "junk," and he should set it aside for further attention and processing. Perhaps it will be sorted in the "bills to pay" pile. And when he opens your mailing, he should be able at a glance to know what he needs to do to get that check back to you or to fill in his credit card number in the proper place.

And don't stop there. Make it easy for him to get his payment back to you. I've seen some organizations *not* include a reply envelope at all, merely an address for Mr. Smith to mail his check to. This is a prescription for disaster. Most organizations provide some preaddressed standard reply envelope. The question is, do you pay for the postage, or do you make him?

One theory is that if you only provide the reply envelope, requiring Mr. Smith to reach into his drawer for his own cache of stamps, it will show him that your organization is really being frugal, and that you really, really need the money—so much so, that you need to save the 44 cents (or 50 cents, or $1.00 by the time this book gets published). Well, some bad things can happen if you do this.

First, Mr. Smith, noticing that he needs to fork over his own stamp, might be resentful—you've already imposed on his generosity; he's responded with a pledge and is ready to write the check, but you're nickel and diming him for a bit more. Or, Mr. Smith might reach into his drawer, and find that he's down to one or two stamps of his own. What is going to get mailed first, his overdue electric bill or the pledge he made to your organization? So, your pledge form sits on his desk until such time that he's made a trip to the post office to replenish his supply. Not good.

Statistically, you will find better collection the easier you make it for the Mr. Smiths of the world to get their money to you. Go ahead and use your standard permit postage-paid reply forms. They look official and legitimate. But if you really want to personalize the process, go ahead and affix a real stamp on the reply envelope.

If Mr. Smith is the kind of guy who would pry the stamp off and use it to mail in that overdue electric bill, you were never going to collect his pledge in the first place. And if he doesn't mail you his check back in your stamped envelope, eventually he'll have to throw that envelope away, and be forced into the position of feeling guilty about wasting the money of a needy nonprofit organization.

Guilt is a very significant philanthropic motivator. It's awkward to exploit personally, or over the telephone—much easier through the mail.

Reconfirmation Setting aside the issue of collecting overdue pledges, and the implementation of reminder systems and collection strategies, is there anything else your organization can do to "shore up" the integrity of telephone pledges at the beginning? Telephone pledges are more ephemeral and delicate than a pledge on a handshake or a written pledge or contract.

Some organizations find an instant reconfirmation of the pledge useful in solidifying pledge integrity and avoiding the wishful hearing of too-eager fundraisers that can result in uncollectible pledges.

In some cases, after an initial confirmation by the telephone representative, the call can be switched or handed to a supervisor or manager for an "additional thank you." The supervisor or manager can once again thank the prospect for his or her generosity and review the salient variables: pledge amount, payment time frame. Granted, this can sometimes be a bit awkward, coming after a phone call of several minutes, and can strain the prospect's attention and goodwill further. The costs (personnel time and prospect goodwill) need to be weighed against the measurable improvements in collection rates.

Some organizations even generate a second, separate call to the prospect that evening or the next day to reconfirm salient aspects of the pledge. This, of course, can increase costs yet further, not to mention what may be perceived as yet another intrusion by the prospect into his private space. Each organization in considering its own constituencies needs to weigh the cost-benefit of reconfirmation strategies.

Refusals

I have something I need to gently break to you. In telephone fundraising, unless you're calling into a highly distilled list of current or recently lapsed donors, you're going to experience more "nos" than "yeses." I'm sorry, but didn't your mother tell you when you were a kid this wasn't going to be easy?

In the case of calling a list of nondonors affiliated with your organization in some way, you will still generate a lot more refusals than pledges, and in the case of cold-calling a list of completely nonaffiliated prospects, you're going to experience really, really, really a lot of refusals.

Refusals Defined

Exactly what is a *refusal*? A refusal is a decision by a prospect *not* to give money to your organization as a result of your telephone solicitation. No more, no less.

It does NOT mean that he or she will NEVER support your organization, next year, next month, or perhaps even tomorrow. It's just she has decided not to give *right now*. That means usually, in the majority of instances, "refusals" are still prospective donors for your organization! They are still prospects that have value. Please treat them as such.

Refusals occur after you have made your *bottom line* proposal, that last rung on your giving ladder below which you will not fall, be it $50, $35, or even $25. And Mr. Smith, your prospect, responds with phraseology similar to the following:

No, I can't do even that much this year.
I'm sorry, I can't.
I can't do anything at all this year.

I won't do anything at all.
No!

. . . or even more ambiguously:

Even an amount like that I'd have to think about.
I'm sorry, I can't commit to any amount right now.
I'm sorry, I just don't want to be pinned down.

While some of the statements above might fall into the gray area of an unspecified pledge defined a bit later in this chapter, most often they are statements by the prospect indicating not that he or she *can't* give anything to your organization, it's just they don't *want* to, at least not right now, not tonight, not during this phone call. They simply would rather say they "can't" rather than they "won't"—it's easier for them.

How Telephone Fundraisers Should Handle Refusals

I remember years ago one of our new telephone fundraisers, whom we'll call "George," came to us with significant commercial telemarketing experience. George had an extensive background cold-calling to sell products to prospects whose names were taken right out of the phone book. We were hoping he could make the transition to fundraising, appealing to constituents of an organization and their goodwill.

George had a very aggressive approach, one that had worked well for him as a telemarketer but did not serve him well as a fundraiser. His grating, brusque telephone demeanor would quickly rub prospective donors the wrong way. During the course of a phone call, he would take a prospect to the breaking point, and sensing he had irritated the prospect to the point where he would hang up, he would beat him to the draw, and quickly hang up on the prospect before he did on George!

In this way, somehow, he psychologically came out the winner—an effective coping mechanism for dealing with refusal after refusal. Needless to say, this employee did not last the afternoon.

In dealing with telephone fundraising to affiliated constituents, you have already imposed, called unannounced, interrupted them from what they had been doing right before the call, assertively made proposals for funding, appealed to their goodwill, and despite your best efforts, they have decided not to support your organization. While you might wish as a telephone fundraiser they would have a little empathy for you, it's *you* who must have the empathy for *them*.

It's incumbent upon you to leave Mr. Smith in as upbeat and positive frame of mind at the end of the call as possible, such that he can still be a constituent for your next appeal:

Mr. Smith, I understand [you can't give this evening], but thanks for taking the time to speak with me about XYZ organization, and have a terrific evening!

Depending on the relationship of the prospect with your organization, refusals can be even more personal:

Mr. Smith, I sure understand, but thanks so much for taking the time to speak with me—and please continue to enjoy our performances this year. We hope to see you at the theater soon!

. . . or for an educational institution:

Mr. Smith, I understand, but thanks so much for speaking with me tonight about ABC College. Remember, alumni weekend is October 20, and we'd love to see you make it back!

. . . or for a prior donor:

Mr. Smith, I understand your situation this year, but keep us in mind, and we truly are grateful for all of your past support! Thanks again.

In unscripted or less scripted formats, like Call Guides and Call Outlines, a skilled fundraiser may even have picked up some personal detail earlier in the conversation, perhaps a reason for the prospect's refusal that can personalize and engender goodwill at the end of a call:

Mr. Smith, I understand, but thank you so much for taking the time to speak with me about XYZ Organization, and please accept my best wishes for your daughter's success at college! Have a great evening!

Moreover, fundraisers should be made to realize that receiving a refusal is not a negative reflection on themselves or their character. Sure, they might have done a better job in the phone call, have been a little more persuasive and compelling or a little more insightful in dealing with the prospect. But at the bottom line, refusals are an occupational hazard, the bane of telephone fundraisers, and something they simply have to accept. Help your staff with the perspective that each refusal merely takes them one step closer to a pledge.

The .300 hitter in baseball is considered pretty darned good, in the top 10 percent of all players. But even a .300 hitter fails 70 percent of the time! That's the way it is in telephone fundraising, too.

And from the perspective of your nonprofit organization, handling refusals well is a chance for your organization to continue to build friends and constituents. Handling them poorly will slightly poison the well for your own future donor development, not to mention what has become the delicate and sensitive ecology of the entire telephone medium over which substantial regulations have arisen—thanks to callers like George.

Unspecified Pledges

What about *unspecified pledges*? Isn't this a *third* possible outcome of a telephone fundraising call? There seems to be a bit of confusion and range of definition of this subject. But for purposes of telephone fundraising, allow me the temerity of simplifying things and setting forth the following rule:

> **Telephone Fundraising Rule**
>
> An "Unspecified Pledge" is a pledge to pay an unspecified amount of money on or by a specified date.

Let's take each element. First, an "unspecified" is indeed a pledge: a verbal promise that in theory if not in practice has the same level of commitment as a specified pledge.

Second, it is a promise to pay an amount of money to your organization or some asset of determinable monetary value. It is indeed a "promise"— not a "maybe" or an "I'll think about it"—but a solid promise. It's just the prospective donor cannot, will not, does not want to divulge to you the amount of money he or she intends to give over the telephone.

Third, it is a promise to pay the pledge on or by a specified date. It's not an open-ended, "will send it in sometime," "sometime later," "anytime," "in the future"—that mythical spot in the time-space continuum where all good things must happen.

Ideally, the promise to pay the unspecified amount should be optimal, by return mail if possible, just as you would have negotiated with a specified pledge. Deferral of payment of an unspecified pledge has the same downside as those of specified pledges: the longer the deferral, the less chance of collection.

For example, consider the following situation:

Fundraiser: *Okay, Mr. Smith, I'll send you out a blank pledge form that you can fill in with the amount along with a reply envelope. Can we count on getting your pledge back to us, say in two weeks? That would help us a lot!*

Mr. Smith: *No, I can't commit to a date, but I will send you back a check if you send me a pledge form and reply envelope.*

Fundraiser: *Mr. Smith, the fiscal year end of our campaign is June 30. Can we at least count on you to get your contribution in by that date?*

Mr. Smith: *Sure, that shouldn't be a problem.*
Fundraiser: *Okay, then I'll mark this for June 30 . . .*

This is still an unspecified pledge, but its deferral is to the outer limit of the campaign. The chances of collecting on this are much less than a prospect saying:

Look, send me the form and the reply envelope. I'll get you back a check right away.

What about the following situation?

Fundraiser: *Mr. Smith, do you think you can get your check back to us at least by June 30? That's the end of our fiscal year, and it would be terrific if we can count your gift towards our goal this year!*
Mr. Smith: *No, I can't commit to any date whatsoever, either June 30 of this year, or even next year, or the year after, or even by June 30, 2052. But send me out the pledge form, and I'll take care of it.*

Technically, this is a refusal, though it's incumbent on the fundraiser to follow through with Mr. Smith's request, and to mail him a pledge form and reply envelope, even though his definition of "taking care of it" may be to toss it in the trash. Still, surprises sometimes do happen!

What an Unspecified Pledge Is Not

The following instances are *not* unspecified pledges:

Prospect: *Look, why don't you send me something out, I'll take a look at it, and I'll take care of it?*
Fundraiser: *Okay, Mr. Smith, should I sent that to [confirmation of prospect's address]?*

. . . or

Prospect: *I need to think about what I can do, so can you send me out a pledge form?*
Fundraiser: *I'll be happy to get one out to you Mr. Smith—is your address still [confirmation of prospect's address]?*

Remember, each of these examples have occurred *after* you have fallen to your bottom line ask of $50—or even $35 or $25, depending on your giving ladder. Consequently, neither of these examples is anywhere near an unspecified pledge. These are all indefinite noncommitments, and the chances of collecting anything form these is next to nil.

Statements by prospects involving phrases like these present the fundraiser with a formidable challenge:

I'll do my best.
I need to think about it some more before I commit.
Send something to look over.
Send me something and I'll take care of it.
I need to discuss this with (my wife, my husband, my partner, my spiritual guide, etc.).

It's the final objective of telephone fundraiser to encourage prospects to make a decision *now*, over the telephone. That decision will be either a "yes" or a "no." Prospects who make a decision to pledge a specified amount of money will likely honor their commitments. Prospects who do not—do not.

If, through a negotiating process, a prospect cannot make an *impulse* decision on a gift at the bottom of your organization's giving ladder, be it $50, $35, or even $25, then she is a refusal. Save your postage!

Many prospects would prefer deferring their decision on making a pledge into the next decade or beyond. Strategies for encouraging them to make a decision, right *now*, over the telephone, are discussed in Chapter 11.

Teaching telephone fundraisers the importance of securing specified pledges as opposed to unspecified pledges is one of the great challenges of training. I understand why callers veer into the unspecified ranges:

- They don't want to appear pushy.
- They are overly empathetic with the prospects.
- They are loath to accept a refusal—unspecifieds are so much nicer!

Indeed, I wish I had a quarter for every fundraiser who, when faced with a recalcitrant prospect who does not want to make a decision, says:

Fundraiser: *Okay, I understand, Mr. Smith. I'll tell you what, can I send you out an unspecified pledge? Then you can decide what you want to do.*
Prospect: *Sure, that would be fine.*

Of course it's fine with Mr. Smith. You can send him anything you like, you're paying for it!

Collection Rates

Even unspecified pledges qualifying under the tighter more restrictive definition mentioned earlier in the chapter have far, far lower collection rates than specified pledges.

Depending on the organization, the degree of affiliation of its donors and pledgers, and, of course, the professionalism and skill with which you've solicited, collection on carefully confirmed specified pledges can range from a minimum of 55 percent to as high as 85 percent, sometimes even a little higher if you're dealing with current donors.

My experience with collection rates on unspecified pledges: about 5 percent. Perhaps your organization can do better.

Summary

Adequately confirming pledges is key to their collection. Lots of pledges and a high pledge rate are nice statistics to look at on daily and weekly reports. But sooner or later, the chickens will come home to roost. Indeed, some organizations for financial reporting purposes have a category for pledges as receivables on their balance sheets for their full, undiscounted amounts.

You need to *collect* on those promises. A lot depends on it: the integrity and success of your telephone fundraising program, the ability of your organization to do its good work in pursuit of its mission thanks to the dollars you raise, and last but not least: your job.

 Telephone Fundraising Rule

Pledges are nice. Collecting them is nicer.

Dealing with Objections

U p to now I have described situations where prospects simply "can't give that amount," and your job as a fundraiser or as a negotiator was pretty simple: You make proposals and fall to a level of giving that Mr. Smith *can* give to your organization.

Sure, you may have had to make a compelling case and expend some energy in moving Mr. Smith from a state of ambivalence to a pledger. But he never uttered the words that are the bane of telephone fundraisers anywhere:

I can't give anything at all.

Objections Defined

Enter the world of the *objection.* An objection in telephone fundraising is defined as "a declaration by the prospect that he or she can't or won't give anything at all."

This is a declaration that must be listened to and dealt with by the fundraiser. Objections are a block in the path of the call process. You cannot run over them or ignore them. If you do, it's like running over Mr. Smith personally. Not only is it rude and not at all empathetic, it is callous and counterproductive. You will never get pledges if you do.

An entire book could probably be written on telephone fundraising objections, how and why they occur, how they relate to philanthropic motivators, and examining in a detailed way how to move a prospect from an initial, seemingly intransigent "no" to a "yes," either of the enthusiastic kind or the somewhat more reluctant but still firm kind.

Indeed, philanthropic objections can occur in any medium, not just the telephone. It's just that in the media involving two-way communication, either a personal visit or a telephone call, you get the opportunity to find out what the objections are right away and to instantly respond!

Objections Can Occur at Any Point in the Call

Objections can occur at any stage of the phone call (see Figure 11.1). They can occur at the introduction stage:

Fundraiser: *Mr. Smith, this is Alice Jones with ABC Organization. I'd like to speak with you about . . .*

Mr. Smith: *If you're calling about my making a donation, I'm sorry but I can't afford to give anything!*

Objections can occur during the "Rapport" stage (see Figure 11.2):

Figure 11.1   Objection 1

Figure 11.2   Objection 2

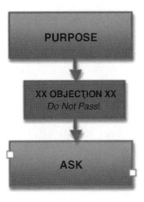

Figure 11.3   Objection 3

Fundraiser: *Your past support has been terrific, Mr. Smith, and we really are grateful to you . . .*

Mr. Smith: *Well, thanks for your thanks, but I'm not going to be able to give anything this year!*

Objections can occur either during or right after you make your mini–case statement for Mr. Smith's funding, in the purpose section of the call (see Figure 11.3):

Fundraiser: *. . . so the threats to our environment are greater than ever. I'm sure you agree, Mr. Smith!*

Mr. Smith: *I agree that what you're doing is important. It's just that I can't renew my support this year.*

Frequently, objections will surface right after the first ask, or the sight-raise proposal (see Figure 11.4):

Figure 11.4   Objection 4

Fundraiser: *So Mr. Smith, how do you feel about increasing your support to XYZ this year at the Benefactor's level for $500!*

Mr. Smith: *Alice, I hate to say this, but I'm not interested in giving anything at all for XYZ this year.*

Generally, the earlier in a call an objection surfaces, the more difficult it is to deal with it. However, regardless of where they occur, the following telephone fundraising rule applies:

Telephone Fundraising Rule

Telephone fundraisers *must* respond to their prospects' objections before being granted a license to proceed with the fundraising call.

Objections Examined

Let's take a look at each element of an objection.

A Declaration by the Prospect

An objection involves a statement by the prospect. You can't read Mr. Smith's mind; he must tell you what's on it. Also, he may not be forthcoming with a lot of information, and you may have to go hunting for an objection when you suspect one is hanging out there, invisibly blocking your path to negotiation.

Can't Give Anything

The statement the prospect makes indicates it's not the specific amount of money you have proposed (if you've gotten that far in the call), it's a "no" to *any amount* you have proposed or will propose. "Can't give anything" means nothing, zilch, nada, not even one dollar and twenty-six cents!

Won't Give Anything

This is a statement the prospect makes that indicates that regardless of the amount of money you have proposed, Mr. Smith is *unwilling* to give *anything* to your organization, even though he *could*. That is, he has some underlying complaint or issue that has led him to withhold all philanthropy to your organization. He may have the capability of giving modestly or substantially, but he *will* not. Sorry!

What Objections are NOT

Objections are *not* instances in which the prospects wish to delay making a decision with statements involving any of the following:

I can't make a decision right now!
Can you send something out?
Let me think about it.
I have to discuss this with (a third party)!

These are simply strategies the prospect is employing to defer making a decision on a pledge either temporarily or indefinitely. He is on the fence, or just doesn't have the resolve to tell you "no" straight out.

It is true, these kinds of statements may be masking an objection, either an "I can't" or "I won't" type of objection that you may need to uncover through some gentle probing. But barring your uncovering a hidden objection, ways of dealing with these instances of delaying or running out the clock are discussed later in this chapter.

Discovering Objections

Recognize When You Have an Objection

Sometimes fundraisers don't even know that they have run into an objection—they have to listen carefully lest they run right over one and find themselves falling into a pothole:

Fundraiser: *So, Mr. Smith, how do you feel about a gift of $250 this year to XYZ?*
Mr. Smith: *I don't think so . . .*
Fundraiser (interrupting): *Well then, how about just $100?*
Mr. Smith: *No, like I was saying . . .*
Fundraiser (interrupting): *Mr. Smith, we really, really need your support, can you do at least $50, or maybe $35?*
Mr. Smith: *No, no, no!*

Sometimes all you need is to just give Mr. Smith a chance, and he will tell you what is separating you from his philanthropy:

Mr. Smith: *As I was trying to tell you, I can't give anything at all this year. I've been out of work for the last three weeks with back surgery and can't support you this year.*

If this information had surfaced right after the first proposal, then the fundraiser could have explored options with Mr. Smith, rather than simply running right over him. But the fundraiser above plowed over the prospect, without listening, and at this point in the call Mr. Smith's back isn't all that's hurting!

I have heard instances where fundraisers were merely intent on making their pitch, so they ran over objections in an even more callous way:

Fundraiser: *So, Mr. Smith, how do you feel about renewing your last gift of $125?*

Mr. Smith: *I'm sorry, I just can't commit to anything right now. We've just had a death in the family and I can't.*

Fundraiser: *But it's critical we reach our goal tonight! Can we count on you for just $50 or $75?*

Mr. Smith (irritated): *Look, my wife died on Tuesday, it's going to take a while for us to sort things out. Goodbye.*

Sadly, situations in telephone fundraising like the above do occur, and in this case the telephone call may have done irreparable harm to a prior relationship. Mr. Smith deserved a little empathy, and instead you gave him grief.

Uncovering Objections When One Isn't Readily Apparent

Frequently, in spite of your having set the basis for robust two-way communication earlier in the call, Mr. Smith may be somewhat parsimonious in expressing himself, so that you're not certain what he means:

Fundraiser: *So Mr. Smith, how do you feel about making a gift of $1,000 this year?*

Mr. Smith: *I'm sorry. I just can't this year.*

Does this mean that Mr. Smith is going to give at least *something*, he just simply "can't" give at the $1,000 level? Or does it mean something else? One effective way of probing what he means is what we've discussed earlier in the call, repeating back to him *exactly* what he said, in effect, to ask him to elaborate:

Fundraiser: *Mr. Smith, you say you just can't give $1,000 this year?*

And more often than not, the prospect will elaborate:

Mr. Smith: *No, I can't give anything this year. My daughter just left for college, and we're struggling with the tuition. We didn't qualify for as much financial aid as we thought.*

Now our fundraiser has some facts of the situation, facts that she can deal with to empathize, and perhaps find a lower level that may fit into Mr. Smith's budget.

As we've discussed earlier, one of the most difficult things for fundraisers to do in these situations is to *shut up*. Solicitors are geared up to solicit, to keep those proposals flowing; after all, remember the fundraising theorem: $P = f(A)$, the more you ask, the more you will receive.

But, being silent is often a prompt to the prospect to provide a little more information, out of her courtesy to you, to elaborate on her situation. After all, 999 times out of 1,000, the prospect doesn't wish your organization ill; he or she wants you to succeed. After being asked to give, she may even feel a little guilty about having to say "no."

Other times, you may have to be a little more direct in following up Mr. Smith's indefinite statement:

Fundraiser: *So, in light of the emergency, Mr. Smith, how do you feel about contributing $250?*

Mr. Smith: *I'm just not interested.*

Fundraiser: *You say you're not interested, Mr. Smith?*

Mr. Smith: *That's right.*

Fundraiser: *Mr. Smith, is it the amount, or something else?*

Mr. Smith: *You know, I'm really ticked off about XYZ's handling of the relief efforts last year. I felt they were late out of the chute and seemed to spend more money on advertising than on the relief effort itself.*

So, the fundraiser uncovered an "I won't give" type of an objection, rather than an "I can't" objection. It may be that the organization received other similar complaints and is able to counter Mr. Smith's perception with some facts and good news to sway him. Regardless, by asking some gentle follow-up questions, that is, "probes," the fundraiser is in a much better position now of dealing with this situation than if she simply "ran over" the prospect:

Mr. Smith: *I'm just not interested.*

Fundraiser: *Well, then, how about $125?*

Mr. Smith (somewhat irritated): *Not this year . . .*

Fundraiser: *Can we count on you for just $25 or $35?*

Mr. Smith: *Goodbye.* (Hangs up.)

Two Types of Objections

Objections are not an amorphous list of detailed complaints existing on your organization's objection sheet, along with detailed responses or rebuttals to them—an effort to persuade the prospect to change his opinion, to get him to turn around (although I am flattered to have seen "objection sheets" used by nonprofits around the country that have word-for-word responses that we developed years before at my old company—imitation is the sincerest form of flattery!)

Objections come in two flavors, vanilla and chocolate—or shall we say, two species: *financial objections* and *willingness objections.*

Financial Objections

These are the objections involving the statements by the prospects relating their inability to give anything at all to your organization *now.*

I can't give anything.
I can't afford to give anything.
I can't afford to give anything right now.
I can't afford to give anything because (any of a hundred reasons).

Keep in mind that most telephone pledges are *impulse* decisions to give, as a result of the stimulus of the call. Indeed, the whole issue of "impulse philanthropy" is one that should be further explored—what motivates people to give on the spur of the moment, from donating to a solicitor on a street corner, to finally saying "yes" in the course of a phone call.

Regardless, the money given is a *discretionary expenditure* by the donor, paid out of or short-term credit, or a short time later out of reserves drawn from disposable income—like a checking account.

I grant you, this may not be quite true for capital fundraising programs, where you are appealing to a loyal, affiliated constituency, the program is launched by an awareness campaign, and letters are sent to prospective donors asking them to consider the kind of gift they can make, well in advance of the fundraising call.

But for *annual* gifts, it's Mr. Smith's *perception* how much free cash he has for discretionary expenditures that will determine how amenable he is to your proposals and entreaties—and giving money away may be the *last* thing Mr. Smith has on his discretionary list, well below the new flat-screen TV and the January trip to Barbados.

Coupled with this, as human beings I believe we are self-programmed to say "no," simply because if you said "yes" to each and every demand on your resources, you would not survive!

The key here is the prospect's *perception* that you are dealing with him as a fundraiser, and that *perception* may differ from the factual reality of his financial situation. Reality is difficult to impossible to change—but altering perceptions is something that a skilled fundraiser can frequently accomplish.

There are *two* factors a prospect weighs in determining his overall ability to give, on an impulse, from discretionary resources:

- The prospect's perception that current expenses are too high to give to you

- The prospect's perception that current income is too low to give to you

Sure, it would be nice if you had a balance sheet and income statement for each prospect you call, and when Mr. Smith says "I can't afford to give anything," you could discuss the *real* financial details:

Fundraiser: *Mr. Smith, I can see from your latest income statement that your dining out budget alone was $3,800 last year, so sir, with due respect, can't you afford to give us $100 this year, or even 1 percent of your dining out budget, a measly $38?*

But that's not realistic. You have to rely on what Mr. Smith says to you based on his perceptions to be able to deal with these objections.

Objections Dealing with a Prospect's Expenses

If prospects state specific reasons why they can't afford to give anything, or if you can encourage their disclosure through gentle probing, the financial objections you uncover will run the gamut almost from cradle to grave:

I'm in grad school.
I'm paying off school loans.
I'm saving for the down payment on a house.
We just had a baby.
I just started a new business.
I'm paying tuition for two private schools.
I'm paying college tuition for three kids.
We're dealing with aftermath of an accident (or natural disaster).
I just lost of lot of money due to (fill in the blank).
I've had a lot of health expenses.
My spouse just died.

. . . and so on, ad infinitum.

Objections Dealing with the Prospect's Loss of Income

Here again, prospect's objections may vary according to where he or she is on life's journey:

I'm an intern with very limited income.
I just landed my first job.
I'm going back to school and am working part time.
I just lost my job.
My spouse just lost her job.
They've cut back on my hours.
Business has been way down this year.

Interest rates are so low, it's affected my income.
I'm retiring and will soon be on a fixed income.
I've been retired and am on a fixed income.

How to Deal with Financial Objections

In sales, and even in fundraising, dealing with objections usually involves coming up with a *rebuttal*, a term that I've never been totally comfortable with in philanthropy. I think of rebuttals as occurring in debates, or legal arguments—and that last thing we want is to engage Mr. Smith in an argument!

I prefer thinking in terms of helping the prospect find a *solution* to his or her financial issue or problem: the problem of what is separating his or her philanthropy from you. This means you're going to have to understand Mr. Smith's situation, *show* him you understand it, and come up with a solution: a proposal that is *credible* given his financial circumstances.

Answering Mr. Smith's objection, and providing a solution comes in several stages. For example, let's take the objection, "I have kids in college":

1. Hear the objection in its entirety and understand it.
   Mr. Smith: *I'm sorry I can't give, I'm up to my eyeballs in tuition.*
   Fundraiser: *So, you have kids in school, Mr. Smith?*
   Mr. Smith: *That's right, I've got two kids in college, one at State, the other at Princeforth.*
2. Empathize with the prospect.
   Fundraiser: *Two kids in college—you must be very proud, Mr. Smith!*
   Mr. Smith: *Proud, yes—but needless to say, I don't have a lot of spare dollars to give away these days!*
   Fundraiser: *Well, I can certainly understand how making a large gift would be out of the question. College tuition can be quite a burden these days . . .*
   Mr. Smith (interrupting): *You got that right! It's absolutely insane!*

   At this point in the call, there is a real danger of the fundraiser losing perspective and *sympathizing* with Mr. Smith as opposed to taking a step back and analyzing the financial situation from *your* point of view. Mr. Smith is involved in circumstances involving thousands, perhaps tens of thousands of dollars of outflow, probably incurring some indebtedness as well. Even in a situation like this, couldn't he at least *participate* in your fundraising effort with some kind of gift? Just few dollars against thousands and thousands?
3. Perspective, urgency, pivot, and propose.
   Fundraiser: *I can certainly understand that a large gift might be out of the question this year, given the thousands you must be paying out in tuition . . .*
   Mr. Smith (interrupting): *You got that right!*

Fundraiser: *But this is a critical year for ABC as well, we have only about $2,000 to reach our goal that will ensure that we'll continue doing our important work, so in light of this and your tuition expenses, how do you feel about a much smaller gift, even $125?*

It's like you are saying:

Mr. Smith, I can certainly understand things from your point a view, you can see that I do! But just take a moment and understand our needs, our situation, weigh them in your decision, and considering them. But taking into account your finances, can't we agree to come down a bit, to a level that you know you can afford?

And then comes the critical element: laying another proposal on the table. Good news, you're *allowed*, you have a pass around that objection block and didn't just try to plow through it. You've taken the time to understand Mr. Smith's situation, you have empathized with him, and countered with a credible proposal that takes into account his unique circumstances.

Telephone Fundraising Rule

Making a proposal after hearing and understanding a prospect's objection *is* the solution. And it puts you, the fundraiser, back in control of the call.

Let's take another example, following a 1–2–3 system for providing a solution to providing a solution to financial objections: *I just lost my job.*

1. Hear the objection in its entirety and understand it:
   Mr. Smith: *I'm sorry I can't give. I lost my job last month and am really cutting back on all of my expenses.*
   Fundraiser: *My goodness, I'm sorry to hear that Mr. Smith. What field are you in?*
   Mr. Smith: *I'm in pharmaceutical sales.*
2. Empathize with the prospect
   Fundraiser: *Well, how are things looking? Do you have any prospects?*
   Mr. Smith: *Yes, I've just had my third interview with World Pharma, and it looks pretty good.*
   Fundraiser: *Well, congratulations, best of luck with that new job—and I can certainly understand how making a large gift might be out of the question right now . . .*
   Mr. Smith: *Yeah, maybe next year I'd be able to support again like I have in years past.*

3. Perspective, urgency, pivot, and propose

Fundraiser: *But, Mr. Smith, this is such a critical year for us, too. With the business downturn, we've lost some of our corporate funding and would really appreciate it if you could do at least something this year—in light of this, could you manage even a small gift, say $50 or $75?*

Mr. Smith: *Yeah, I suppose I can manage that.*

Avoid one way of dealing with financial objections: offering up the prospect of substantial deferral:

Mr. Smith: *I won't be back to work for another six weeks, at least.*

Fundraiser: *That's okay, Mr. Smith, our fiscal year doesn't end for another five months, June 30. What I can do is put you down for $100, send it out now, and you'll have plenty of time to get it back to us. How does that sound?*

It sounds to me like the nonprofit organization will have a difficult time collecting that $100!

Phrases like "in light of," "considering what you have said," or "taking into account your situation" are ways of pivoting from Mr. Smith's stated objection and restating your needs in an urgent way to moving to a counterproposal.

Last, the *urgency* you provide prior to the pivot should be moderately high to very high. Your proposal should be preceded by a good reason to motivate the prospect to set his financial issues aside, even at least partially, for your needs. If you do, and Mr. Smith buys in and begins to empathize with *your* needs, you have significantly increased your chances of getting a pledge.

As has been said before, your urgency shouldn't be over the top and needs to factual and appropriate:

Fundraiser: *Mr. Smith, I understand you don't want to give, but unless I get a few more pledges tonight, I might be fired!*

While the fundraiser may be telling the truth in this highly urgent appeal, I'm sure you agree it falls into the "over the top" and "inappropriate" category.

How Far Do You Fall Down the Giving Ladder after "Providing a Solution" to a Financial Objection?

When you're faced with an absolute "I can't give anything" objection, how far should you drop on the giving ladder?

If you're dealing with a simple two-ask strategy, the amount of money you propose after pivoting from the objection is more than likely at the bottom of your giving ladder: $75, $50, $35, or $25. If the prospect says "no" once again, your call has concluded.

With a three-ask strategy, it's a little more complicated. What you want avoid is the "crashing elevator" syndrome:

Fundraiser: *Mr. Smith, how do you feel about a gift of $500 this year?*

Mr. Smith: *I'm sorry I can't give anything this year. I've got two kids in college, and just can't do anything for ABC College.*

Fundraiser: *Mr. Smith, it's great you've got kids in college, and no one knows more than you what a good education costs! Can't do you a little something this year, even $25 or $35?*

Mr. Smith: *I'm sorry, I just can't this year.*

By falling to the minimum and crashing through the floor of the giving ladder, the fundraiser omitted the strategic second ask, based on what he thought Mr. Smith could afford, but was unwilling to give. One way of softening a second proposal, but getting one in so you have some place to go on a final ask is to "show" the installment:

Fundraiser: *Mr. Smith, how do you feel about a gift of $500 this year?*

Mr. Smith: *I'm sorry I can't give anything this year. I've got two kids in college, and just can't do anything for ABC College.*

Fundraiser: *Mr. Smith, congratulations on your kids—you must be very proud! Certainly no one knows better than you what a good education costs, and that's why we need your help more than ever this year at ABC College. In light of this, can you give just $50 now, and maybe in six months, $50 again?*

The second proposal was actually for a level of $100. And by following the three-ask optimal strategy, it still leaves enough room for the prospect to fall the one of the bottom rungs of the giving ladder:

Mr. Smith: *I'm sorry, I just can't.*

Fundraiser: *As you know, the alumni challenge grant will match dollar for dollar every new gift we receive this evening. It would be a shame if you couldn't at least participate! In light of this, can we count on your for just $50, or even $35? Which is more comfortable?*

This strategy can be employed wherever you are on the giving ladder, but the general rule in dealing with objections: Do not fall any lower than the rung immediately above the bottom on a counterproposal using the three-ask strategy of negotiation.

Willingness Objections

Willingness objections are very different in origin than financial objections. In this case, money is not the issue for Mr. Smith. He could give if he wanted.

But he doesn't want to. These are the less common of the two major types of objections and can present fundraisers with some unique challenges.

Most willingness issues fall in one of three categories:

Specific Problem or Complaint   Your organization has done something to displease Mr. Smith. Technically, he may be a constituent in one way or another. He may have even given in the past. But not now, not this year. He has a beef that must be addressed. Chances are you're the first person he will have spoken to about this complaint. Congratulations. You're elected to deal with it.

Every organization has its own unique set of problems and circum-stances. You need to know what the problems are in order to prepare your fundraising staff to deal with them, lest they flounder in their prospects' breeze of discontent.

Problems with Affiliation   Mr. Smith may be unwilling to give because he is a nominal constituent. Your records may show that he has given in the past, but he doesn't remember the circumstances or why. Or, he may be generally aware of the work of your organization, somehow got on your list, gets your e-newsletter, but cannot be characterized as an advocate for your cause. Or, perhaps he ought to feel closer to you, but just doesn't. He might be an alumnus from the Class of 1962, but you've done nothing to cultivate him. In fact, from his perspective, the only time he hears from you is when you want money.

Last, you may be a nonprofit that serves a geographic area, perhaps a city or state, like a performing arts organization. Mr. Smith may simply have moved far away, to another area of the country, and is ready to support their civic causes but no longer yours.

It bears mentioning that oftentimes prospects who say "I can't give" in reality are *really* saying "I won't give." It's a nicer way of refusing a telephone fundraiser. It's as if Mr. Smith is saying:

Look, the problem is not with you, it's with me. I just can't afford to do anything for you.

Instead of saying:

Look, I just don't care enough about you.

It's up to telephone fundraisers to sense this unstated objection by finding out if the prospect has a lukewarm embracing of your cause. If so, get the prospect excited about you!

Quid Pro Quo   This is the rarest variety of willingness objection, but it bears mentioning. Here you are dealing with a prospect who is, at least initially, absent eleemosynary motives, and his interest in your organization is self-serving. He'll give, but he wants something in return, value for value. These kinds of objections are among the most difficult to deal with, the most sensitive, and the most entertaining.

Again, the types of quid pro quos sought by constituents can be as varied as the organizations and prospects themselves, and are very difficult to prepare fundraisers for, item by item.

If you're an organization that has a membership program, with stipulated benefits at various levels, or you simply have a donor recognition program with increased prestige the higher the gift, you may have some leverage with those prospects who have mostly self-directed philanthropic motivation.

Strategies for Dealing with Willingness Objections

Countering a Misperception with Facts

Your organization may have some invalid rumors circulating about, or there may be a commonly held belief that is inaccurate. For example, let's take the case of the disaster relief organization mentioned previously:

Mr. Smith: *You know, I'm really ticked off about XYZ's handling of the relief efforts last year. I felt they were late out of the chute and seemed to spend more money on advertising than on the relief effort itself.*

Fundraiser: *You know, Mr. Smith, I've heard that, too, but the truth of the matter is that we were able to send cargo planes with food and medical supplies within 48 hours of the quake—just as soon as the runways were cleared for landing. And on top of that, we only spend about 2 percent of our budget every year for advertising, and that's essential to communicate to you and others about the work we're doing and the need for you to give! In light of this, I hope you feel we're doing a good job—so can we count on you to renew that $500 gift this year?*

Mr. Smith: *Well, Alice, I wasn't aware about the issue with the runways—okay, I'll go ahead and renew!*

Sometimes enlightening prospects with the facts isn't successful as in this case with a symphony orchestra's new concert hall:

Mr. Smith: *I'm not interested in giving anything! I am so unhappy with the new concert hall. The acoustics are mediocre, but on top of that, you're artificially amplifying the sound of the orchestra to compensate. That's terrible! I can see the microphones you have scattered about. Just awful!*

Fundraiser: *Mr. Smith, I understand the issues with the acoustics. We are looking into improving them and hope to do that sometime in the near future. But I can assure you, we are not amplifying the sound of the orchestra in any way, it's . . .*

Mr. Smith (interrupting): *What do you mean, I can see the microphones, about a dozen of them spread about!*

Fundraiser: *Mr. Smith, those microphones are for our live concert recordings and for our radio broadcast. They aren't for amplification of the . . .*

Mr. Smith (interrupting) *Look, I don't care what you say, I can see what I can see. I'm not interested in giving money to you anymore. Goodbye.*

You can't win them all. But you never want to get into an argument with a prospect over the "facts."

Mr. Smith: *I won't give because the new concert hall has electronic amplification of the orchestra.*

Fundraiser: *Mr. Smith, I can assure you the microphones you see are only for recording purposes, not amplification.*

Mr. Smith: *I'm sorry, I'm a purist, and I can see and I can hear. You are amplifying the sound of the hall because of its acoustical design flaws.*

Fundraiser: *We are not.*

Mr. Smith: *Yes you are.*

Fundraiser: *Are not!*

Mr. Smith: *Are so!*

Fundraiser: *Are not!*

Mr. Smith: *Are so!*

Better to move to the *deflection* technique mentioned below.

Telephone Fundraising Rule

Responding to objections does not involve arguing with the prospect. No!

It's difficult to prepare fundraisers for any but a few of the most commonly held objections raised by constituents; moreover, it's almost *always* impossible for a lowly telephone fundraiser to fix anything himself, except in a few rare cases:

Mr. Smith: *Look, why should I give to you? For years the school hasn't even been able to get my name right. I'm Mr. Frances Smith, not Ms. Francis Smith. I've written you several times and the mail keeps coming, wrong, wrong, wrong. If you can't get my name right, how do I know you'll spend my gift wisely?*

Fundraiser: *Mr. Smith, no problems. I'm making the change in your record as we speak. Just a moment—there's it's done! Fixed.* Mr. Frances Smith, the third. Now, Mr. Smith, about your membership in the Benefactors Society, we'd love to have you come back to the school for the Benefactors Ball in October. What do you think?

Deflection of the Prospect's Willingness Objection

Occasionally, the prospect will raise a willingness objection that is unique and that you don't have the facts to counter. Or worse, it may be a situation or complaint about which nothing can be done. In these instances, you have to ask the prospect to lay aside his or her grievance for the greater good. For example:

Mr. Smith: *I don't want to give anything because I feel you wasted money building that wretched new student activities center. The design is flawed, its location is horrendous, and it's the ugliest structure I have ever seen.*

Obviously, our resourceful fundraiser is in no position to wave a magic wand and redesign and resite the structure to Mr. Smith's liking. The best she can do is ask him to set aside his grievance for something more important:

Fundraiser: *I understand your unhappiness with the student activities center; however, I hope you won't let that one issue stand in your way of supporting a truly great school. Our architecture department is still #1 one in the state, and we're ranked by* U.S. News *as one of the top regional universities in the Midwest, but we can only keep that ranking with gifts from our alumni. In light of this, can you at least participate in the Annual Fund this year with a gift of $100?*

Or take the issue of the disaffected orchestra subscriber who simply won't let go of the issue of amplification:

Mr. Smith: *Look, I don't care what you say. I believe those microphones are for amplifying the sound of the orchestra!*

Fundraiser: *Well, Mr. Smith, I will certainly pass your comments along to the executive director. Your concerns are very important to us, but I hope you will not let that one issue fall between us! Any gift you make this evening not only will help us find and keep the finest musicians in the world, but it will also help us bring classical music into the schools and the community, and that's really important, I'm sure you agree! In light of this, can we count on you for a gift of just $125 or $150, for which we would be truly grateful!*

Mr. Smith: *Well . . . okay. We'll make it $150, but let that executive director know there are some unhappy people in the balcony section, and we want something done about those microphones. They even look hideous!*

Fundraiser: *I'm writing down your comments and I'll make sure that our director gets a chance to see them. But Mr. Smith, thank you SO much for that $150 gift! For your convenience should we put that on Visa or Mastercard?*

Sometimes the most powerful thing a telephone fundraiser can do is simply to hear out the prospect's complaint. Just allowing Mr. Smith to vent and to get things off his chest, with your lending a sympathetic ear, will be enough to calm him and get him thinking about *you.* Your listening makes him feel *valued.*

Reflection by the Prospect on a Positive Relationship with Your Organization

If you are calling a prospect that has a long-established relationship with your organization but has become disaffected for one reason or another, you might ask her to reflect on and recollect happier times, and what made him value your organization in the first place.

Mr. Smith: *Look, since I graduated from XYZ, I've gotten involved in a number of other charities and causes, and you're simply not high on my list.*

Fundraiser: *Let me ask you, Mr. Smith, do you feel that having a college education was important to you? Do you feel you received a good education at XYZ? Well, Mr. Smith, since you graduated in 1970, we're a much finer school today than ever before, the kind of place that every alum can be proud of, and that's why we're hoping you'll put something back into the school I hope you feel gave you something important. In light of this . . .*

In your desire to have him reflect on the positive, it may be social reasons and not the education upon which he will positively reflect:

Mr. Smith: *Oh yeah, I had a great time at XYZ College. I think I was drunk the whole first year, but then I pulled it together, got decent grades, and graduated. But wow, those parties were terrific!*

Fundraiser: *I'm glad you had a great experience here . . . I sure am, too! But at the end of it, if we work hard and party hard, having a diploma from XYZ is really important, you know something valuable and respected, I'm sure you agree! In light of this, Mr. Smith, can we count on you to show your support with smaller gift, say the Donor's Level, for $100?*

Or let's take the situation where an alumnus has a personal complaint and even may have sought a quid pro quo:

Mr. Smith: *Look, I'm not interested in giving to the medical school. I told the Dean I'd be happy to make a substantial gift, but my son, Daniel, was denied admission despite top grades and test scores. You let him in, and I'll give.*

Fundraiser: *Dr. Smith, I don't know all the particulars of your situation. Let me congratulate you, though, it sounds like your son is really special. But let me ask you, how was your experience at XYZ Medical School? Do you consider yourself successful today? Well, I hope you can set your disappointment aside for a moment and help keep XYZ one of the top medical schools in the country with your participation in this campaign . . .*

Hopefully, the prospect will look back on the total relationship he had with your organization and reflect that it is a positive one. The issue he has with you at present is minor, a bump in the road. Get him to focus on the big picture.

Telephone Fundraising Rule

Encourage prospects to focus on the positive. Eschew the negative. You'll get more pledges!

You'll notice the same 1–2–3 technique we discussed earlier in dealing with financial objections applies to answering or providing a "solution" to willingness objections as well:

1. Hear the objection in its entirety and understand it.
2. Empathize with the prospect.
3. Perspective, urgency, pivot, and propose.

Rather than putting Mr. Smith's objection in "financial perspective," as we discussed earlier in the chapter, with willingness objections we seek to put the objection in "emotional perspective" based on the prospect's positive, happy prior relationship with you.

How Far Down the Giving Ladder Do You Fall after Encountering a "Willingness" Objection?

Perhaps you don't fall at all. This issue wasn't money; it was something else, and hopefully you were able to deal with the issue and set it aside. Let's take the example of the "relief effort" quoted earlier:

Fundraiser: *So, Mr. Smith, how do you feel about making a $500 gift to the emergency relief effort?*

Mr. Smith: *Look, I'm not interested in giving anything this year. I feel you were way too late in the response to the tsunami, and you spent way to much money on promotion and advertising.*

Fundraiser: *I've heard that, too, but the truth of the matter is that we were able to send cargo planes with food and medical supplies within 48 hours of the wave—just as soon as the runways were cleared for landing. And on top of that, we spend less than 5 percent of our budget every year on media advertising, and that's essential to communicate to the general public about the work we're doing! Thousands of people have responded to those ads with donations, which is good news, I'm sure you agree! In light of this, I hope you feel we're doing a good job—so, Mr. Smith, how do you feel about that $500?*

If Mr. Smith can't afford $500, he will tell you, and then you are free to negotiate down, if necessary.

Now you are ready to deal with any objection thrown your way!

Deliberation, Delay, and Deferral of Decisions

What happens if our prospect, Mr. Smith, doesn't say "yes" or "no" and doesn't volunteer a specific objection, either of the financial or willingness variety? Instead, he wants to defer making a decision. *Now* is not the time to decide on supporting your organization. *Later* is better—much later, perhaps. Perhaps indefinitely.

These are prospects who are unwilling to make a decision, are incapable of making a decision, or sometimes legitimately can't make a decision.

We all know the variations and the nuances:

I can't make a decision now.
I don't want to make a decision now.
I don't want to make a decision over the telephone.
I don't want to be pressured into making a decision now.
I want to think about it.
Let me think about it.
I need to think about it.
I need to discuss this with:
   My wife
   My husband
   My partner
   My family
   My business partner
   The board of directors
   My spiritual advisor
Can you send me something?
Do you have anything to send out that I can take a look at?
Send me something and I'll consider it.
Send me something and I'll take care of it.
I only give through the mail, not over the telephone.
I just don't know right now what I can do.

These statements invariably occur in the negotiation region of the call, after you have made an ask of a specific amount. The "delay/defer" can occur between the sight raise and your second ask, if you're pursuing a three-ask strategy, or between your first ask and the second and final ask if you're pursuing a two-ask strategy of negotiation (see Figure 11.5).

Or it can occur between the second ask and the close in a three-ask negotiating strategy (see Figure 11.6).

These are *not* objections, hence they should be shaded a "cautionary yellow," rather than the red "STOP" indicated by absolute financial and willingness objections discussed earlier. They can fairly easily be slid through or around by a skillful telephone fundraiser by simply negotiating!

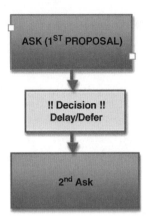

Figure 11.5   Delay 1

For example, let's assume our fundraiser just asked Mr. Smith to consider making a gift of $100 to XYZ Organization:

Fundraiser: *So, Mr. Smith, how do you feel about a gift of $100 this year to XYZ?*
Mr. Smith: *I'll tell you what, let me think about it.*
Fundraiser: *Mr. Smith, a gift of $100 is an amount you need to think about?*
Mr. Smith: *Yes, I can't commit to that over the telephone.*
Fundraiser: *Mr. Smith, we're nearing the end of the campaign, and we urgently need to know how much we can count on from our friends! This year, can you pledge just $50 or $35—and after you have a chance to think about it, if you can give more, that would be terrific! So which is more comfortable, $50 or $35?*

Or let's consider one of the variants of the "send me something" deferral of decision:

Fundraiser: *Mr. Smith, in light of what you have said, how do you feel about joining the Sustainers with a gift of just $125!*

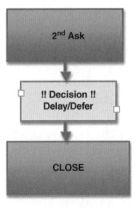

Figure 11.6   Delay 2

Mr. Smith: *Alice, can you just send me something out, and I'll take care of it?*

Fundraiser: *Mr. Smith, I'll be happy to send you out a pledge card and a reply envelope, but you can help us a lot by letting me know what the minimum you know right now is possible for you. That way we can see if we're on track to hit our goal! So, would the minimum be the Sustainers, or would the Donor level be more comfortable, at $50 or $75?*

Mr. Smith: *Okay, let's make it $50.*

Fundraiser: *Mr. Smith, that's terrific! Thanks so much for your $50 pledge, I'll send out a pledge card and a reply envelope for the $50 . . .*

The sense of dealing with deferral and delay of decision is like this:

So, Mr. Smith, I can understand how you might need more time to make a decision on the ($ amount) that I have just suggested, but there's real urgency at our end to know a specific amount that you can commit to right now, so in light of that, can you let me know if ($ next lower amount) is good for you?

Dealing with Deferrals and Delays

Essentially, you can deal with deferrals and delays of decisions in much the same way that you dealt with objections, in the 1–2–3 system mentioned earlier, with only steps 2 and 3 necessary, because there is no objection:

1. **Empathize with the prospect**

    Show the prospect that you understand his or her desire to defer the decision on a gift *at the level you have mentioned.*

2. **Perspective, urgency, pivot, and propose**

    Perspective

    In contrast to the method of drawing an *objection* into perspective, the perspective employed by the fundraiser when faced with a prospect who wishes to defer is that the *amount* of money you had just proposed is an amount about which Mr. Smith needs time for deliberation, NOT the need for deliberation, deferral, and delay of ANY amount.

    That is, when Mr. Smith is telling you, "I need to think about it," he may be disingenuous and may be employing a technique to terminate the call. After all, he's uncomfortable talking about money. This is going to cost him. He doesn't want to give now. Later perhaps, but not now. Yet he doesn't want to tell you "no" outright.

    However, you are choosing to frame the issue in another way—that the deliberation he is requesting is simply for the *amount* you proposed, and not a need for deliberation for *any* amount.

This puts you back into control and allows the fundraiser simply to fall to the next level giving at which Mr. Smith might *not* need to deliberate, delay, or defer.

Urgency

The urgency attached to your request for a specified pledge at a lower amount must be real and believable. You need a good reason for Mr. Smith to commit to something NOW. Your organization will need to decide what reasons are truthful, accurate, and compelling.

Some ideas in the "We need to know now because . . ." category:

- We're nearing the end of the campaign and want to know if we are going to be able to reach our goal.
- We're just $x short of our goal this evening and you can help put us over the top!
- We need to know the minimum we have coming in so we know if we'll be able to meet our budget for the coming year.
- We need to know the minimum we have coming in to avert our crisis (program, funding, etc.).
- We need to know if we'll be able to get every dollar of the challenge grant. It would be a shame if we didn't make the goal, I'm sure you agree!

Pivot and Propose

Pivot and propose are the last elements of countering the "delay"—you must finally lay another number on the table for Mr. Smith to accept or reject:

Fundraiser: *So, Mr. Smith, we're short only $500 tonight, and it will really help us to know the minimum you feel comfortable giving right now if we're going to reach our goal!*

Mr. Smith: *I'm sorry. Please send something out and I'll consider it.*

The above example represents a missed opportunity by the fundraiser, who could have and should have made another proposal. Just as you do with objections, get a number back on the table. Unless you do, you've lost control.

The Baseline Pledge Strategy

In spite of your best efforts, Mr. Smith may raise the same deliberate/delay/defer tactic again, and at this point you may have to fall to the bottom of your giving ladder. One effective method is to cede apparent control of the call to Mr. Smith, making him feel for a moment that he is in total control:

Fundraiser: *Mr. Smith, it's really important we know now the minimum we can count on if we're going to make our goal. Sir, can you tell me what the minimum is*

*you can pledge tonight? Even $50 or $35! Of course later, after you have a chance
to think about it, and if you decide you can give more, it would be terrific. So, which
amount is more comfortable?*

This is called a *baseline* pledge negotiation. It accomplishes several
things:

1. It prevents an unspecified pledge by default.
2. It temporarily makes the prospect feel he or she is in control (you can
even ask the prospect, "You tell me what is the minimum" and
proceed to suggest the baseline amount).
3. It secures a pledge, although of modest amount, when you might not
otherwise get one.

Of course, Mr. Smith's protestations for his deliberation, delay, and
deferral may merely be a screen for an unstated "willingness objection"—
specifically, that he really isn't sufficiently moved by your cause to make even
a modest gift. In these cases, what you have is a "refusal." Sorry, but it's
better to know now!

Other Negotiating Strategies

"Agree to Send Something" Strategy

One of the most common deferral and delay strategies employed by
prospects is the "send me something out" (presumably through the
mail), followed by the phrase, "I'll consider it," or "I'll take care of it,"
which we've briefly touched on earlier.

How many times have we heard less skilled fundraisers accede to the
prospect's request?

Mr. Smith: *Alice, can't you just send me something out, and I'll take care of it?*
Fundraiser: *Okay, Mr. Smith, what I'll do is send you out a blank pledge form and a
return envelope. Is your address still . . .*

How painful it is to hear this scenario, time and again when a more
productive option was available:

Fundraiser: *Of course, I'll be happy to send you a pledge form and a return envelope!
But Mr. Smith, it would really help us know tonight the minimum you'll be able
to send back so we'll know if we're able to meet our budget for the upcoming
year . . . What's the minimum you feel comfortable with—even $50 or $75?*

Not only did Alice agree to Mr. Smith's request, but she combined it with
the "baseline pledge strategy"!

The Legitimate Call-Back

For every rule, there seems to be an exception—so many, in fact, that "rules" become "guidelines" and then "guidelines" become "recommendations" and then "recommendations" become "suggestions" and so on, to the point that one begins to wonder if reverse psychology may be more effective: "Don't Say This or That" to ensure that fundraisers *will* in fact "Say This" and "Say That."

So, in the spirit of reverse psychology and exceptions to the rule, let me offer one more fundraising rule:

Telephone Fundraising Rule

Sometimes, it's desirable to arrange a call-back with a prospect (in rare instances).

Whew. Okay, I laid it out, but don't go crazy with it, or you and your fundraising staff will be doing nothing but call-backs! There are several criteria that must be met before you invest in the additional administrative hassle and personnel cost of calling the same prospect twice, or three times, or more.

1. The amount the prospect is considering must be substantial.

   What is substantial may be relative to your organization and the specifics of a fundraising program. In an annual giving program, the cutoff might be $1,000 or $500. Calling back for $100 hardly seems worth it if the fundraiser can secure a commitment for the next amount down, $50 or $75, right now in *this* call. For capital campaign solicitations with multiyear commitments, the cutoff would be relatively higher.

2. The prospect must be sincere.

   This is asking quite a lot from a fundraiser to discern, particularly one relatively inexperienced in the "slippery ways" of many prospects. But if Mr. Smith is honestly sincere about considering a substantial gift, but simply needs to check with his wife, complete his tax return, wait a few days to see if his bonus comes through, or to confirm that his vintage Mercedes 230SL doesn't need a new engine, then go ahead and arrange a call-back.

For example:

Fundraiser: *Mr. Smith, how do you feel about a gift of $1,000 this year for XYZ?*

Mr. Smith: *You know, before I do anything, I'd have to check with my wife, Shirley.*

Fundraiser: *Mr. Smith, that's an amount you and she can seriously consider and discuss?*

Mr. Smith: *Yes, it's just this time of year I know she likes to give to her favorite charities, among them her college, and I just don't want to step on her toes, if you understand what I mean.*

Fundraiser: *Well, Mr. Smith, I can give you a call back after you've had a chance to discuss with her that $1,000 commitment. Would later this week, say Thursday night, give you enough time?*

Mr. Smith: *Well, can you just send something out, and I can take care of it after I talk with her?*

Fundraiser: *Mr. Smith, I'll be happy to send you out a pledge form and reply envelope, but it would really help us a lot to know in advance if you can do that $1,000 so we can add it to our pledge totals . . . in fact, I might even do a backflip here on the phone room floor if you are able to come through with that!*

Mr. Smith: (Chuckling) *Okay, call me next Thursday evening.*

Fundraiser: *Around 7 PM, does that work for you?*

Mr. Smith: *Fine, around 7 PM.*

Fundraiser: *Thanks so much for considering that, and good luck with Mrs. Smith. We're rooting for you!*

Mr. Smith: *Thanks, but it should be fine.*

In another circumstance, Mr. Smith may not be as genuine:

Fundraiser: *Mr. Smith, how do you feel about a gift of $1,000 this year for XYZ?*

Mr. Smith: *You know, before I do anything, I'd have to check with my wife.*

Fundraiser: *Mr. Smith, that's an amount you and she can seriously consider and discuss?*

Mr. Smith: *Well, no. It's just before I do anything I always check with my wife.*

In the above instance, this situation simply puts the fundraiser back into "negotiation" mode to find that level of giving Mr. Smith can be serious about—ideally an amount low enough that he doesn't need approval from a third party—a purely discretionary decision on his part.

And now, the corollary to the "Telephone Fundraising Rule" stated above:

Telephone Fundraising Rule

Avoid "call-backs."

Summary

The percentage of calls in which you will encounter an objection will vary based on many criteria. Are you dealing with donors, lapsed donors, or never-givers? How affiliated is your prospect group? Can they be classified as constituents? Has your organization entered a rough patch with problems in the local newspaper or the national press?

Or are you trying to build a constituency from scratch and have a prospect list that you've purchased or traded for of individuals who *might* have an interest in what you're doing? If that's the case, you can count of investing a lot of telephone time in "friend raising" as well as "fundraising" to do that spade work necessary to make potential donors take interest in what you do and feel valued about how they can help.

Regardless of your circumstances, the more objections you encounter, the tougher it's going to be to achieve results. If you're dealing with a lot of "willingness objections" because your organization is perceived as having done things it shouldn't have, or not acted when it should have, be prepared for your phone program to do a lot of heavy lifting. There's no way around it; it will cost you more money than merely renewing happy donors, pledge after pledge, like shooting fish in a barrel.

Dealing with objections = increased phone time = increased expense = decreased net. These are the facts of life.

But using the phone in such circumstances can be a terrific opportunity for you, one on one, to rehabilitate your image, shore up your donors and prospective donor base, and engage in a lot of very positive public relations that can ensure your success in the long term.

Remember, there are only two media at your disposal that enable you to deal with objections instantly, on the spot: personal visits and two-way telephone conversations. This is your chance to do it, up close and personal.

One last rule about using the telephone for fundraising:

 Telephone Fundraising Rule

Think long term. You owe it to your organization. You owe it to your donors and constituents.

Writing, Refining, and Testing Your Script

W hat should you do if you are charged with the unenviable task of writing a winning telephone fundraising script? Your script will be used by a dozen, a score, a hundred, or more telephone fundraisers. What you write is the "Law." The words, phrases, and procedures you create will be used by others. There is no higher authority than YOU.

That may be a bit of an exaggeration, but one thing is certain: You are not going to find your script text in a burning bush somewhere. You will need to write it yourself. And what you first come up with may need refining and then testing. The final test, of course, will be its effectiveness in helping your fundraising staff garner pledges over the telephone.

Step 1: Writing the First Draft

Before you begin to write your script, you need to assemble necessary materials—background info on the organization, details on past development performance, an analysis of the database to determine if any segmentation and separate subscripts are appropriate, an analysis of past giving and levels and ranges, and the objectives of the current fundraising effort. If you already work for the organization you are fundraising for, you already know much of what you need in the way of background information to help others effectively represent your organization. If you're a "hired gun," you will need everything from brochures and videos that have been created by the organization to annual reports to fundraising reports created by the development office.

When you think you're ready to represent the organization yourself, then you're ready to write your first *draft*.

Step 2: Writing the Final Draft

After your first draft is complete, you need to carefully read it so you can take the next step—polishing your script into a final draft. Review your script for word counts and syllable counts. Remember the "principle of parsimony," saying in as few words as possible what you want to communicate, avoiding multisyllabic words that are not easily understood over the telephone, and creating text that is speech friendly as opposed to being more appropriate for written letters. Evaluate the appropriateness of the tone. Try reading your script aloud several times to yourself to see how the words roll off your own tongue. By standing up, script in hand, and walking around the room, gesticulating, let the thespian emerge in you. Remember, what you are writing will be *spoken* by others. Try to simulate for yourself the live interaction of caller with prospect. By imagining the scenario, you may discover you will need to make some changes, even at this early stage.

You may find that some phrases work and some are obvious mistakes. A phrase such as *"pandemic political partisanship"* that you included in your written draft may look great on paper but when spoken aloud you find this phrase a tongue twister. Therefore, you rewrite and opt for the new phrase: "selfish interests." This new phrase is cleaner and easier to say. Besides, you just saved yourself eight whole syllables (11 − 3)!

It may be helpful to time the script section covering your fundraising purpose. Are you making a 30-second speech? Can you say what needs to be said in fewer words, condensing it down to two or three powerful sentences? Rule: Every two sentences or statements insert a tie-down question, an open- or closed-ended question that tries to elicit agreement by the prospect. Every point of agreement, every "yes" response, helps create a positive environment for a pledge!

Step 3: Role-Playing

Role-playing is another method to help you to rewrite and finalize your script. Use the assistance of another staff member or administrative assistant in a dramatic reading of your budding masterpiece. One of you can play the role of the "prospect" and the other the role of the fundraiser. Get their opinion on how good the script sounds. Any sentences that seem wordy or unclear can be rewritten. Edit the script until you are completely satisfied that your message is coming across quickly, clearly, and effectively.

In addition to or instead of a staff member, try role-playing the script with one or more of your experienced top fundraisers, one whose opinion you value and who has come up with good ideas in the past that have worked. See how the script rolls off his or her tongue, see how compelling it sounds. When you've passed that test, you're ready to go LIVE.

Step 4: Live Calling Test

You can pursue several different strategies to test your script. You can test the script with one or two of your top fundraisers, with a larger group, or with the entire staff. By doing so, you see how your script performs across a group of fundraisers who have a variety of accents, speech patterns, and tones.

Step 5: Fine-Tuning the Script

You need to evaluate the script once it is placed into action. The answers to the following questions will help in your evaluation of the script.

Are your callers getting through to prospects?

Are callers being granted permission to speak, or are they being hung up on?

Are their efforts at building rapport (if this is an objective) being rewarded, or do they need to pursue another strategy?

Is the "purpose," that mini–case statement you have written, having an impact on the prospects?

Are prospects at least listening? Do you sense their assent to your premise?

Are you sensing "buy-in" with positive reactions, statements, or further questions—or are you greeted with silence and indifference?

Are you successfully laying the groundwork for your fundraiser to get to an "ask" and lay a foundation for a successful negotiation?

Are you reaching your statistical objectives, whether they are measured in pledge rate, average gift, income per contact, income per hour, contacts per hour—or some combination of all of the above?

The monitoring and the feedback you get from your staff may indicate that a midcourse correction is warranted. So, it's time to go back to the writing desk. At worst you may need a total rewrite and a new set of tactics. Other times you may benefit from just a "tweak" here and there: For example, you were using the word *leadership* when the word *stewardship* was better instead.

Or you may find that the tone you set was too formal. For example, you were asking to speak to Mr. James P. McDermott, when the more casual "Could I speak to Jim McDermott, please?" would have been more appropriate. Finding that right "tone" to reach out to your constituency is key to connecting. And connecting with them is key to being successful.

Furthermore, in your auditing, you may find there are subgroups in your overall prospect list that need to be treated differently. Perhaps they need a different "purpose" or overall strategic approach. You may make a decision to pull that segment out of your overall prospect pool and create a unique script for it.

Summary

Whether you're new at creating a telephone script or call outline, or whether you're dealing with a professional, the veteran of scores of campaigns—don't expect your scriptwriter to deliver perfection, like Moses coming down from the mount with a perfect script inscribed on stone tablets.

Finding a successful formula is an evolution, and finding what works is often a result of educated guesses and trial and error. You may find that one script approach works great with one list segment, such as "lapsed members," and doesn't work so well with other list segments. You may find yourself having to jettison one approach for a completely new one. But this is one of the great advantages of the telephone medium: It allows you to change, turn on a dime, and fine-tune your way to success.

CHAPTER 13

Conclusions and Final Words

In the nearly 30 years since I first got into the telephone fundraising "business" back in the winter of 1980, a lot has changed.

Back in the olden days, prospects were a lot easier to get on the phone and less reluctant to take calls from nonprofit organizations seeking support. As we have pointed out, the medium worked, and word spread: "Raise more money by calling your donors; don't just rely on direct mail." It's hard to believe today, but sometimes prospects were *eager* to personally talk to someone from an organization they cared about or from which they had been separated by a period of time. This was a chance for them to reconnect.

Organizations that merely had dipped their toes into the telephone fundraising medium and found they had success decided to make more calls. Early on, the theory was that people didn't give merely because they had never been personally asked. So, the more calls you made, the more pledges your organization received, and the more money you raised. Just the immediacy of a voice from your organization calling Mr. Smith by name was sufficient to achieve some modicum of success.

The observation that $P = f(A)$ seemed to be all that mattered.

Volunteer phonathons that had been loosely organized, using for a brief period an organization's administrative offices, morphed into semi-permanent, in-house facilities, some of the more advanced among them creating phone banks with a dozen or dozens of phones, paid staff, and data sheets on individual prospects enabling callers to note results of their attempts to reach a prospect, and when they did, note the results of the contact.

Callers used primarily touchtone phones and could be seen dialing feverishly away in order to reach as many people as they could in a given amount of time. Sometimes they even developed sore index fingers from all of that punching! Ah, I see some of you veterans out there smiling; you remember those days?

Success bred success, as organizations opted to make more calls but could not do so with their limited facilities. So they hired outside consulting firms to create and manage in-house efforts or gave their lists to groups of boutique telefundraising firms that had sprouted up to fill the demand for calls and expertise.

Commercial telemarketing companies experienced in selling products and services ranging from landscaping to toilet paper began to look at the market for nonprofit fundraising. The nature of their efforts, with low close ratios, necessitated their making many, many more calls per hour in order to achieve cost-effective results, factoring in the cost of labor. Many of these larger companies introduced sophisticated call management software and systems, along with electronic automated dialing and, later, sophisticated predictive dialing systems capable of dialing thousands of prospect records per hour.

The objective was $P = f(A)$ . . . keep dialing, keep contacting, keep asking, keep raising money.

It was unfortunate that in this phase arose some ethically challenged telemarketing companies that charged their nonprofit clients on a commission basis, with contributions flowing directly to them and not to the organization they were representing. Stories of nonprofits receiving little or no proceeds from these kinds of relationships, coupled with increased complaints to state attorneys general offices and consumer affairs departments about caller misrepresentations and aggressive tactics, led to a wave of regulations by various states. These broad nets thrown to regulate the activities of the "bad apples" caught everyone, good and bad, increasing the costs of telefundraising for everyone through often-complex registration, bonding, and reporting requirements.

Still the calls kept coming. The sheer volume of them was such that a common complaint by the Mr. Smiths of the world was, "You're the third call this evening. Why must you all call at the same time?" Needless to say, the bloom was off the rose, and the ringing phone came to be regarded with apprehension and irritation to a degree surpassing the dozens of pieces of "junk" Mr. Smith may have received in that day's mail. The consumer began a counteroffensive with "do not call lists," answering machine screening, or simply choosing not to answer the phone at all.

Around 1990 it was even predicted by some fundraising experts that in ten years, telephone fundraising would disappear altogether as a significant component of nonprofits' integrated fundraising strategies.

But that hasn't happened, despite sometimes lower net results from phone programs due to lower pledge rates and average gifts. With declining results more organizations are realizing there has been a missing factor to the $P = f(A)$ formula: the "Q" factor.

"Q" = Quality

Like everything else in fundraising, the *quality* of what you are doing is an important factor in your results. It's the *quality* of your grant proposal that captures the attention of the funders and can set your proposal apart from everyone else's.

It's the *quality* of your presentation in the personal meeting you may have set up with Mr. Smith to discuss his major gift to your capital campaign giving effort. In your meeting, you not only sounded and looked good to Mr. Smith, you made your organization look good as well. He was swayed. Count him in.

And it was the *quality* of your letter copy that raised more money than any direct mail piece you had done before. People read it and were moved—they gave.

It was the improvement in the *quality* of your web site, less cluttered, professional looking, and more attractive, with the "Donate Now" button right up front, that increased web site hits and dollars given.

And, improving the *quality* of your telephone conversations with your constituents is the single most important thing you can do to improve the gross *and* the net income of your telephone fundraising efforts.

If you've found just *one* idea in this book that can help you land that one pledge that otherwise would have gotten away, or increase the support of that $50 giver to $250 or even $500, this book will have more than paid for itself. Moreover, if you're able to reconnect and develop a relationship with that lapsed constituent nearing retirement, who knows what good things can happen? Thanks to your call, he may hang up feeling very good about you and the work of your organization. You may have done the spade work for a future major gift. Who knows? You don't until you make that call.

So, before I "hang up," let me leave you with this thought:

$$P = f(A * Q)$$

Your pledge results will be a function not only of the number of "asks," but the overall "quality" of the calls you make. You can significantly improve that quality with some care and sensitivity to the scripts and call outlines you provide your telephone fundraisers.

Be innovative. Experiment. One of the great aspects of the telephone medium is that you're not locked in. You can change, edit, and turn on a dime. Those of you who are responsible for creating materials for fundraisers and managing phone programs, please, come up with your own solutions, maybe write your own book. There are dozens of good books on the topic of writing effective fundraising letters, and we're nearing a dozen books on the topic of fundraising over the Internet. Why not the topic of telephone fundraising? Ah, is that my publisher I see smiling now? More books, more books!

For those of you who didn't know much about telephone fundraising but managed to wade through this book, I hope you leave with a bit more understanding and appreciation that there is depth to the medium, that the same fundraising "rules" apply to it as with anything else in fundraising, and that there's a fair amount of nuance and psychology involved in using the medium effectively.

For those of you who are "old hands" and know all this stuff already, or know more than I remember and have forgotten, I hope you've had a chuckle or two.

Appendix

SAMPLES AND SCRIPTS

A. Sample Giving Ladder

Following is a sample giving ladder:

$2,500
$1,000
$ 500
$ 250
$ 125
$ 50
$ 35/25

B. Friends of Furry Folks Sample Scripts

Volunteer Call Guide for a No-Kill Animal Shelter, "Friends of Furry Folks"

SAMPLE VOLUNTEER CALL GUIDE FOR A NO-KILL ANIMAL SHELTER, "FRIENDS OF FURRY FOLKS"

> **TIPS:** Be upbeat, confident. Speak clearly and not too fast. Don't worry about folks saying "no" — plenty of our friends will say "yes"! Since all of them are on our mailing list, each should already be aware of our important work. And please remember to smile!

STEP 1: IDENTIFY THE PROSPECT

Ask the person who answers the phone to speak to the prospect on your list. If he or she is unavailable, ask when would be a better time to reach the person. Thank the person.

STEP 2: INTRODUCE YOURSELF

When you have the prospect on the telephone, introduce yourself. You can say you are a volunteer with Friends of Furry Folks Shelter and are calling to raise money for the new "Shelter Fund."

STEP 3: EXPLAIN THE NEED FOR THE NEW SHELTER FUND

Some "talking points":

- If the person you are talking to is a past donor, thank him or her for their generosity. Explain why the new "Shelter Fund" campaign is so important.

- With the downturn in the economy, there are more abused and stray cats and dogs on our streets every day!

- With the coming winter, many of these animals that once had homes face cold, sickness, hunger, and unimaginable suffering!

- The Shelter Fund will enable us to house 100 more stray dogs and cats in need of loving homes.

- It will help us provide the personnel, food, and medical care these poor animals so desperately need.

STEP 4: ASK THE PROSPECT FOR A GIFT

Ask the prospect if he could consider making a gift of $250 as a Sustainer to Friends of Fur, or a gift of $100 as a donor.

STEP 5: IF THE ABOVE AMOUNT IS TOO MUCH

Ask the prospect to give as much as she can: $50 will shelter and feed a dog for five days, and $35 will do the same for cat. Find an amount that fits their budget. Explain it's so important she help our furry friends as winter approaches!

STEP 6: IF THE PROSPECT SAYS "YES"

Confirm the amount of his gift. Inform the prospect you will mail out a donation form and a postage paid reply envelope for his check. Confirm his mailing address. Thank, thank, thank the donor for their contribution!

LAST STEP: IF THE PROSPECT SAYS "NO"

Thank the prospect for her time. Be sure to mention that she can follow our work on our new web site www.FRIENDSOFFURRYFOLKS.ORG and wish them a good evening.

"THANK YOU SO MUCH, GOOD-BYE!"

Sample Hard Script for a No-Kill Animal Shelter, "Friends of Furry Folks"

Identify	Hello, may I speak with (name of prospect)?
Introduction	Hello, (name of prospect), this is (your name) with Friends of Furry Folks. I'd like to speak with you a moment about our shelter.
Explain Needs	(name of prospect), first of all I want to say "thanks" for your past support of the"Friends"—it helps us care for hundreds of cats and dogs each year. As a cold winter approaches, you know what terrible suffering strays in our city face! Right now our shelter is nearly over-crowded, and we soon won't be able to take in any more animals! But your gift tonight to our new Emer-gency Shelter Fund will help us feed and shelter more than a hundred additional strays until we can find them the loving homes they deserve.
Ask	(name of prospect), some of our friends are able to make an emergency gift to the Shelter Fund of $125 or more. Can you do something like that this year?
Second Ask	(name of prospect), it's urgent that every one of our friends helps the Emergency Fund tonight! How do you fee about a smaller gift of just *(pick one)*: $50 or $75? $50 or $35? . . . which is more comfortable?
Confirm	(name of prospect), thank you so much for your gift of ($ amount). I'll send out a note confirming your ($ amount) gift, and a reply envelope for your check. Should I send that to *(read street address and city, state, zip completely)*. And (name of prospect), do you think you can get your check back to us by (today's date + 14 days) (name of prospect). Thank you again for your ($ amount) gift, and have a great evening.
Unspecified	(name of prospect), thank you for your willingness to give to the Emergency Shelter Fund. I'll send a pledge form and a reply envelope so you can send us your check. Should I send that to *(read street address and city, state, zip completely)* (name of prospect), thank you again for your ($ amount) gift, and have a great evening.
Refusal	(name of prospect), thank you for taking the time to speak with me. Please feel free to drop by the shelter anytime and take a look at the great work we're doing. Have a good evening.

Sample Soft Script or Call Outline for a No-Kill Animal Shelter,
"Friends of Furry Folks"

Identify	Hello, may I speak with (name of prospect)?
Introduction	Hello, (name of prospect), this is (your name) with Friends of Furry Folks Shelter. I'd like to speak with you a moment about some things happening at the shelter!
Rapport	(name of prospect), first of all I want to say "thanks" for your support of the "Furry Folks Fund." You know, in the past year alone, you've helped us feed and shelter over a thousand stray dogs and cats here in Nicetown! (name of prospect), when did you first hear about the terrific work we do here? [DISCUSS RELATIONSHIP] You must be an animal lover yourself—do you have dogs or cats? [DISCUSS] Thank goodness we have a no-kill shelter in our community, don't you agree! [DISCUSS]
Purpose	You know, (name of prospect), with the bad economy, more strays are coming through our doors than ever—you see, many folks just can't afford to keep their pets, so they turn them out into the streets of Nicetown, to fend for themselves, which is really sad, isn't it? [RESPONSE, DISCUSS] But, (name of prospect), we're overcrowded already and may soon have to turn animals away! To get through the cold winter, we urgently need to add places for a hundred more strays through the Emergency Shelter Fund—until we can find them homes.
Sight Raise	(name of prospect), some friends have been able to help this emergency by joining what we call the "Loving Hands" with a gift of $250 or more—is anything like that feasible for you this year? [DISCUSS]
Counter	(name of prospect), I know that's a lot of money, but we need every one of our friends to help us tonight. In light of what you've said, may I suggest the: "Dog's Best Friends" group with a gift of $125? "Feline Friends" group with $75?
Close	It's urgent that every one of our friends helps the Emergency Fund tonight! We need to add the additional cages and staff by the end of November so we don't have to turn a single dog or cat away! So, [name of prospect], can we count on you to join the "Friends of Fur" with just (*pick one*): $50 or $75? $50 or $35? . . . which is more comfortable?

Confirm	(name of prospect), thank you so much for your gift of ($ amount). Should we put that on your Visa or MasterCard? [note: this will ensure the money will be helping the animals immediately]
If "yes" to Credit Card:	Terrific, may I have the card number? [RECORD] The name as it appears on the card? [RECORD] And the expiration date? [RECORD] (name of prospect), we'll put through a charge tomorrow in the amount of ($ amount).
If "no" to Credit Card:	I'll send out a note confirming your ($ amount) gift, and a reply envelope for your check. Should I send that to *(read street address and city, state, zip completely)*. And (name of prospect) do you think you can get your check back to us by (today's date + 14 days)? [RECORD DATE] [name of prospect] thank you again for your ($ amount) gift, and have a great evening!
Unspecified	(name of prospect), thank you for your willingness to give to the Emergency Shelter Fund. I'll send a pledge form and a reply envelope so you can send us a check. Should I send that to *(read street address and city, state, zip completely)* (name of prospect), thank you again for your ($ amount) gift, and have a great evening!
Refusal	(name of prospect), thanks for taking the time to speak with me. Please feel free to drop by the shelter anytime and take a look at the great work we're doing. Have a good evening.

C. Health Foundation's Talking Points[1]

Health Foundation
(City/State)
IDC Communicator Talking Points

Letter signer:	Name:
Campaign Focus:	Annual Fund, supporting patient care excellence, community partnerships, and innovation in care (Medical Home Model).

---

[1] Contributed by Gregg Carlson, Chairman and CEO, IDC.

(*continued*)

Letter signer:	Name:
Reason for Support: (Why are we calling?)	To ensure that Health Foundation is able to meet the health care needs of its members and be an involved and responsible member of the community. • Patient care excellence. Health Foundation is committed to providing the best health care available with the patient as its central focus. Your support helps us do that. • Gifts to Health Foundation are put to use in the areas of the greatest need—unless donors wish to designate where their gift should be used (e.g., hospice, etc.). • Gifts to the Health Foundation help to fund community partnerships where we work with schools, health care providers, and throughout the community on issues that need direct attention. • One example of our community partnerships is our work with childhood immunizations. (State) has a ___% immunization rate, one of the lowest in the country, yet concerns are rising about the safety of vaccines. • Health Foundation is working with schools and parents to address both concerns and increasing access and education. • Gifts to the Health Foundation help fund innovation in health care—staying at the cutting edge of knowledge, research, and advancements in health care. • The Medical Home Model is an innovation that focuses on Doctor/Patient relationship and prevention of disease—gives the patient direct access to the health care team, increases communication (e.g., via e-mail). Looking at implementing across all of Health Foundation.
Introduction:	Hi, my name is _____ and I'm calling to follow up on a letter you received from (Name).

(*continued*)

Letter signer:	Name:
Relationship Building:	How long have you been a member with Health Foundation?
	How has the care you've received from Health Foundation been?
	How long have you lived in the (State) area?
	How familiar are you with Health Foundation's work in the community beyond just taking care of patients?
Challenge:	Health Foundation Physicians have issued an important challenge—they will match every gift, dollar for dollar, up to $200,000.

D. InfoCision Management Corporation[2]

Four Easy Steps to Scriptwriting Success

Writing an effective telephone marketing script can be a daunting task. In today's climate, getting to the point quickly and making a favorable impression on your prospect is more critical than ever. However, by following four simple rules, your scripts will always be fresh and effective. Your telephone marketing goals will be much more easily accomplished if you *identify the emotional trigger, engage your prospect, paint a picture with words,* and *make an assumptive ask* for the sale.

Identify the Emotional Trigger   It really doesn't matter whether you're selling—telephone purchases and donations are made on *impulse.* These are dictated characteristically not by logic but by feelings of *emotion.*

There are over a hundred emotional states to consider when writing a fundraising script: sympathy, fear, anger, guilt, security, self-worth, sense of belonging, etc. Once you've identified that emotional trigger, you've found the link that connects your prospect to your appeal.

Engage the Prospect   Next, you need to find out what's on your prospect's mind—and there's no better way to do so than by *asking* him. By initiating a dialogue, you bring your potential client directly into the decision-making process. Here are a few ways to start a dialogue:

---

[2] Contributed by Steve Brubaker, senior vice president for Corporate Affairs, InfoCision Management Corporation.

- Ask a qualifying question
  The qualifying question is a filter to weed out the prospects that simply have no opportunity to respond favorably to your appeal.
- Ask a leading question
  Differing from a qualifier, the leading question has a sharper edge and mixes in a bit of guilt and persuasion into the question. For example, maybe you are calling aggressively for a political candidate with a green platform. The qualifying question might be, "Mr. Jones, do you believe the environment should be our primary concern in the upcoming election year?" whereas the leading question might be, "Mr. Jones, we don't want our grandchildren to inherit a filthy, polluted atmosphere—do we?"

See the difference? One question seeks your opinion objectively and the other is more likely to lead to a specific answer or even draw a manageable objection.

Paint a Vivid Picture It is not enough for a prospect to simply hear your script—he must have a graphic mental image of what your message is all about. There are a few devices to consider that will make this imagery possible.

- Create a sense of belonging by tying your product to a club or organization.
- Give your prospect a sense of status by focusing on the positive image and feelings that your product or appeal will generate.
- Try using bundle marketing to add value to your product. Nothing makes a product more attractive than tossing in a free premium.

Ask Assumptively Most important—always assume the prospect will respond affirmatively. Nothing conveys more confidence in your script than believing in the quality of your product or appeal. More often than you might expect, a confident, assumptive ask is sometimes the sole difference between a failed presentation and a successful one.

E. The Taylor Institute for Direct Marketing[3]

Inspiring the Next Generation of Industry Leaders (InfoCision Management Corporation)

If you were to fill a room with direct marketing experts and ask them to raise their hand if they have a degree in direct marketing, what do you think you would see? A good guess would be not many hands in the air.

---

[3] Contributed by Steve Brubaker, senior vice president for Corporate Affairs, InfoCision Management Corporation.

So what gives? Well, for starters, at last count, only 42 out of the 4,100 U.S. colleges and universities reported offering a direct marketing program with at least 50 percent or more of the course content spent on direct marketing. None of the schools reported requiring hands-on experience with direct or interactive marketing companies.

Since Lester Wunderman first coined the term *direct marketing* over 40 years ago, learning the profession has pretty much been done through on-the-job training, trial and error, and seminars.

Knowing how academically underserved the profession was, Gary Taylor, founder and chairman of InfoCision Management Corporation, the second largest privately held teleservices company, thought it was time to elevate the profession. With a donation of $3.5 million from Gary and his wife, Karen, the University of Akron College of Business Administration launched the Taylor Institute for Direct Marketing in the fall of 2004.

Located on the campus of the University of Akron in Akron, Ohio, the Taylor Institute for Direct Marketing is the only fully accredited four-year degree in direct marketing and offers the most sophisticated direct marketing educational program anywhere in the world. Created to provide students entering the field with valuable skills, the Taylor Institute offers a variety of major and minor programs of study covering all facets of direct marketing. The classes balance theory with practicum, so students get the hands-on experience they need to be successful.

Direct marketing is the most focused of all means of mass media communications and is significantly more highly targeted today than ever before. This unique learning experience allows students to gain practical, hands-on experience in all components of direct marketing such as project ideation, analytics, creative, and campaign evaluation. Using state-of-the-art laboratories and tools, they manage and develop marketing-based print, website, broadcast, and other media products/campaigns for real clients in a real-world, professional environment. Upon graduation, students can expect to be employed in direct marketing and marketing departments for large and small firms, advertising agencies, web-development firms, and, especially, in their own entrepreneurial businesses.

Never has the old adage "providing the right customer with the right product, at the right time, for the right price" been as true as it is today. Marketing is going through turbulent times as the old tried-and-true methods of reaching consumers are falling short, forcing marketers to change fast or close up shop.

Technology and consumer power have forever changed how marketers connect with their customers. As consumers increasingly embrace the growing variety of communication channels, direct marketing is poised to become even more sophisticated as spending on eMarketing, mobile marketing, social media, and word-of-mouth or viral marketing will continue to grow.

Consumers now control the game, and what better resource for an evolving industry than the Taylor Institute for Direct Marketing—the only one of its kind, dedicated to the profession.

F. Mal Warwick Associates Sample

Scripts and commentary prepared by Joe White, President, Left Bank Consulting, jwhite@sharegroup.com. Reprinted with permission from *Mal Warwick's Newsletter: Successful Direct Mail, Telephone, & Online Fundraising* (http://ga1.org/malwarwick/join.html; Copyright © 2008 by Mal Warwick).

Mal Warwick Associates

2550 Ninth Street, Suite 103, Berkeley, CA 94710-2516, (510) 843-8888, (510) 843-0142, www.malwarwick.com

---

Rating the writing: how to assess a telephone fundraising script

Writing a telephone fundraising script is a lot like writing a fundraising letter. (It's a lot different, too!) What the two forms have most strikingly in common is that they're based on years and years of accumulated knowledge about what works and what doesn't—when real people receive your letter or your phone call. And much of what we've learned in the course of all those years is likely to be surprising to anyone new to fundraising. (The fancy word is *counterintuitive.*)

Recently the good folks at *CASE Currents*—the monthly magazine for development officers at colleges, universities, and private schools—asked me for an article about how to write an effective telephone fundraising script (sometimes called a "conversation outline"). In taking up their challenge, I developed the following assessment tool. It appeared along with the article in the May 1996 edition of the magazine.

I'm indebted to my colleagues at the Share Group, and especially Joe White, for the benefit of their many years of experience. Their comments are reflected below.

Rate script on each criterion, circling the rating, with 5 = best, 0 = worst.

#	Criterion	Rating	Weight	Total
1	Opening is respectful and involving. Builds rapport and leads to conversation.	0 1 2 3 4 5	x 1 =	
2	Message is simple and straightforward, easy to understand. Includes a minimum of detail.	0 1 2 3 4 5	x 1 =	
3	Simulates a real conversation. Uses the singular personal pronouns, "you" and "I."	0 1 2 3 4 5	x 1 =	
4	Written in natural language. Easy to read aloud. Uses contractions, short sentences, no ten-dollar words or acronyms.	0 1 2 3 4 5	x 1 =	
5	High-energy. Communicates enthusiasm.	0 1 2 3 4 5	x 1 =	
6	Talks about donor benefits, not institutional needs. Encourages participation. Seeks the donor's agreement on the case.	0 1 2 3 4 5	x 5 =	
7	The "Ask" is unmistakably clear. Asks for a specific amount of money or other explicit act.	0 1 2 3 4 5	x 4 =	
8	Ask is repeated in a natural progression, from high to low, emphasizing additional benefits with each subsequent offer. Facilitates negotiation of the gift.	0 1 2 3 4 5	x 3 =	
9	Establishes urgency—i.e., makes the case to take action now. Refers to a concrete campaign goal.	0 1 2 3 4 5	x 2 =	
10	Formatted and designed for easy reading. NOT written in capital letters. Uses white space, indents,	0 1 2 3 4 5	x 3 =	

bullets, underlining, or other visual
cues to make script easy to follow.
Color-coding for multiple scripts.

11	Makes best use of segmentation opportunities, with variable message for different interests.	0 1 2 3 4 5	x 5 =
12	Pledge amount is confirmed. Seeks commitment from donor to send money within a specific period. Mailing address (and possibly other information) is verified.	0 1 2 3 4 5	x 2 =
13	Payment procedures are clearly explained. Donor will understand exactly what will happen and when.	0 1 2 3 4 5	x 1 =

SUBTOTAL THIS PAGE

TOTAL

First, total your 13 ratings. (Remember: 0 x 1 = 0!)

Then, to evaluate your score . . .

With as many as five points available for each of the 13 criteria, and weighting factors that total 30, a perfect score is 150 points. You may translate a numerical score into a letter grade as follows:

Rating	*Letter Grade*	*Meaning*
140–150	A+	No more need be said.
120–139	A	Give that writer a pat on the back!
100–119	B	Shows lots of promise.
70–99	C	Needs some improvement.
40–69	D	Requires a lot of work. Maybe better to start from scratch!
0–39	F	Uh oh!

G. Joseph H. White, Jr.'s "What's in a Phone Script?" Article

In the following article, veteran telephone fundraising specialist Joe White, president of Left Bank Consulting, an international telephone fundraising consultant based in Toronto, critiques the three sample scripts appended to this text. These are actual scripts that were used in nonprofit fundraising campaigns. Only telltale names have been changed to conceal the organizations' identity.

SAMPLE #1 — Fundraising Script—Lapsed Donor Reinstate/March 2008

INTRODUCTION

Hello (PROSPECT), this is _____ calling from XYZ Agency on behalf of the Animal Group. I'm a paid solicitor, and the XYZ Agency is a professional fundraiser, who will receive as costs, expenses, and fees, a portion of the funds raised through this solicitation campaign. This call may be monitored or recorded to ensure quality.

FIRST ASK

I would first like to thank you for your past support of the Animal Group's work to protect animals. As a supporter of the Animal Group, you no doubt know about three unique ways in which we serve animals and the people who care about them. These are our Rescue Services team; our mobile programs, which include adoption and spaying and neutering; and the hands-on work we do to make sure that even pets with behavior issues have the chance for a good home.

The Animal Group is unique among animal welfare agencies in having an entire department dedicated to mobile animal rescue services in the field. Our highly trained specialists respond to pets and wildlife that are injured, trapped in trees or on ice or by fire, and other dangerous situations. (Last winter, for instance, we safely extricated a kitten who had crawled inside a car engine and gotten trapped— we had to painstakingly take apart the engine!)

Our Rescue Team has an incredible arsenal of humane traps, nets, and other specialized equipment that no other organization in the area has.

Your support is vital to the Animal Group's ability to offer these important services. Would you help us reach out to help more animals in need in 2008 and renew your support with a gift of ($3 x HPC or $100)?

SECOND ASK

I understand . . . (Repeat and reflect objection). That is a lot to ask, but we would not ask if the need were not so very great.

Two of the most critical tools the Animal Group has are our Spay Vehicle and our Mobile Adoption and Rescue Vehicle. What's unique is that they both take services out to people in their own communities throughout U.S. state/territory/colony.

The Spay Vehicle is a mobile surgery unit that's dedicated to performing spaying and neutering for low-income pet owners who could not otherwise afford these procedures for their pets.

We also have a specially equipped, state-of-the art vehicle called the Mobile Adoption and Rescue Vehicle that can safely and comfortably transport 43 animals at one time. We can use it to provide temporary shelter for animals during natural disasters and other emergencies. Right now we're using it to take animals out of the shelter to communities where they can meet people who might adopt them—and this activity will pick up as the weather gets nicer.

We are proud of the work we are doing—because it really helps animals—but we need your help. Can you help ensure we are able to continue these programs by renewing your support with a gift of ($2 x HPC or $50)?

THIRD ASK

I understand.

In addition to our work in animal rescue, the Animal Group offers state-of-the-art programs in animal behavior. We work with hard-to-place animals in our shelters to make them adoptable, and also with pets once they've gone home with new families.

The worst thing that can happen to an animal is to be returned to a shelter—especially when often all that's needed is some counseling that will solve a pet's behavior issues, like food-aggression or separation anxiety, for instance. Our Pet Behavior Hotline is a free service where people can turn for help. We also offer behavior counseling, obedience classes, and our staff conducts workshops locally, regionally, and nationally to show other shelters how to offer behavior programs, which really work.

Knowing that these programs provide badly needed services to pet owners that can keep pets from being returned to shelters and help make adoptions work out, can you help ensure we are able to continue our animal behavioral services by renewing your support with a gift of ($(MRC or $25)?

GIFT CLOSE

Great! The best way to process your gift is on Visa or MasterCard—this way the Animal Group can put your money to work right away. Which card would you prefer to use?

IF NO TO FIRST CC ASK

I understand. The reason I asked for a credit card is that it's the most efficient way to process your contribution—there's less administrative time, paperwork, and postage involved and more of your contribution goes towards our programs. Would you help in this way?

IF STILL NO

That's fine. We'd be happy to process a check pledge. I'll send you a card and reply envelope in the mail. It will have space for your credit card information, if you're more comfortable giving that way through the mail.

FUNDRAISERS: MAKE CERTAIN TO TAKE ALL CREDIT CARD INFO BEFORE RECORDING BEGINS

RECORDED CONFIRMATION OF PLEDGE AMOUNT AND TYPE

Let me confirm this again, please . . .

CHECK: You have agreed to make a (pledge/contribution/gift) of $_ to the Animal Group.

Is that correct? (*Note: must get a yes or no response.*)

We'll send you a card and reply envelope in the mail—it has the Animal Group logo (with the red barn) in the upper left-hand corner so you can identify it easily. May I count on you to return your gift within 3 to 4 days/the same day/the next day/within 2 days of receiving the envelope?

Note: *If initial time frame is not possible: or (specific date 2 weeks from today/in 2 weeks); 3rd ask is for (within 4 weeks or specific date 4 weeks from today)*

Return date must be an exact time frame. If they do not make such a commitment, it is not a valid pledge and should be recorded as a refusal.

CREDIT CARD: We'll send you a confirmation for your gift of $__ to the Animal Group. I have recorded that we will charge it to your (Visa/MC). Is all that correct? *Must get yes or no.*

ADDRESS CONFIRM FOR ALL PLEDGES: And let me just confirm your mailing address. Are you still at (read address on screen)? *Must get yes or no.*

CLOSE/DISCLOSURE YES: Just one last thing—I need to let you know that donations to the Animal Group are tax deductible. Thank you again for your contribution.

CLOSE/DISCLOSURE NO: Thank you for your time (today/tonight), (Mr./Mrs./Ms. Prospect). I hope you'll consider supporting us again in the future.

Sample #2 — Fundraising Script/Donor Reinstate TM Appeal, Sept. 2006

INTRODUCTION

Hello (PROSPECT), this is ___ calling from Telemarketing for Change on behalf of the Citizens for FREE HYDRO. I'm a paid solicitor, and Telemarketing for Change is a professional fundraiser, who will receive as costs, expenses, and fees a portion of the funds raised through this solicitation campaign. This call may be monitored or recorded to ensure quality.

I'm calling to give you a brief update on our work, especially concerning the recent rate increases for Mega Edison and Giant Electro customers. Is this a convenient time to talk? I promise to be brief.

FIRST ASK

First of all, I want to thank you for your past support of FREE HYDRO. With the support of utility rate payers like yourself, FREE HYDRO has had a long history of successfully fighting to keep electricity rates affordable for county residents. Since 1984, FREE HYDRO has saved customers about $10 billion.

But now we face a new battle, and we need your help. You may have read recently that your Utility (NOTE TO FUNDRAISERS: reference information on the dialer screen to learn whether the donor is a customer of Mega Edison or Giant Electro) will be pushing for a rate increase (26%, $160/year for Mega Edison customers; 55%, $338/year for Giant Electro customers) because the utility is now purchasing power via an auction process. These are increases that many households simply can't afford.

So, FREE HYDRO is working in two ways: FREE HYDRO is working through the courts, appealing to the state appellate courts to overturn the hike, as well as pushing for legislation in (State Capital) that will extend the current rate freeze another three years, to protect consumers from these unfair rate increases. FREE HYDRO is building a statewide coalition of community groups, residential customers, and political leaders to extend this freeze. But we need your help. We are calling past supporters of FREE HYDRO and asking them to help with a generous contribution of (2 x MRC, or $100 minimum), making you a FREE HYDRO Consumer Champion. Is that something that you could do?

(IF YES, go to CREDIT CARD ASK, below; IF NO, continue . . . . . .)

SECOND ASK

I understand, that is a lot to ask for. I only start at that level because there are those who can help at that amount, and I'd hate to miss them by not asking.

As soon as word of these rate hikes came down, FREE HYDRO sprang into action in a way that no one else can: FREE HYDRO's Action Center on our website has information on citizen lobbying. We've been working to get word out about these unfair rate hikes into the press, and working to hold politicians accountable to the needs of rate payers all over the state, as opposed to utilities that are awash in profits right now, before any rate hike has gone into effect.

When the State Legislature created FREE HYDRO in 1984, aside from a small seed stipend, it was mandated that no state funds could be used to run the organization. So, we've accomplished all of our work through the generous support of rate payers like you, who understand that working together we can make a difference fighting rate hikes, unfair regulations, and many other activities.

Can you help with a contribution of (1 x MRC, or $50 minimum),

(IF YES, go to CREDIT CARD ASK, below; IF NO, continue . . . . . .)

THIRD ASK

I know there are a lot of good organizations out there, but we are asking because the need right now is so very great. If we don't do anything, these new rate hikes will go into effect on January 1, 2007. But we've seen in the past that when everyone works together, we can make a difference. If you could support our work with a small, $25 contribution, it will go a long way to freezing these utility rates. Can you help at that level?

(IF YES, go to CREDIT CARD ASK, below; IF NO, continue . . .)

IF NO

Well, thank you in any case for your time. Maybe you can help us at another time. Bye bye.

CREDIT CARD ASK

<u>1st</u> CC ASK IS ''ASSUMPTIVE'': Great—thank you so much! We're processing gifts today using (accepted credit cards) . . . which would you prefer to use?

<u>2nd</u> CC ASK IS ''EXPLANATORY'': I understand. The reason I asked for a credit card is that it's the most efficient way to process your contribution—there's less administrative time, paperwork, and postage involved and more of your contribution goes towards our programs. Would you help in this way?

IF STILL NO

That's fine. We'd be happy to process a check pledge. I'll send you a card and reply envelope in the mail.

FUNDRAISERS: MAKE CERTAIN TO TAKE ALL CREDIT CARD INFO BEFORE RECORDING BEGINS

RECORDED CONFIRMATION OF PLEDGE AMOUNT AND TYPE

Let me confirm this again, please.

1) CONFIRM PLEDGE AMOUNT, TYPE, and RETURN DATE (for check pledges)

CHECK: You have agreed to make a (pledge/contribution/gift) of $__ to FREE HYDRO. Is that correct? (*Note: must get a yes or no response.*)

We'll send you a card and reply envelope in the mail—it has a (*describe envelope*) on the outside of the envelope so you can identify it easily. May I count on you to return your gift within 3 to 4 days/the same day/the next day/within 2 days of receiving the envelope?

Note: If initial time frame is not possible: or (specific date 2 weeks from today/in 2 weeks); 3rd ask is for (within 4 weeks or specific date 4 weeks from today)

Return date must be an exact time frame. If they do not make such a commitment, it is not a valid pledge and should be recorded as a refusal.

CREDIT CARD: We'll send you a confirmation for your pledge/contribution/gift of $___ to FREE HYDRO. I have recorded that you have asked to have it charged to your (Visa/Amex/MC) account. Is all that correct? *Must get yes or no.*

2) CONFIRM ADDRESS: And let me just confirm your mailing address. Are you still at (read address on screen)? *Must get yes or no.*

3) DISCLAIMER/TAX STATUS LANGUAGE (when applicable): Just one last thing—I need to let you know that donations to FREE HYDRO are NOT tax deductible.

4) THANK DONOR FOR THEIR GIFT AND SUPPORT! Thank you for your generous gift of $___ and for your support of FREE HYDRO—your help makes our work possible!

MAKE SURE THE DONOR HANGS UP FIRST!

SAMPLE #3 — COMMUNITY COLLEGE FOUNDATION FUNDRAISING SCRIPT, FALL 2007

This is the college's 45th Anniversary. A great time to make a $45 gift to Community College!

INTRODUCTION

Hello, this is (FULL NAME) calling on behalf of XYZ Community College Foundation.

I'm calling to thank you for your support of the College and the Foundation. With your help last year we beat our goal of $700,000 to support important college programs like scholarships and professional development—programs that keep our college a top-level institution.

Thanks to <u>you</u> and other generous supporters, the Foundation provided more than $100,000 in scholarships last year. <u>Your</u> generosity helps keep XYZ COMMUNITY COLLEGE affordable for everyone who wants to attend. Unfortunately, this year the Board of Trustees raised fees that will cost the average student about $30 per semester.

This year we have to do a bit more because the #1 reason students don't attend college or drop out is money (financial circumstances). We want to raise another $30,000 for scholarships to offset the fee increase and keep needy students in college. I hope you can help before the end of December.

TOP ASK (Make sure to ask high!)

Can you join us by making a gift of $100 (or $50 more than last gift)? Your generosity will help a needy student with financial aid or buy books for the library.

And a lot of people find it convenient to put their gift on their credit card. The Foundation accepts Visa, Mastercard, Amex, and Discover.

IF YES, go to CLOSE.

SECOND ASK (Give more good info/Restate urgency)

I understand—not everyone can help at that level but we have to ask just in case! President XYZ has made it clear that a community college education MUST BE accessible to everyone. So we need your help to make sure <u>all</u> students in the area have these opportunities. Here's how we use your contribution to the Foundation:

- Providing financial aid to students in need.
- Providing professional development for faculty and staff.
- Ensuring President XYZ has the funds for new academic programs and initiatives.
- Purchasing new books/journals for the library.
- Offering scholarships for older, nontraditional students.

For example, the Career Resource Center is available for students, alumni, and people in the community to explore career options. This is really important because 90% of COMMUNITY COLLEGE alumni still live in the area.

Can the XYZ COMMUNITY COLLEGE Foundation count on your help tonight? Can you make a tax-deductible gift of $45 in honor of our 45th Anniversary?

IF YES, go to CLOSE.

THIRD ASK (Stay urgent—give final, compelling reason to give!)

I understand. I'm sure we can find an amount that is comfortable for you—we want as many people as possible to participate. We are close to our goal and you can help close the gap before the end of the year. Can you help with a gift of $30 (or match last gift)?

REFUSAL

Mr/s _____, I do appreciate your time and hopefully you can help at a later date. We will continue to serve our fellow citizens in our community for many years to come. When you receive a letter, perhaps you can make a contribution at that time.

CREDIT CARD ASK/CHECK CLOSE

Great, thank you so much for your gift of $____; it will really help. Which (credit) card do you want to use today/tonight (XYZ COMMUNITY COLLEGE accepts MC, Visa, Amex, and Discover).

IF NO: Processing gifts on credit card allows us to put your money to work right away AND saves money because we don't have to sending mailings. (Wait for donor to respond.)

IF STILL NO: I understand, we will send you a pledge notice in the mail. You should receive the envelope in 3 or 4 days. Can you please mail your check so we receive it before the end of December? Your gift is fully tax deductible.

1) CONFIRM PLEDGE AMOUNT—repeat the GIFT AMOUNT

2) CONFIRM METHOD OF PAYMENT AND CREDIT CARD NUMBER

3) CONFIRM ADDRESS

4) THANK DONOR FOR THEIR GIFT AND SUPPORT!

FAMOUS LAST WORDS: Thank you so much for your help . . . it means a lot to us!

ADDITIONAL INFORMATION/TIPS FOR SUCCESS

- Know these names: John Smith is president of ABC COMMUNITY COLLEGE. Jane Smith is executive director of the COMMUNITY COLLEGE Foundation. Jane Smith is the chair of the COMMUNITY COLLEGE 2007 Annual Fund Campaign. Alice Smith is the president of the COMMUNITY COLLEGE Foundation.

- Contact name is John Doe or Jane Doe—both can be reached by phone at 222-222-2222 if the donor has a question. Address is XYZ COMMUNITY COLLEGE Foundation, 22 Main Street, Anywhere, USA.

- Gifts to COMMUNITY COLLEGE Foundation are tax deductible to the full extent of the law.

- Budget of COMMUNITY COLLEGE (the College) is over $17 million. Approximately 5,000 students attend COMMUNITY COLLEGE—mostly from Blue County, but 25% are from Red County and 10% from nearby Mississippi and Utah.

- COMMUNITY COLLEGE was founded in 1962.

- The state has 15 community colleges; COMMUNITY COLLEGE is the smallest. Red County is the most rural area in Utah and the poorest.

- COMMUNITY COLLEGE lost over $5 million in budget cuts from the state over the past few years.

You are NOT expected to know everything about COMMUNITY COLLEGE. Be honest with people you speak with—this is a small community! *The Globe* is the local community newspaper.

Critique of Sample 1

There are a number of problems with this script. First, the wording is awkward. Take the first sentence as an example: People don't speak like this. Thanking donors at the start of a phone script is basic and required. Making assumptions about what donors "know" is a mistake ("you no doubt know"). Instead, use the personal connection to deliver something different, new, and interesting. Lots of donors don't read your direct mail or newsletters or those precious letters you sweat over so long!).

This script does not engage the donor—it is all about what the charity is doing and the script tends to whine on. The sentences are TOO long: 39 words, 27 words. Shorten your sentences, be conversational. You lose donors with scripts that drone on like this one.

The first ask is third person. What a waste! Fundraising is people asking people. What exactly does "reach out to more animals" mean—getting their e-mail addresses?

I would prefer the script helping the caller to make a personal connection with the donor, such as "We really appreciate your support of our programs to help animals we both love. Do you have a companion animal, a dog or cat?" Using this technique helps make a human connection. Callers just have to make sure not to lose control of the phone call by letting the donor chatter away for 20 minutes about Fluffy.

The wording of the second ask is awkward. When you write phone scripts take a few minutes to read them out loud to pass the "conversation test." Would you really say something like this? Scripts need to provide callers with support. Concise language that can frame the discussion.

Finally, the script just continues to be all about the organization. I don't think there is a single "you" in this script. It should be full of phrases such as "You understand," "You helped make this possible," "You love animals," "Thank you, you, you."

Critique of Sample 2

I don't think calling people for "a brief update on our work" is very compelling. In this script, why not lead with "I'm calling to talk to you about the pending increase in electric rates. The increases are outrageous." Interject some emotion—that's what turns people on.

It's good to remind donors (especially lapsed ones like those addressed in this script) that they have benefited (saved money) because of the group's efforts.

Ten billion dollars is hard for most people to grasp. Instead, I'd say, "FREE HYDRO has saved rate payers like you and me about $120 per year." Wow! This gets their attention and their gratitude.

The first sentence in the third paragraph is 52 words long! This does not resemble any conversation I'd be likely to get into. See if you can shorten this sentence, make the information punchier. For example: "FREE HYDRO is working to help YOU by suing in court if we have to. We're lobbying the politicians. We're putting pressure on the decision makers."

When you're trying to come across as having a personal, one-on-one conversation, don't use the third person ("We are calling past supporters of FREE HYDRO and asking them to help with a generous contribution . . . ").

Write instead something like "I'm calling you because you have supported us to keep utility rates down. I'm calling you for your help again now to . . . "

In the second ask, don't apologize for asking for financial support. Be proud: You're working for a great and important cause. Make sure your scripts get this across. (What kind of statement is this? " . . . and I'd hate to miss them by not asking.")

Try this instead: "This is a great cause. I'm sure if you were able to, you might consider a gift of that amount. I'm sure we can find a good level for you."

Notice the language "working to hold politicians accountable" versus "we're holding politicians accountable." Why double verb it? Be direct, assertive, proud, confident. People give to urgent, exciting, dynamic causes.

The third ask is lame. I'd rather go right to "Thanks very much for your time. Before I go, will you match last year's gift of $25 to help us make a difference?" You've done all the explaining and this person just wants to get off the phone by this time. Give her a chance to feel good, get it over with, make a gift.

Critique of Sample 3

I like this script. It thanks the donor and reminds him or her of the goals and importance of the college. The next paragraph really sets the problem: The Board of Trustees raised fees and it is hurting low-income students. The script is short and uses nuanced language like "we have to do a bit more." We can all do a bit more: not very threatening. The third paragraph keeps the focus on "needy students" and puts a date in the donor's mind: the end of December.

Mentioning the credit card in the ask is almost assumptive—as though the donor has already agreed to make a gift and now it is just whether it is on MC or Visa.

The script keeps the focus on the students who benefit. This is the "feel-good" approach. The script also makes very clear HOW the contribution is used—nice and concise with action verbs.

The second ask uses a great technique: the "symbolic ask" that seeks to create a logical/emotional connection that makes it easier for the donor to nod "yes," which is close to saying YES to a contribution.

The third ask is right to the point: short. "Help us reach our goal." "You can close the gap." "You can put us over the top." "Match your last gift." These are all designed to make it easy to say YES.

Remember that 70 percent or more of calls end as refusals. Staying on the phone, connecting with donors on a personal level, and getting them nodding/agreeing during your call is what good fundraisers should do. The script is a tool that guides and offers them examples of language that can facilitate getting to Yes.

H. XYZ College Alumni Script[4]

Answering Machine

Good ___, this message is for (TITLE FULL NAME). I'm calling in reference to a letter sent to you by Jane Smith on behalf of XYZ College Foundation. We will try calling you again.

Introduction

Good evening, may I speak with (TITLE FULL NAME)? **(If not available, find a good time to call back.)**

(NON-DONOR)This is (YOUR FULL NAME) calling on behalf of XYZ College Foundation. I'm calling to follow up on a letter sent to you by **Jane Smith**. Have you received the letter? (If **NO**, go to **DID NOT RECEIVE LETTER**.)

(DONOR/LAPSED) This is (YOUR FULL NAME), calling on behalf of XYZ College Foundation. First, I wanted to thank you for your previous support and the great difference loyal donors like you help make in the lives of current students. I am also following up on a letter sent to you from **Jane Smith**? Did you receive her letter? (If **NO**, go to **DID NOT RECEIVE LETTER**.)

Received Letter

Great! As you know, **Jane** wrote about the great impact her XYZ College experience made on her life. Jane mentioned her gratitude for the scholarship she received from XYZ College Foundation and how the Foundation is committed to helping students open doors to their future by providing financial aid, scholarships, and educational resources. How do you feel about these initiatives? **(PAUSE and go to ASK if AGREE, or if questions, then DISCUSS and go to BONDING)**

Bonding Questions

1) Why did you choose to attend XYZ College? How did you find the experience? Would you recommend XYZ College to others? Why/ Why not?
2) What are you doing nowadays (record business information/phone number if given).

Ask/Agrees

With Need   In the letter, Jane mentioned many alumni are supporting the XYZ College Foundation by making a pledge of four installments of $___ for

---

[4] Contributed by Mr. Anthony Alonzo, Advantage Consulting, www.advantageconsulting.com.

a total gift of $___, between now and June 30, 2010. How do you feel about this idea?

(Go to CONFIRM ONE or deal with OBJECTIONS/TAILOR ASK.)

Confirm One That's great! Thank you for your pledge of **$ (total amount).**
(IF INSTALLMENTS . . .) in (**# of installments**) of $___ each payable by the end of the fiscal year, June 30, 2010.

Confirm Two XYZ College Foundation greatly appreciates your generous contribution of $___. Is your address still . . . ? **(READ COMPLETE AD-DRESS and CHECK SPELLING if a new address is given)**. Do you have an email address you would like us to add to your record?

Confirm Three As a follow up to our call, you will receive a thank you note, along with a pledge card and a self-addressed envelope. Will you be sending in your gift (or first installment) of $___ when you receive your envelope? (If NO, arrange for an appropriate date.) Confirm additional installment dates.

Matching Gift By the way, does your employer, or your spouse's employer, have a matching gift program? **(If YES . . .)** May I have the name of the company for our records? To utilize your employer's matching gift program, please contact your Human Resources Department and send in the necessary forms with your gift.

Planned Giving Some donors we've spoken with have expressed an interest in leaving a legacy at XYZ College through their will, trust, life insurance, or other deferred gifts. Would you be interested in receiving some information on how you can make a gift this way?

Hand-Off to Supervisor/Good Bye

Pledge: Oh, my supervisor is walking by and would like to thank you personally.

No Pledge: I really enjoyed speaking with you, thank you for your time.

Objections/Tailor Ask

Cannot Afford I understand. The amount mentioned in the letter was only a suggestion. We certainly understand that everyone is in a different situation. Some alumni I've spoken with this evening have decided to make **(cut full ask in half)** a pledge of four installments of $___ for a total gift of $___? How do you feel about this idea? **(Go to CONFIRM ONE or CONTINUE)**

One of our goals for this effort is to increase participation. When we reach out to corporations and other foundations, the private support XYZ College Foundation receives from alumni and friends, like you is even more important. To secure foundation and corporate support, the Foundation must show that its alumni and community members are behind them. With this in mind, how would you feel about making a gift of four installments of $___ **(half of the total amount above)** for a total gift of $___? **(Go to CONFIRM ONE or CONTINUE.)**

We are firm believers that there is strength in numbers and if everyone works together the Foundation will ensure deserving students receive the support they need to earn their degrees. Some alumni have decided to show their appreciation for XYZ College Foundation by making a one-time, vote of confidence gift of $___. How do you feel about this idea? **(Go to CONFIRM . . . GOOD-BYE.)**

Not Interested   If you don't mind me asking, I am really interested in why you feel this way? (DISCUSS).

Did Not Graduate   I will certainly make a note of that and update your record.

Problems with XYZ College   This effort is designed to let you voice your opinion. We would like to hear your ideas and feedback regarding improvements that XYZ College Foundation can make. **(DISCUSS and RECORD COMMENTS)**

This campaign is really about the students and providing them with the opportunity to receive a solid education. I've spoken to others who have considered a pledge in this light. They have chosen to make a pledge of four installments of $___ for a total gift of $___, between now and June 30, 2010. How do you feel about this idea?

Other Priorities   I am glad to hear you support other charitable efforts. We are hoping you will share your giving with XYZ College Foundation, as well. How would you feel about making a more moderate gift of four installments of $___ for a total gift of $___ between now and June 30, 2010? (FIND A COMFORTABLE AMOUNT and CONFIRM)

Send Me an Envelope/Will Send Something in on their Own   I understand your desire to support XYZ College Foundation through the mail. Once you have confirmed an amount you are comfortable with, we will send you a pledge card and self-addressed envelope to make it easy for you to send in your contribution. Some alumni I've spoken with have decided to confirm a gift they feel comfortable with now, knowing they can always increase their gift and send in more once they receive their envelope. How would you feel about confirming a pledge of $__, knowing you can always increase it?

I Need More Time   I understand. May we call you back **(DATE and TIME to within one week)**?

If Prospect Asks to be Removed From the List   I can take care of that for you but first I want to make sure I am removing you from the appropriate list. Would you like to be removed from just the calling list? **(IF NO)** Did you want to still be informed of any upcoming activities and updates but not solicited for contributions? **(IF YES)** Ok, great! I will just remove you from the solicitation list. You will still receive updates from XYZ College Foundation.

Did Not Receive Letter   IS YOUR ADDRESS STILL? (UPDATE INFORMATION ON FILE) . . . The letter had two purposes: First, to let you know I would be calling. Secondly, **Jane** wrote about the supportive environment at XYZ College and how the self-confidence and skills she gained there are contributing to her current career.

   Jane mentioned her gratitude for the scholarship she received from XYZ College Foundation and the great impact it made on her life. She also wrote about the Foundation's commitment to helping all deserving students open doors to their future by providing financial aid, scholarships and educational resources. How do you feel about these initiatives? **(PAUSE discuss; proceed to ASK if agrees with needs or to BONDING)**

Develop Your Own Script

DEVELOP YOUR OWN SCRIPT OR CALL OUTLINE

Create your own effective script or call outline using the following template, with simple 1-2-3 prompts for each stage of an effective telephone fundraising call.

IDENTIFICATION STAGE

Ask the person who answers the phone if you may speak to the prospect.

Use the prospect's first and last name.

Answer honestly what the call is about to a screening prospect, but be brief.

INTRODUCTION STAGE OF CALL

Introduce yourself

Use first and last name

Relate yourself as close to the organization as honestly possible.

RAPPORT STAGE (optional)

Thank the prospect for his or her past involvement, participation, and/or giving.

Reinforce prospect's relationship with your organization.

Ask the prospect open or close-ended questions to develop two-way communication.

PURPOSE STAGE (THE CASE)

Make the case for your organization: why you need money, why the prospect should give.

Be compelling, convincing, with firm conviction in your cause.

Be succinct as possible, seek prospect's agreement through "tie-down" questions.

THE ASK

Make a proposal to the prospect
for a contribution or a membership.

The proposal should be for a
specific dollar amount.

Ask for an amount that may be
greater than you think the
prospect is able or willing to give.

COUNTER PROPOSAL (optional)

Listen carefully to the prospect's response to your first proposal.

React and respond to any questions, objections, or issues the prospect may raise, and reinforce the urgency and need of your organization for support.

Make a counterproposal based on your pereception of the prospect's maximum ability to give.

THE CLOSE

Listen carefully to the prospect's response to the previous proposal.

React and respond to any questions, objections, or issues the prospect may raise, and reinforce in the most compelling way you can why the prospect should give.

Make a final proposal based on your perception of the prospect's abilty and willingness to support. For previous donors seek a renewal or upgrade of their prior gift.

CONFIRMATION OF PLEDGES

Thank the prospect for the specific dollar amount of the pledge!

Confirm: name, address, due date of pledge, payment type, and if possible, e-mail address.

Thank the prospect, again and again!

REFUSALS: HANDLE WITH CARE

Thank the prospect for his or her time in speaking with you.

Wish them well, and reinforce any connection they may continue to have with your organization.

Be upbeat, considerate and understanding... they may be a prospect for you next time!

Afterword

THE CHALLENGE OF TOMORROW:
TELEPHONE FUNDRAISING AND THE INTERNET

TED HART, ACFRE

The fundamentals of organizing and soliciting potential donors have not changed measurably since the telephone was first used to seek support. However, the advent of the Internet and strategies to incorporate its use into the work of charities promises to unleash a dramatic change in the telemarketing landscape of the future.

Few people look forward to receiving unsolicited telephone solicitation for support; however, data shows that charities can still count on the telephone to enhance and deepen the donor relationship they seek and, in so doing, raise more money than they would without the use of the telephone.

One opportunity open to many charities in the Internet age is to begin developing various *online* volunteering and gift solicitation tools into their telephone fundraising and outreach efforts and to do this in a way that does not rely as heavily on expensive paid staff or outsourced telemarketing calls.

Online Phone-Banking Tools

Before deploying any Internet-based telemarketing enhancement, charities should first develop and motivate a community of supporters for online giving and advocacy. As this is successful, then provide tools making it possible for volunteers to make calls from their own homes using online phone-banking tools. The introduction of these tools can incorporate several strategies:

1. Update current donor records
2. Identify likely supporters
3. Motivate and deepen relationships
4. Solicit gifts

This expanded use of the Internet will be used in various combinations of the above opportunities to enhance the outreach and cost effectiveness of charity efforts using the phone.

During the 2008 presidential campaign, Barack Obama's team provided tools such as these to their legions of supporters using MyBarackObama.com and other web sites. The result was more than 9 million calls made via the online phone-banking tools provided. In this case, campaign volunteers helped "clean" the campaign database before local campaign teams ever made contact. By taking a first pass through the voter list, Internet volunteers verified voter data from their homes, culling bad data on voters who had moved or died and saving local volunteers' time. This is just one use of such tools that could dramatically enhance supporter relationships with the charity while reducing the cost of making such calls with paid solicitors.

Warming Calls

Unlike other solicitation tools, outbound telephone calls interrupt the prospective donor and essentially demand his or her immediate attention. Therefore, charities and their paid or volunteer solicitors must pay particular care to be sensitive to the prospective donor whose life is being interrupted. Some lessons learned in the past give us a window to what will lead to more successful attempts in the future. For example, calls should not be made at inconvenient hours such as dinnertime or early morning. A carefully written script should be developed to get the most value from the time and money spent on each call and to avoid angering or annoying the person receiving the call.

Warming calls are a suggested strategy. These are calls made principally by volunteers that are not meant to solicit gifts but instead to provide opportunities to enhance data and/or to introduce issues, concepts, or topics the donor may not be aware of. In some cases, more elaborate calling scripts that include answers to every objection a prospect might mention can enhance the value of the dialogue.

While some might find efficiency in using prerecorded messages rather than "live" callers, this method of outreach should be discouraged. In its place calls use that are meant to build upon other communication already started either online or offline. While telephone numbers can be dialed at random, warming calls would only build upon relationships already under development via other fundraising and communication strategies.

The value of the telephone should not be underestimated as a medium to deepen the relationships charities seek with their donors. In many cases the voice heard on a telemarketing call maybe the very first voice the donor has heard in relationship to the charity she supports. The donor solicitation funnel moving donors toward additional support will continue to be enhanced by telephone outreach efforts.

While some estimates suggest that telephone fundraising calls can cost four times as much as a direct mail piece, it is also true that they can generate as much as two to six times the response. The additional benefits are that contact can be confirmed and response can be secured, all while having a direct opportunity to enhance a relationship. Direct mail contact cannot be confirmed, and only if a gift is made can any sort of response be known.

Looking Ahead

As noted before, few people actually enjoy having their lives interrupted by telemarketers. So when we look at the future of telephone solicitations, it is easy to be pessimistic. However, those who have developed the skills necessary to target their prospects both in demographics and message will continue to show strength in the medium.

An expanding global fundraising sector will be enhanced by the ability to provide multilingual telephone fundraising, particularly as VoIP services and international telephone rates continue to reduce the cost of making such calls overseas.

As online phone-banking tools grow in their utility to charities, not only will volunteer utilization grow but so too will the ability to utilize part-time, flexible, and stay-at-home workers grow, further reducing cost and increasing effectiveness of these efforts.

Hallmark of Success

In the future, a charity's use of the telephone will be enhanced by its ability to coordinate with and use state-of-the-art marketing research, direct mail, print advertising, the electronic media, the Internet, and a combination of both paid and volunteer efforts.

Taking the considerations above into account, it can be anticipated that several driving forces will continue the expansion of the use of the telephone in fundraising:

1. Continuing demand for convenience and the need to speed up donor interaction
2. Continued improvement in the capabilities and efficiencies to be found in Internet-based technologies and telecommunication
3. The increased utilization of sophisticated software and the development of more extensive and more creative databases about donors and potential supporters
4. Continued increase in the cost, and decrease in effectiveness, of other traditional forms of fundraising solicitation
5. Increased knowledge of how to develop and operate successful telephone fundraising and outreach programs (as shown throughout this book)

In Conclusion

Looking to the future, charities can expect to see even more integration of traditional fundraising techniques such as telephone solicitation with new Internet-based databases and technologies. As broadband expands and services like YouTube and social networking sites grow, the opportunities to engage a donor population using multiple media are enhanced. Smart strategies of integration between the various tools available both online and offline will provide for a rebirth for the use of the telephone for fundraising solicitation.

About the Author

Ted Hart, ACFRE, is considered one of the foremost experts in online fundraising and social networking for charities around the world, having founded the ePhilanthropy Foundation and P2PFundraising.org. Ted is sought after internationally as an inspirational and practical speaker and consultant on topics related to nonprofit strategy, both online and offline. He serves as CEO of Hart Philanthropic Services (http://tedhart.com), an international consultancy to nonprofits/nongovernmental organizations (NGOs). He is founder and chief executive of the international nonprofit environmental movement called GreenNonprofits (http://greennonprofits.org), dedicated to helping nonprofits and NGOs around the world to learn how to become part of the much-needed global environmental solution. He has served as CEO of the University of Maryland Medical System Foundation and before that as chief development officer for Johns Hopkins Bayview Medical Center. He has been certified as an advanced certified fundraising executive by the Association of Fundraising Professionals. Ted is author of several published articles, is an editor, and author of the books *People to People Fundraising: Social Networking and Web 2.0 for Charities* (Hoboken, NJ: John Wiley & Sons, 2007); *Nonprofit Guide to Going Green* (Hoboken, NJ: John Wiley & Sons, 2009); *Major Donors— Finding Big Gifts in Your Database and Online* (Hoboken, NJ: John Wiley & Sons, 2006; *Nonprofit Internet Strategies: Best Practices for Marketing, Communications and Fundraising Success* (Hoboken, NJ: John Wiley & Sons, 2005); and *Fundraising on the Internet: The ePhilanthropy Foundation.Org's Guide to Success Online* (Hoboken, NJ: John Wiley & Sons, 2001). He is a contributing author to *Achieving Excellence in Fund Raising*, 2nd ed. (Hoboken, NJ: John Wiley & Sons, 2003). Hart is a graduate of the University of Rochester and the State University of New York at Brockport, where he received his master's degree in public administration (MPA). He has also served as an adjunct faculty member to the Master of Science in Fundraising Management program at Columbia University.

He resides in the Washington, D.C., area with his daughter, Sarah Grace, and son, Alexander Michael.

Index